"Authors Cécile Roche and Luc Delamotte extrapolated years of collective experiences, case studies, learnings and growth in the functional area of Engineering. In their book *The Lean Engineering Travel Guide: The Best Itineraries for Developing New Products and Satisfying Customers*, they lay out for the reader a cafeteria style learning within the guide as well as a holistic approach around the important nuances of Engineering/Product Development/Design. The journey of developing People, Purpose, Problem solving, Process design and improvements never has a destination but rather a relentless pursuit of growth measured by our work. This can facilitate the reframing of non-value-added activity, that was once a conditioned norm. The authors navigate through their travel guide with multiple points of interests that take a deep dive into the P's noted above. I would recommend not only to Engineering but to other genres inside an organization to see how the importance of cross functional groups can align to a true north! Lots of experiences to be learned from the authors as they share their wisdom in a nice visual way to learn."

— **Tracey Richardson, Author of** *The Toyota Engagement Equation*

"Cécile Roche and Luc Delamotte have written a unique book that I would have found very useful when I was employed as an engineer working in R&D and new product development. Well-written and grounded in the fundamentals, the book provides many practical examples that will help engineers correctly understand and successfully apply Lean to engineering work."

— **Professor Bob Emiliani, Connecticut State University, author of many famous books on Lean**

"Cécile Roche and Luc Delamotte describe the levers of Toyota's Toyota: the merging of the technical and social components of a learning organization. Toyota is a company found in engineering and innovation, and one committed to developing its people at every level as problem-solvers. *Lean Engineering* creates the link between the technical skills required to create customer value and thrive into the future and the social skills leaders need to foster engagement and capability to do so. If you are an engineer, a leader with a technical background or managing technical teams, or a lean practitioner seeking the roadmap to an effective lean system, *Lean Engineering* is the guide that will enable you to create an enduring learning organization."

— **Katie Anderson, author of** *Learning to Lead, Leading to Learn: Lessons from Toyota Leader Isao Yoshino on a Lifetime of Continuous Learning*

T0341135

The Lean Engineering Travel Guide

Lean is an essential way of working in a world that is accelerating and becoming more complex. It revalues the human dimension in the company by encouraging individual thinking and initiative and gives meaning to teams that are more and more challenged by competitiveness and innovation.

This book is designed as a travel guide. The first part includes all the traditional sections from the 'front end' of a travel guide, including some basic vocabulary, tips, and a historical section about some of the pioneers of Lean in Engineering. The journey begins in the second part, which explains a number of Lean Engineering practices in some detail and the best itineraries to develop better products, discussing the underlying intentions and offering advice for implementation. Numerous concrete cases illustrate this part with case material drawn from the authors' own experiences. Part Three is a brief guide to where and how to get started.

Currently, there are no books on Lean Engineering written by practising engineers who have themselves experienced the adjustment of Lean principles to the business and challenges of new product development. The authors describe tools and practices that have already been widely tested and improved by many engineers with different cultures and skills in the Thales Group and other companies. Lean Engineering as the authors describe it has thus been able to demonstrate its effectiveness for several years. In addition, the authors describe new unique practices invented within the framework of their activities and which thus do not exist anywhere else (e.g., Causal Influence Diagram (*CID*), Pull-Scheduling Board).

The Lean Engineering Travel Guide

The Best Itineraries for Developing New Products and Satisfying Customers

Cécile Roche and Luc Delamotte

Foreword by Olivier Flous

Routledge
Taylor & Francis Group

A PRODUCTIVITY PRESS BOOK

First published 2024
by Routledge
605 Third Avenue, New York, NY 10158

and by Routledge
4 Park Square, Milton Park, Abingdon, Oxon, OX14 4RN

Routledge is an imprint of the Taylor & Francis Group, an informa business

ISBN: 978-1-032-46495-4 (hbk)
ISBN: 978-1-032-46494-7 (pbk)
ISBN: 978-1-003-38194-5 (ebk)

DOI: 10.4324/9781003381945

Typeset in Minion
by Deanta Global Publishing Services, Chennai, India

'All men by nature desire to know.'

Aristotle – Metaphysics

This book is dedicated to all the teams at the Thales group
with whom we work to deploy Lean Engineering, to the many
managers who adopt new Lean practices, and finally to all
the members of the Lean Academy of Engineering.

Contents

PART ONE   In the Land of Engineering

PART TWO   Map, Territories, Pathways

List of Figures

Foreword

Can we still think of 'Lean' as something fresh and new? For a system with roots going back more than 70 years (yes, *way* before the digital revolution), you may think everything that can be said about Lean has now been said. Lean earned its reputation in the domain of industrial production – where it has become a globally recognised benchmark for improving operational performance. But, surprisingly, it was only around 20 years ago that Lean started to appear in the world of engineering too, and has been enjoying a kind of renaissance ever since. Thanks in part to the work of Allen Ward people have begun to realise that the management and learning system invented by Toyota is not just about increasing the productivity and quality of products leaving the production line. Rather, the Lean system can also work upstream – on the definition, design, and development of products so that Lean can also be applied, for example, to the continuous capture of knowledge, or the methodical resolution of problems, or the pace of processes. In fact, the application of such principles in the world of software development has greatly enhanced agile methods.

People often forget that engineering is essentially a creative activity (rather than a production activity), and this creative aspect gives the application of Lean principles to engineering a distinctly fresh feel. Few books have set out to describe these principles, practices, and how to deploy them in the world of engineering. But in this book, Cécile Roche and Luc Delamotte will do exactly that: in their 'day jobs', they have scrupulously applied the principles they recommend. They will share the vast knowledge they have acquired in the field and make it available for anyone willing to engage with this process where the aim, quite simply, is excellence.

When we decided to deploy Lean in many of the engineering divisions within the Thales Group, we did so because we believed the competitive edge of engineering lies in a collective approach to a range of issues: solving problems (rather than alleviating symptoms), capitalising knowledge in reusable form (in components and processes), controlling technical debt, understanding trade-offs associated with design alternatives, and more. In short, we wanted to put the business at the heart of the improvement process, and not simply add a bunch of control structures where the control is illusory and the only reality is more bureaucracy.

Lean provides a powerful framework to put rigour and discipline at the heart of engineering. It is not so much a control system as a people development system. Behind what looks like common sense and simple practices is a coherent and powerful system. It is brought in progressively, challenging bad habits on the way. Specialist Lean coaches are essential to support teams during this process, giving them the tools and insights to implement an approach that is highly specific to each of them as individuals.

Interestingly enough, it seems that the digital revolution has a particular resonance with Lean. It is no coincidence that the value creation process applied by the majority of digital companies is called *Lean Startup* (4). Rapid development and testing cycles (in which we constantly adapt to observations about product usage to maximise value creation) are at the heart of the Lean approach. With the emergence of digital platforms and DevOps for software, the pace is accelerating (with several versions of a product put into production each day) and product feedback becomes simpler and faster by picking up usage data straight off the platform.

Within this book, there are many real-life illustrations of implementing a Lean approach in engineering organisations. While there is plenty of detail, we also hope you find it concise and engaging. My warm thanks go to Cécile and Luc, whose aim here is to inspire you to implement such an approach within your own organisation. Do that, and you may have a great journey ahead of you.

Olivier Flous
VP, Engineering & Digital Transformation – Thales Group

Preface

Cécile Roche

I started my Lean journey many years ago, working in my original field of product development. I am an electronics engineer by training and spent many years studying and testing systems, equipment, and components. I started with an exciting (but one-off) adventure with a splendid parallel supercomputer project and then developed specific components for visualisation systems and, finally, for airborne radio equipment. From the outset, I wanted to improve the way I approached these developments by testing different methods, so I explored simulation tools for a while, followed by different approaches to specifying. I then became interested in validation and integration, finally spending a lot of time in working groups, defining, and optimising development processes.

I still have good memories of this period, and we did some great work. But there was always something missing. I remember the frustration of spending endless hours on project management rather than on actual engineering, especially as we engineers were so often accused of ignoring the real-world constraints of programmes, schedules, and budgets in favour of playing with technology and having fun. But it didn't feel like I was having much fun at the time. I felt there had to be a better way: an approach that could reconcile both aspects, strengthening the creative engineering process while respecting management constraints. For a long time, though, I was torn between these two approaches as if they were systematically incompatible.

My first approach to Lean reflected this. I thought for a moment that simply 'chasing waste' and removing unnecessary activities would free up time to focus on the product and engineering. But I soon found there is no such magic wand, and doing things well does not necessarily equate with doing things right. Then I had the chance to really learn about Lean in our very own factories with a very good teacher, Michael Ballé, who is still my *sensei* (an expert coach in Lean) and whom I must thank once again.

This was a return to first principles, via an approach applied to my own industry, and it made me think differently. In writing my earlier books (1)(2), I really wanted to share a fundamental discovery: *Lean is first and foremost a continuous learning system for everybody in the company.*

Today, however, I want to go back to what got me (and so many colleagues) excited about engineering in the first place: a passion for the product. It's easy to lose sight of this, and just thinking about the product feels in a sense like going home, after a career-long journey that seems to have involved so many dead ends and arduous roads. And then, just thinking about all these explorations, detours, and the discoveries that I made along the way, the concept for this book – as a kind of metaphorical 'travel guide' to the land of Lean, seemed to make a lot of sense.

There's a paradox in this: the better I got to understand the principles of Lean in production, the less I wanted to adapt the tools of Lean Manufacturing to engineering. Instead, I began to see a very specific kind of Lean, but still based on an identical set of underlying principles. I then had the chance to test these approaches and learn more with different teams – all of whom were equally endowed with huge measures of curiosity and open-mindedness. And we found that it works! Then Luc joined my team, and others since, and our mission now is to make continuing progress with our engineering teams and share our collective learning.

For the past few years, I have also had the opportunity to participate in, and then lead, the Lean Academy of Engineering. Each month a small group of people from several companies (from Small Medium Enterprise [SMEs] to large corporations) representing a variety of industries meet in one of these companies to explore the practices presented in this book. Interest in this has been building over the last five years, and we are now beginning to observe some quite spectacular results. And when I say results, I'm mainly talking about growth. The practices sound simple enough: to understand the concept of value for customers, to change the long-term vision of products, and to develop employees' knowledge, their reflection, and critical thinking. And the results are significant. We see SMEs gaining the loyalty of more demanding customers, design offices boosting their ability to innovate and pitch new ideas, and bosses rethinking how they see their business. Of course, there are also those who will stay stuck where they are locked in by a rigid business structure or perhaps a rigid mentality. The practices all seem simple enough. But getting in the habit of thinking about continuous improvement can be harder.

Sharing experiences over the years with all our fellow travellers on the Lean journey has taught me an important lesson: life in general (and engineering in particular) is full of apparent trade-offs, and we spend much of our time trying to resolve them: how to design a small yet powerful battery? How to be both rigorous and innovative? How to trust someone and not be let down? With time, I have understood that *the Lean approach, far from being an off-the-shelf solution to problems, is a way of identifying the most important of these trade-offs and working collectively to reconcile them.* This implied a radical change in my way of thinking.

I have lost count of the number of times participants at the Lean Academy have asked me for a reference book which sets out all the stages of this learning. There are plenty out there (and we cite many of them in this book). However, it seemed to us that the progress made by some of our Academy members, and the results they achieved within their firms deserved to be shared. That is what prompted me to write this book – a project that's been maturing within me for many years. And I want to warmly thank Luc for joining me in putting into words all that we have learned.

Luc Delamotte

Before my own Lean journey began, I held various engineering roles within many different practices – and I also made many mistakes.

I started my career as a systems engineer in telecom satellites. After several years spent writing specifications, definition files, technical proposals, reports, and meeting minutes, I became the technical manager in charge of design for a two-way broadband satellite terminal.

We were predominantly system engineers and software developers inspired by Open Source practices.[1] We were lucky to have an expert programme manager who spoke to us about the customers and the product and regularly challenged our technical choices. I realised then that making the right product was more important than just applying the right process. A bit like Lockheed Martin's 'Skunk Works' (autonomous

---

[1] See https://fr.wikipedia.org/wiki/Open_source

teams developing innovative projects outside the official framework), we had drastically lightened our own processes. Too much so, perhaps.

During that period, we all learned a lot: we developed standards, filed patents, validated our concept, and enjoyed ourselves. But the painful truth is that we lacked rigour and the quality of the product suffered. I understood later, first with my discovery of Agile, and then of Lean, that process does not need to be a straitjacket and that more rigour does not necessarily make you less agile.

I then took the lead of the systems engineering department for satellite navigation solutions, as a line manager running a team of experienced engineers. Essentially, though, I was no more than a resource manager. My days were filled with monitoring workload curves, resource loadings, meeting minutes, and progress reports. I took part in coordination meetings and reviews of work packages and resources. My diary was constantly overbooked, and I had precious little time to devote to my team members. Without a shadow of doubt, they deserved more and better.

Since then, I have learned two essential things about the role of tech department heads: you need time to develop each individual team member. But you can't do that until you have mastered every aspect of your own discipline.

Having been a technical manager, and then a department manager, I was appointed software project manager for a large and complex programme. Finally, I thought I would get a chance to apply my learning. A coach trained about 40 people, including me, in Agile frameworks and methods (Scrum and XP). I felt as though he was bringing in everything I had missed during my previous experience: underlying principles, the right mental attitude, effective tools, and discipline. I decided to vacate my office and set up my workstation alongside the teams in the open workspace.

It was then that I discovered the power of visual management. A whole bunch of simple charts and graphics, owned by the teams and intended for sharing information, turned out to be a gold mine for a project manager. I finally had at my fingertips all the essential facts and data of the project (rather than other people's opinions). No need for individual reporting nor endless progress reviews. Decisions could finally be made quickly and objectively.

On the software side, developments were accelerating, but we soon saw the limitations of this fairly local improvement, as it did not include upstream and downstream processes (such as system engineering and integration). I got a little deeper into Lean and understood we were missing at least one key point: customer-driven continuous flow.

We then offered customers a quarterly visit to our premises to test out each major delivery. To be ready on time, we had to synchronise the entire workflow around these events. After many adjustments and discussions, a so-called 'pull, flow and cadence' was put in place, using *Kanban Boards* to track and display progress visually. The acceleration of the process was tangible. Support from the business line manager was decisive in bringing down a final line of resistance to what was seen by some at the time as a risky experiment.

Understanding the principles, implementing the associated practices, and then seeing the improvements come to fruition was a revelation. I had just started my journey into Lean, and I had travelled with an extraordinary team. But at the end of the project, that team was disbanded. It seemed unthinkable to turn back – to abandon what I had learned and to somehow stop making further progress I had become completely hooked. So I joined Cécile's team to extend my Lean adventure and accompany those who wanted to start it elsewhere in our group.

It is, therefore, my great privilege to share with you what I have learned from my Lean journey. And I hope this will be as much of an inspiration for you as it was for me.

Acknowledgements

This book is above all the fruit of the many experiences that the wide variety of situations and products of the Thales Group has allowed us to conduct.

First of all, we would like to thank Olivier Flous, who, as *VP, Engineering & Digital Transformation* of the Thales Group, published the Golden Rules of Engineering, which were the foundations of the implementation of Lean Engineering, and whose objective is that Lean methods and practices become 'fundamentally a part of engineering' and we are progressing every day on this path!

We warmly thank all those with whom we have been able to learn, test and progress within the Group, in particular the Lean core team and all its representatives in the different countries or regions, and all the engineering teams with whom we work on a daily basis. Thanks to them for the many exchanges and for the moments of joy shared.

Warm thanks to Sharon Craggs for her precious help in the English translation.

Finally, we warmly thank Johanna Guillaume who drew the map of the country of engineering and who put her talent at the service of our travel dreams. Thank you, Johanna, for interpreting our vision of Lean Engineering country so well!

Introduction

You might be asking yourself whether it even makes any sense to talk about Lean in the context of engineering or development. Well, the vocabulary is a little different, depending on the country and culture, but the most important thing is the product – using the word here in its broadest sense: namely, what gets delivered to a customer. It can be a device, a service, a system – any element that will help a customer (or user) to solve their problems. True success in Lean Engineering is always accompanied by a real passion for the product. We, the authors of this book, work in an industrial group where people are really passionate about products. The products vary, just as the customers vary and the domains of activity vary. These are ideal conditions for continuous learning. This book has been built on these various experiences, and those of other companies with which we work, as well as on thought and reflection, observation, research, and exchanges that help us learn and grow.

The product delivers value. To offer customers the products that excite them and make them loyal is about understanding what it is they value. This is a necessary condition for any company to grow. Then, to ensure profitability, the company must recoup a part of that value created for customers. And finally, committing to be sustainable means creating long-term value for all stakeholders and for society in general. Engineering is at the core of value creation and, indeed, has a direct impact on all these elements.

Innovation is the true way to create value, so long as you can bring innovation to market to fit the pace of customer demand. The big challenge is how to adapt quickly to a rapidly changing world – without being distracted by passing fads. We have seen how electronics, information technology, and all kinds of other technological changes have been game-changers throughout our industrial history. Today, digital transformation is forcing companies to rethink their business model and the way they innovate. By developing peoples' ability to deal with new problems and transforming the knowledge gained into great products, Lean is particularly well suited to face these changes: it has the capacity to make digital technology a powerful lever of value creation.

In writing this book, we had in mind the idea of a 'travel guide' as the broad framework of our approach. This felt apt because for both of us, the progression in Lean Engineering has felt like a journey that we started many years ago, each of us with different starting points and different paths.

For one of us, the starting point was process improvement through successive workshops and resulting action plans. For the other, Agile for software development was the trigger. Both of us came to realise that the roads we had travelled were either dead ends or too slow – not allowing us to evolve to keep pace with the market, competitors, and the economic environment. Here's why:

Systematic use of process improvement tools, such as Value Stream Mapping (VSM) to highlight wastes and every other limiting factor – and eliminate them – can lead to errors and misunderstandings:

- The focus is on the process, not the product. What is the point of doing the wrong product in the right way? It can even allow you to miss out on the worst kind of waste possible: doing the wrong product!
- Chasing waste (e.g., delays, rework, non-quality, multiplication of meetings, barriers to communication) without looking at the root causes is a bit like putting a plaster cast on a wooden leg. The same symptom can have different causes, and therefore different solutions. Thus, the solution proposed for one problem may not have the desired effect on others. Moreover, focusing only on symptoms greatly limits what we can learn about what's going on.
- A process improvement project may give the feeling that improvement is a separate activity from the daily normal work, which is carried out alongside or even after the normal activities have been completed (as with a post-mortem analysis). This also leads to a differentiation between the one doing the work and the one proposing the improvement. The former is not encouraged to understand how to improve one's work, while the latter is not led to test the validation of one's proposal. Moreover, each improvement risks being understood as 'the best way' to do the work, which leads to a loss of team ownership and commitment. Finally, the improvements will never be considered as continuous but as decontextualised actions to be carried out in addition to normal activities.

Similarly, the deployment of agile methods (e.g., Scrum, XP) in development projects for software-based systems also has its pitfalls:

- Limiting improvement to software developments alone may create friction at the interface with upstream and downstream activities. This is counter to overall flow improvement and unfairly limits the positive impact of agile methods.
- If developing the system simply goes lockstep with various software development iterations, then customers are taking a backseat. But it is they who pull the flow and should set the pace for system deliveries.
- If you deploy the same method everywhere (like Scrum) and scrupulously respect the 'four values' and 'twelve principles' of the Manifesto for Agile Software Development – irrespective of the situation or context – then you can end up acting *against* your desired objective: to become agile. *A 'uniform deployment of agility' sounds like a contradiction in terms.*

We felt there had to be a better way. Having spent five years implementing a Lean approach for production activities, we had seen the real benefits – not only on the industrial performance of the company but also on the motivation of its people. What's more, the improvements were sustained. We began to understand that Lean could be a performance lever *outside* its traditional domain of production.

Several things convinced us to extend the Lean approach to engineering activities. The first came from our production teams. Many of the difficulties observed in production have their roots in the product engineering itself (for example, insufficient product definition, poor consideration of industrial capacities, or over-investment in industrial equipment due to a lack of upstream awareness). So it makes sense to work as early as possible in the product life cycle to reduce these difficulties.

Further elements backed this up.

One of these came from project management, where several Agile teams were collaborating with system teams that did not practice Agile themselves. It was hard for them to observe the positive impact of Agile on system performance while, at the same time, they noticed recurring difficulties in maintaining a common repository for all teams (for sharing engineering artefacts, reviews, and suchlike) and also difficulties with effective collaboration.

Another trigger was the decision to launch an ambitious performance plan for all of the Thales Group's engineering, our primary activity, and spearhead of our business. Lean could be part of that plan and thus contribute to increasing engineering performance.

Finally, although perhaps it should have been cited first, was our encounter with A.C. Ward's book (3). It is a book we recommend to everyone, and is worth reading and re-reading. Each chapter gives you the feeling that the author personally knows the situation in your company – and how to improve it. The book has changed the way we look not only at Lean but also at engineering: a conception of Lean in development that is not just a simple adaptation of Lean Manufacturing. Ward's book became the 'bible' for our VP, Engineering & Digital Transformation, and became our guide in building the engineering performance plan.

It was around this time the authors' Lean paths intersected. Luc, with his engineering expertise and experience in Agile and Lean, joined the team that Cécile was leading.

The idea of writing a book about Lean in Engineering (in the form of a travel guide) came to us somewhat later. We wanted to show how Lean, wherever it applics, is a journey, not a destination. We also wanted a format that would allow us to deal with the subject in its entirety – while at the same time leaving the reader to choose their topics without losing the continuity of the narrative.

A travel guide is first and foremost a book to make you want to get moving. Then, once you arrive, it helps you familiarise yourself with the basics of the local language, customs, and culture and accompanies you on your journey of discovery. You can use it to get detailed explanations, or simply more general information. It can even help you find your way back if you are a little lost.

Travel guides also allow readers to organise their own itinerary and discover for themselves all kinds of surprises and hidden corners. We – the authors – are still on the road, pursuing our own Lean journey, and there continues to be no shortage of discoveries in our own work.

We hope this guide will make you want to embark on your own Lean journey. It has been designed to get you on your way and give you the lay of the land as you progress. For more experienced travellers, we hope to leave you with a renewed appetite to continue your journey and, perhaps also, to discover amazing new things.

Reading Tips

This book is organised in the form of a travel guide. You can read in a linear fashion from front to back if you want, or you can dip in and out, picking up whatever interests you. With this in mind, we have included plenty of cross-references between chapters, allowing you to move between topics according to what you're looking for.

There are also numerous footnotes citing the books, publications, blogs, and articles we have used. The bibliography is devoted to Lean, and more particularly to Lean in Engineering, again, linked by references throughout the text. Finally, an index of keywords provides an easy reference to the pages where the main concepts are detailed.

Part One, *In the Land of Engineering*, includes all the traditional sections from the 'front end' of a travel guide, including some basic vocabulary and a historical section. This section will talk about some of the pioneers of Lean in Engineering, who were around long before the Lean 'brand' first appeared.

Part Two, *Maps, Territories, and Pathways*, explains a number of Lean practices in some detail, discussing the underlying intentions and offering advice for implementation. We have illustrated this part with case material drawn from the authors' own experiences.

Part Three is a brief guide to where and how to get started.

And throughout the book you will find sidebars and boxes, taking you a little further into certain subjects and adding some enlightening anecdotes to get you thinking.

Bon voyage!

Part One

In the Land of Engineering

When you come to apply Lean principles to engineering and development, you begin to see just what a radically different approach this is.

It is not something that can be simply 'bolted on' to your existing design and development processes. Rather, it is about designing and developing according to practices that will *always* lead to continuous improvement. It means agreeing on trade-offs (e.g., cost versus performance) and the problems inherent in solving them. It means unlearning old habits and developing new ones as well as critical thinking skills. It is not an additional task, or responsibility, or administrative burden on the daily activities of your teams and their managers. *It is another quite distinct way of doing all of these at once.*

Lean is driven by common sense and clear-headed logic. But it can feel counterintuitive and sometimes hard to get everyone on board week in and week out. You'll hear comments like 'I completely get it – but I just don't have the time', or 'I can't improve my process if they don't improve theirs first', or even 'It's too simplistic, how can this work?' or, most typically, 'Once we have fewer problems, we'll have time to look at this properly'. There's a whole raft of ways people will want to turn your common sense initiative into some kind of expensive luxury. Meanwhile, even those who are broadly supportive may still find this new way full of uncertainty: 'But where do we start? How do I get my managers on-side? And what's the return on investment?'

We can return to all of these questions later in the book. But first let's take a look at exactly why Lean is just so different from anything else. And how you can maximise your chances of making it work.

1

Why This Journey?

There's a lot of talk about Lean. In manufacturing, of course, the concept has been around for decades. However, Lean Engineering or Lean Product Development feels more like an exciting new frontier. Consultants have been ready to cash in, some in more useful ways than others. Lean has become something of a buzzword, and like any buzzword, is prone to be overused – sprinkled liberally around the various blurbs on consultancy websites that have otherwise remained mostly unchanged.

Some consultancy groups are trying to get to grips with what it means – but struggle to transcribe the practices of Lean Manufacturing into the world of engineering. One example is the attempt to draw parallels between, on the one hand, Lean Manufacturing's 7 *muda*,[1] and on the other hand, waste in product development. But it's not that straightforward: *muda* are often the symptoms of the two other evils of manufacturing, *mura* and *muri* (respectively, unevenness in the volume of activity and overburden on resources). Thinking backwards, consultants start hunting for waste to improve processes. So it's not so easy to map one bit of Lean theory from manufacturing directly onto the rather different activities of engineering.

Consultants may also want to focus on project management, cutting delays by making productivity gains in the development phase. Others will come up with techniques to engage your workforce, committing to making teams happier, more autonomous, and more 'freedom-based'.[2]

---

[1] TIMWOOD: unnecessary Transport, Inventory, and Motion, on the one hand, and Waiting, Overproduction, Overprocessing, and Defects, on the other hand.

[2] B. Nobles and P. Staley. (2017). *Questioning Corporate Hierarchy*. CreateSpace E-book. 'Freedom-Based Management'.

DOI: 10.4324/9781003381945-2

A few will be ready to talk about your products and your customers. But rarer still are those who can actually bring together all of these factors in one global approach. And that is what we will strive to do throughout this book.

GOING FOR COMPETITIVENESS

Having a competitive advantage means consistently generating higher sales, greater profitability, and better sustainability than competitors. Lean focuses on all three.

Whether we're talking about large groups or SMEs, traditional industries or start-ups, high-tech or services, B2B or B2C, all companies need customers who are fully satisfied with the product to ensure growth. At the same time, they all need efficiency and agility to sustain profitability. And they must all innovate to engage existing customers and attract new ones.

Great products are the result of great teams. Getting excellent, optimised products, designed to solve customers' problems (without creating new ones) while ensuring a controlled and affordable total cost of ownership, is the result of excellence from engineering and manufacturing teams. So this journey into Lean will be of interest to executives, managers, consultants, and others, as well as to members of the engineering teams who, every day, work to develop better products.

Increase Your Turnover

It's a simple enough challenge: if your products are good – meaning they provide value for your customers, then your customers will keep coming back for more, which in turn will attract yet more new customers. At its heart, Lean has strategic implications for organisations to achieving growth and thrive. It therefore must be part of a corporate-level strategy.

Improve Your Profitability

Building the right products is paramount (no customers = no business), but to ensure good profitability, you need to build them right too. Lean embraces the removal of waste (generated by our own errors and misconceptions) to improve the profitability of all of our activities.

And Do It Sustainably

Most managers are motivated to maintain growth and profitability. Lean allows them to import the principles of sustainability into their strategy. Rather than cutting costs, it is about investing in the development of people through *kaizen* (refer to *Vocabulary*): namely, developing their ability to face new problems and unpredictable situations and propose continuous improvements.

But This Is Not Enough

Beyond delivering products quarter-after-quarter and year-after-year, companies must also deliver sustainable solutions that do not harm society or the environment. The action of continuously eliminating waste through *kaizen* is a truly frugal and therefore sustainable approach.

GOING FOR INNOVATION

> *Innovation means offering your customers new ways to solve their problems. Mastering innovation means regularly proposing new features rather than wanting to integrate everything into a single product that becomes difficult to get right.*

Innovation Beyond Creativity

Innovation is a nexus between creativity and the customer. It takes place when creativity successfully meets a customer's need, want, or desire. The vast number of innovative products that fail to meet these goals is a reminder that creativity alone is not enough: creative ideas are pointless unless they are used. The best way to avoid confusing creativity with innovation is to keep testing your ideas with customers. This may lead to minor adjustments, or may even take the whole project in a completely new direction (4).

Breakthrough or Disruptive Innovation?

Breakthrough innovations are more about product innovations. They are mainly done by incumbents in the market. Disruptive innovations are more associated with major changes in the market and the displacement of incumbents by new entrants.

Aim for a Flow of Innovations Rather Than a 'Perfect' Product

Coming up with THE perfect product that solves every problem for every customer is a bad idea. The ability to solve *relevant* problems is what makes a product great, rather than simply the number of features it can offer.

'Feature creep' – the tendency to add too many new features – makes a product more complex and can affect quality, as well as having a detrimental impact on the entire product life cycle, making it too expensive to produce, install, and maintain. Costs rise, and demand falls. Sometimes, people build unnecessary features because they don't know what the market really wants.

It also means your product falls out of step with what your customers want, which is, as you will see below, the worst possible kind of waste for any company. Lean will help you think in terms of product *flows* rather than single 'killer' products. The aim is to bring in innovations at a rate that matches the needs of your market (refer to *Product Takt*).

2

The Journey to Lean

Before leading your teams through this profound change in the way they work, you'll need to know why you want to change, who your allies are, who to talk to, and what you need to say.

A JOURNEY FOR SEVERAL PEOPLE

> *Just as there is no Lean without reason, there is no Lean without people.*

What's the Vision?

First off, you need to know *why* you want to go on this journey into Lean in the first place. It certainly is a different way of working, but it is not an end in itself. So ask yourself this: what is the vision of your company, team, or department when it comes to engineering? We're not talking about methods, or process, or being 'best in class' here. Instead, we're trying to get a sense of what is at stake in your business: and then to help each employee understand their mission, and do a better job – one that lives up to the expectations of your customers and delivers a product that is truly great.

DOI: 10.4324/9781003381945-3

Who Are Your Allies?

Depending on your own area of influence and your room for manoeuvre, you will need to find allies. If you are an executive, who are the key players in your management team? If you run a team or department, who is the manager who will give you 100% support? Which team members will help you identify what to learn? If you are in a support function, what is the scope of your role? What are the means at your disposal? What are your priorities? Asking these questions across your groups or teams can open doors to some rich and exciting discussions.

How to Talk About It?

You also need to think about how to communicate your project to the people involved. The idea of moving to Lean will probably not be enough, by itself, to get your teams energised and enthusiastic. What matters is how you share your own vision: how you explain the *why*. You'll have dozens of conversations about issues, choices, and methods, as well as more everyday communication about what's going on in the field. A two-way flow of information is essential, and a collaborative tool (wiki or equivalent) could get you a large audience for your own communication, as well as allow everyone to share their experiences and ideas. You, of course, will need to be fully engaged in this process. And the emergence of an active community to share feedback on new practices is a sign that you're on the right track.

The basic requirement is to provide an environment that allows the team to collaborate effectively. This often boils down to simply finding a room with walls to post visuals (refer to *Obeya*).

HOW TO BUDGET?

As with any journey, you must plan your budget.

How Much Time Is Needed to Get Started?

For the best chance of getting off to a good start, choose a pilot project which involves teams in the same location. It is way more difficult to learn a new way of working collectively when people are not working alongside each other. When it comes to collaboration tools for remote teams – the COVID-19 pandemic has forced many organisations to increase the portion of remote work – beware of locking yourself into a solution that ultimately won't fit with your new way of working – and could be costly too.

Lean is not about doing more: it's about doing better. However, before you get better, you first need to get started – and allow yourself enough time to do so. If you're already working around the clock to hit a tight deadline, you may feel there is no time to do anything new. Conversely, if you do nothing new, you will get nothing new in return. Doing something new can be painful. And it takes time. How much time?

- You need time to get your teams moving from 'firefighter mode' to what we call 'farmer mode': implementing new practices, learning how to solve problems as they arise, and planning frequent and regular sync points between team members. To get this going, you will need to identify which tasks or activities can be cut back, or even eliminated, and reallocate the time for making improvements. Take meetings, for example. How many people regularly go to meetings just to show up? How long do these meetings last?
- You will also need time to invest in supporting learning. This usually means assigning a Lean coach to help everyone else engage in new learning. Obviously, the workload depends on the size of the project. But the key here is that this investment is not just about the success of the project. It is an investment to help the entire organisation learn over the long term.

Return on Investment

Lean is about competitiveness. So your Lean project must be able to demonstrate a positive return. There are three pitfalls to watch out for:

1. Don't try to quantify a return for every single action within your Lean project. What do your new visual management and collaborative working sessions, for example, bring you in the short term? These two practices teach teams to identify problems and resolve them together. The gain is twofold: in the medium term problems will be solved early enough, and in the longer term the team will be more reactive and creative in solving the problems to come.

2. Don't ask teams to make direct financial gains. You are aiming to develop knowledge that will allow you – later – to achieve the best product at the best cost. Think about all those product developments that were cut for cost reasons, but led eventually to higher production or maintenance costs. Teams, then, need to be mobilised not on cost-cutting, but on improving operational performance, which in turn will have an impact on the bottom line. If you do it this way, the team's efforts will have a *lasting* financial impact through improved performance. And the risk of short-term cost-cutting actions will be reduced.

3. Don't confuse different kinds of gains. A boost in orders due to product improvement is not measured in the same way as recurring cost reductions. You'll need to account for all kinds of gains, but avoid mixing them up: they won't all sit in the same column of an income statement. Remember also to include gains that accrue over the long term (and that contribute to sustainable profitability). It's not just a story about this year's accounts.

The most important thing, to begin with, is to demonstrate on your pilot project which performance has been improved, and what learning has been achieved – including from your possible failures. Soon enough, with the continuous improvement process in place, you will see increasingly clear and lasting results.

HOW TO GET HELP?

> *Lean is a learning system. Two guides to make it yours, the* **sensei** *and the Lean coach.*

Your Tour Guide: The *sensei*

When you go on vacation to visit somewhere new, what kind of guide do you prefer? Is it a traditional guidebook, or maybe a travel app, or how about a real-life human tour guide? If you go for the latter option, you'll end up paying more, but you could also get to discover more – the hidden gems, the off-the-beaten-track places which make your journey truly memorable. Of course, you could end up with a phony, incompetent, or simply unimaginative guide, and what you thought was a tour of an artisan craft workshop turns out to be just another dodgy souvenir store. The problem here is how to distinguish that rarity of a great tour guide from all the mediocre guides pitching for your business – because it's only at the end of the tour that you can know if it was worth it or not.

This exceptional guide – the *sensei* – is primarily intended for those who have decided to start this journey, i.e., the (executive) managers. Their mission is to create the conditions for the emergence of a culture of continuous improvement, particularly through the development of your collaborators. One of these conditions is to make you, as a manager, a Lean leader.

This evolution (transformation?) will require changes in your managerial practices, awareness, and greater cognitive effort. To do this, the *sensei* will help you sharpen your focus to better detect the signals that count – until now made invisible by your observation bias. They will question to make you aware of your preconceived ideas, your cognitive biases, and misjudgements. You will be pushed to rethink your habits and attitudes, which are particularly determining at the decision-making level. For example, repeated *Genba Walks* will help you better observe situational cues and understand the factors that are preventing you from achieving your objectives. With this concrete first-hand knowledge, you will be better able to adjust your decisions and lead improvement initiatives. In short, a *sensei* will teach you how to lead with Lean thinking so that you can in turn teach it to your collaborators (5).

To successfully make you a Lean leader, the *sensei* must have a perfect mastery of Lean principles, methods, practices, and tools, and successful experience of their implementation in many different concrete cases – linking Lean principles and practices. It also requires a thorough understanding of engineering disciplines and processes.

Local Support: The Lean Coach

The word 'coach', a buzzword, is polysemous and therefore subject to ambiguity. To avoid misinterpretation, we use it in a sporting sense. The role of the coach is to train a person and/or a team on the field with appropriate exercises according to the skills and abilities of each person.

As an executive manager, you have decided to start a Lean journey in your company. You are accompanied by a *sensei*, that's good! But you need relays on the *genba* to accompany your teams on a daily basis. The workers should spend their time and energy first on product engineering and improvement, not on finding the right Lean practice by themselves. Having someone who knows the Lean principles, how and when to apply them, and which tools are best suited to solve a particular problem will keep teams new to Lean from unnecessary trials and errors.

A member of the team may well take on the role of coach. The advantage is to have a coach who knows the engineering, the products, and the environment. On the other hand, they will have to spend time training and mastering the elements that will facilitate proper coaching of the teams. In any case, it is always more valuable to have an engineer who trains in Lean to become a Lean coach than a Lean coach who trains in engineering.

CHANGE YOUR WAY OF THINKING

> *To be able to learn, you must let go of existing systems and habits and adopt an attitude of constructive doubt.*

A Lean initiative begins very close to home: it starts with your own way of thinking. Not only it is impossible to ask others to change the way they work if you don't change yours, but you won't be able to stay the course if your own way of thinking does not adapt too (see how the *sensei* can help you).

Don't Be Afraid to Drop Your Old Systems

The deepest challenge with Lean (and it's something many fail to achieve) is to stop believing that the solution to all your problems will come from systems, processes, methods, and plans. *When all the attention seems to be focused on the method, you have to ask yourself: what about the content?* Lean is not about setting up a 'problem management system', nor indeed a 'problem-solving system'. The aim of Lean is much more ambitious: to create a 'problem solvers development system'.

Doubt as the Key to Progress

Doubt means to not know, or to no longer know, what to think. Many of us are very uncomfortable with doubt – admitting that we don't know, or have let go of what we used to believe, or have changed our way of thinking.

One helpful method is to confront our beliefs with something external that is not affected by our thinking.[1] In other words, simply look at the facts. Facts are independent of our ideas. They are impartial and objective.

---

[1] See also Charles Sanders Peirce (1839–1914).

Based on facts, we can formulate questions, draw inferences, and run experiments. We can update our knowledge and establish new opinions.

When production deadlines are pressing, activities like observation, questioning, inference, and enquiry may feel like a waste of valuable time. But these represent valuable ways to learn – and to learn rapidly.

3

Before Travelling

Understanding some key definitions and vocabulary and learning something about culture and legends before travelling make you seem like less of an outsider and will create a more genuine travel experience.

CLARIFICATION OF KEY CONCEPTS

Words like value and waste, or engineering and production, seem so familiar that it may be surprising to consider that they can still be confusing. However, clarifying these different concepts will help you think about them more accurately.

Engineering and Production: Distinct but Interconnected

Of course engineering and production are different activities. But you shouldn't create a solid wall between the two. Throughout a product's life cycle, production and engineering are highly interconnected – and in no

DOI: 10.4324/9781003381945-4

way independent. The point of making a distinction here, however, is that the analytical tools required (and the kind of problems encountered) are often very different. Here's how:

1. **Value definition versus value provision.** While engineering strives to define and create value for the customers, production is organised to make this value available as a product. Fixed from the outset by the product definition, value is added gradually (each time the materials change physically), but the total amount of value added is unchanged by production activities. Moreover, the coordination and content of production activities are a direct consequence of the product definition. While engineering creates product value, it also designs the operational process needed to produce it (3). These are the 'operational value streams' made up of information and material flows. In other words, production is primarily focused on the efficient implementation of the right operational processes (Value Stream), while engineering is focused on defining and developing the right product: so the process is on one side and the product on the other. Of course, processes matter in engineering too, and products matter in production. However, applying the right engineering processes is no guarantee that engineers will create the expected level of value. Defining and developing the *wrong* product, even in a highly effective way, is the worst possible kind of waste in engineering.

2. **Variability versus regularity.** On a production line, tasks are repeated over several cycles. The shorter the cycle time,[1] the more frequent the repetition of the same work sequence. The objective is to limit, or even eliminate, the variability between repetitive tasks to ensure a more predictable process. Contrast this with engineering, where the objective is *not* to design the same element again. Although some activities can be repeated from one product to another, their content and duration will vary, especially in the upstream activities. This variability is partly caused by the diversity in the number and size of knowledge gaps that need to be filled to make the right engineering decisions. It's all about clarifying what you know and what you don't know about customer experience, engineering options, manufacturing processes, and the parts to be

---

[1] Cycle time is the fastest repeatable time in which you can produce one part.

purchased. Seeking to systematically and indiscriminately eliminate variations can lead to a resolution of certain problems too quickly, because it seems too time consuming, and thus a limitation of the acquisition of new knowledge.

3. **Immaterial versus tangible**. The focus of production (with the exception of software production) is on physical and visible elements that can be located in a given place at a given moment in a given quantity. With a trained eye, you can walk into a shop floor or production line and get an immediate sense of the process status and level of Work in Progress.[2] By watching team members at their station, you can even start to tell the necessary operations from wasteful ones. In engineering, however, what's being manipulated is mainly information, passing from human brains to hard drives without being visible. It is hard to know how much information is currently being created, is waiting to be used, is currently being used, or is missing. And it is much more tricky to distinguish essential activities from wasteful ones.

4. **Sequential versus parallel**. The coordination of production activities is sequential by nature. Since each item can exist in only one place at a time, there can be no parallel activities where the object is shared. Conversely, the very nature of information allows simultaneous sharing.

All these differences logically lead to a change in Lean methods, practices, and tools with respect to production and engineering. And that, essentially, is what this book is about.

Value and Waste

The notions of value and waste are very often the first things to be discussed at the start of a Lean journey. In the wrong hands, these can be dangerous concepts – providing cover for 'slash and burn' cost-cutting and short-sighted optimisation. But with the right approach, they will drive a sense of purpose through the entire project.

---

[2] Work in Progress (WIP): any activity started that has not yet been completed.

Some Definitions

Throughout this book, the term 'customer value' has a specific meaning. It is not a marketing term (e.g., *customer lifetime value*, which estimates the profit the company hopes to derive from its relationship with a customer). Rather, it refers to the profit received by a customer as a result of purchasing the product.

The central idea of Lean is often formulated as *maximising customer value while minimising waste.*[3] To get operators to understand the impact of this formula on their daily work, early Lean theorists[4] in the 1990s distinguished three types of activities in production operations:

1. Value-added activities;
2. Necessary non-value-added: to be reduced;
3. Unnecessary non-value-added: to be eliminated.

In this classification, the concept of 'value added' represents 'what the customer would be willing to pay for'. But the notion of *'necessary non-value-added'* is highly problematic, lumping together all kinds of essential and valuable functions: support services, physical and financial infrastructure, and even R&D, not to mention the expectations and objectives of company, partners, sub-contractors, and also society and its representatives such as governments, certification agencies, financial organisations, and more. The inference is that the customer would not be willing to pay for any of this.

Consider, for example, a company's R&D activities. Do they really bring no added value on the basis that a customer would not be willing to pay for the very activities that helped bring the product to life? Of course not.

Similarly, are all the company's support functions failing to provide any added value? A support function should facilitate value creation by ensuring, for example, that the working conditions (in the broadest sense of the term) of those responsible for creating it are the best they can be. It is not the support function itself, but the excess bureaucracy it may generate that destroys value. Conversely, in a bid to save money, support functions face budget cuts, and can then no longer provide the service

---

[3] Definition proposed by the Lean Enterprise Institute.
[4] James P. Womack and Daniel T. Jones. (1996). *Lean Thinking: Banish Waste and Create Wealth in Your Corporation.* Productivity Press.

levels required. As a result, engineering working conditions deteriorate, leading to delays and quality problems.

Here's another example. Environmental compliance activities do not bring direct value to the customer, but by helping protect natural resources, they create long-term value for society. While a minority of clients are already willing to pay for these activities, the majority see no value in them. They are not yet ready, for the moment, to 'pay more to protect more'. So you need to consider the whole system, and not just the paying customer, to determine which are the so-called 'value-added' activities.

The central idea of Lean in Engineering can, therefore, be reformulated as follows: *maximising value creation while minimising waste for the entire system*. And we choose to distinguish two categories of activities:

- **Necessary activities**: everything that contributes to creating value for the system as a whole.
- **Non-necessary activities**[5] or **waste**[6]: anything that can be reduced or eliminated without negatively affecting value creation for the system as a whole.

Value in Engineering

Information or Knowledge?

Knowledge is often considered as a commodity or material to be managed. Thus, 'knowledge management' would make it possible to create, detect, organise, capture, share, and reuse knowledge within an organisation. This set of processes is essentially nothing more than a fancy way of describing *information management* – and they tend to enrich the providers who sell them more than the organisations that use them! Information management has its uses, of course. But let's be clear: it's about information, not knowledge.

Information is data (or a set of data) organised and placed in a context to give its meaning. Data is the raw material of information. The function of *information management* (rather than *knowledge management*) is, as you would expect, to manage information. Its main added value is to allow access to the right information at the right time in the right format and with the right level of quality.

---

[5] http://michelbaudin.com/2013/05/27/absence-of-value-added-in-the-tps-literature/.
[6] By the way, this is the translation of the Japanese word *muda*.

Information becomes knowledge once it is processed by us – by we human beings – enabling individuals to act differently as a result. Knowledge can be observed through actions (procedural knowledge) or through words (declarative knowledge).

While knowledge relates to thought processes,[7] information does not. Knowledge is therefore not an object that can be managed like information. If you think of knowledge as an object independent of a thinking subject, then you tend to prioritise investment in technical solutions. Conversely, if you think of it firstly as an individual capacity, you prioritise investment in people first.

Thus, if *knowledge management* exists in any form, the primary focus needs to be on people's development. In this book, you will find us talking more about a learning system than about a knowledge management system.

Information: The Material of Creation

In upstream engineering activities, it is information (rather than components of products) that gets passed on between activities – and therefore between engineers. Each engineer can be seen as a 'knowledge node' of an information network. They combine the information received (or pulled from the information management system) with their own knowledge. They act accordingly and in turn transmit new information to the next node (and potentially share this with the information management system). The value created by each action and carried forward by the information transmitted depends on two things: the *information* received, and the *knowledge* added.

Thus, a 'necessary' activity (i.e., one that creates value) is one that produces useful and rapidly (re)usable information at the right time and in the right place. It is useful because it helps create knowledge among engineers, enabling them to design and develop the right product. And it is (re)usable because it is captured in a format that allows it to be used effortlessly.

---

[7] K. Popper controversially developed the concept of objectivity to argue that (scientific) knowledge, in its full *objective sense*, is knowledge without a knowing subject. From Popper's point of view, our definition of knowledge would then relate to the *subjective sense* of knowledge. However, even in the *objective sense*, knowledge consists of *thought contents* – K.R. Popper. (1968). 'Epistemology without a Knowing Subject'. *Logic, Methodology and Philosophy of Science III*, 52, 333–373.

To maximise value created, engineering must therefore maximise how it creates useful and reusable information, and accelerate its dissemination at the right time and in the right place.

Waste in Engineering

If you ask engineers to identify the main sources of waste in their activities, they will point to unproductive meetings, email overflow, excessive documentation, unnecessary reports, incompatible tools, and so on. What do these all have in common? They are the most *visible* part of waste associated with engineering. But to see beyond this visible stuff, you need a more precise idea of what you are looking for.

Several authors have tried to classify engineering waste according to the seven *muda* model defined by Taiichi Ohno.[8] Some go as far as adding an eighth *muda*: unused talent. Remember that Ohno produced this list to help recognise waste on production lines. It is tempting to use these *muda* to find their engineering equivalents, but this is a bit of a distraction.

The primary objective of engineering is to design and develop good products that will solve customers' problems without creating new ones. The most severe waste in engineering undermines this objective and can be found in two distinct places:

- **On the customer side**: when the product does not meet expectations; when it leads to a bad user experience; when it fails to deliver the expected value; or when its total cost of ownership is too high.
- **On the company side**: in operational processes (manufacturing installation, maintenance) when the product does not correspond to the company's technical, industrial, or service capacities; when it leads to a bad experience for operators, installers, or repairers; when it generates additional costs to deliver the expected value.

As Eric Ries, author of *The Lean Startup* (4) rightly points out: 'building a product nobody wants is the biggest source of waste'. Similarly, building a product that is too expensive to produce, install, maintain, or recycle is next on the list. If developing the right product is the primary goal, then doing it efficiently comes a close second.

---

[8] Taiichi Ohno. (1988). *Toyota Production System: Beyond Large-Scale Production*. Productivity Inc.

Developing the right product, and doing it the right way. So what gets in the way of this?

1. Lack of knowledge of customers, markets, or the company's internal processes. Engineers have made design decisions without having the necessary knowledge about customer expectations or company capacities. Allen Ward (3) calls this cause of waste *'wishful thinking'*, meaning engineers are deluding themselves about their ability to make the right decisions without having the knowledge to do so with confidence.
2. A disturbed or interrupted flow of information. Here again, Allen Ward identifies two major causes:
   - *Scatter*: the flow of information is disrupted by the organisation (through reorganisation, pressure, multi-tasking, multiplication of meetings, checkpoints, reports) or because of communication barriers (incompatibility between tools, geographical locations, misunderstandings between experts, lack of expertise to process information). The result is that information is dispersed, causing a scattering of activities and engineers.
   - *Hand-off*: the flow of information does not reach its target because of the silo effect and division of tasks (e.g., the person who decides is not the one who has the information). Information gets lost, arrives late, or is useless to the recipient.

From this, you can see that activities which impoverish, ignore, disrupt, or interrupt the flow of engineering information are major sources of waste for both customers and the company.

A major objective of Lean in engineering is, therefore, to continuously develop the ability of workers to identify, generate, and share the information and knowledge needed to make the best decisions – those that effectively solve customer problems without creating other problems, for customers, or for the company.

The Customer as a Co-creator of Value

We have already defined that the company, and in particular engineering activities, creates value in the form of a material good (the product) delivered to the customer in exchange for money. *In a more service-oriented vision, the customer creates value by using the product, rather than destroying value by consuming it.* The product then represents a store of *potential* value, a 'value proposition', and this value begins to emerge as the product is used (the so-called 'customer experience'). The customer, in turn, becomes a creator of value through their 'consumption'. Value is thus co-created in the interaction between the customer and the company, via its product. To take this thought even further, the authors of *Cradle to Cradle*[9] suggest that recycling the product creates a new resource and that the creation of value thus extends even further than is described by the co-creation model.

In the case of services, the product disappears behind the services it supports. Customers no longer buy the product (which remains with the service provider) but the service. *The company becomes a provider of services conveyed by its product (and potentially by another's product!).* This model, which was initiated in the field of IT and software services (for example, Software as a Service (SaaS), or Infrastructure as a Service (IaaS)) can be extended to many other areas. Some armed forces purchase radar surveillance services without owning the radar, which is of particular interest to organisations that do not want to invest in infrastructure that is too expensive to buy and maintain. They can then transform CAPEX (Capital Expenditure) into OPEX (Operational Expenditure).

To get the maximum benefit from services generated by the use of its products, a company needs to design, develop, and manufacture high-quality products while maintaining low life-cycle costs. In this new business model, all direct and indirect expenses related to the product's life cycle are now borne by the company – not by the costumer.

This broader view of value creation is not always easy for engineers to grasp. Beyond the value created by the product itself, they need to find solutions that enable customers, in turn, to create value by providing additional resources in the form of 'value-added' services. In this case, the customer is willing to exchange money for knowledge, skill, and availability of qualified people. It will use and/or integrate these new resources directly with its own resources to create value.

---

[9] William McDonough and Michael Braungart. (2011). *Cradle to Cradle, Créer et recycler à l'infini.* Editions Gallimard collection Alternatives.

Controlling and improving services is a differentiating factor in relation to competitors, but also decisive in increasing the value that can potentially be captured by the company (i.e., profit).

LEAN IN ENGINEERING: A MATTER OF TRADE-OFFS

As we saw in the previous section, the main task of engineering is to define, design, and develop the best product, i.e., the one that is best suited to the needs of the customers. This means it has to do three things:

1. Fully satisfy customers (bring value to them);
2. Achieve the objectives set by the company (bring value to it);
3. Be compatible with the company's technical, industrial, or service capacities and capabilities.

This sounds simple enough, but is usually a real challenge: how to identify the option that provides the best trade-off between these three perspectives?

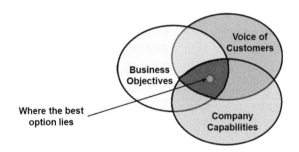

FIGURE 3.1

Trade-offs between needs, objectives, and capabilities.

Throughout this book (and especially in Part Two), you will see how trade-offs impact, in one way or another, every engineer who is faced with a design decision. *Ultimately, most of the big challenges encountered with Lean in engineering come down to a question of trade-offs.*

VOCABULARY: SOME ESSENTIAL WORDS

To really understand Lean in Engineering, let's revisit some of the underlying Lean principles. Here's a chance to brush up on some keywords and definitions.

A Word about Words: Learning and Keeping the Original Terminology

The power of language is enormous. Working in an international environment often allows us to realise that the language we use can actually influence how we think. If a word is vague and ill-defined, then the concept it is being used to express will also be vague and ill-defined. That's why we chose to keep some words in Japanese (or German) rather than proposing a direct translation into English which might not fully communicate the nuances of the original words.

Challenge

The challenge for every employee in a Lean company is to commit to improving every day, that is, to question what they know or think they know, to look for new ways to do their work, and to experiment with new ideas. The challenge is to make the effort to improve beyond the satisfaction of what has already been accomplished. There is no *kaizen* without challenging what one knows and does. However, in order for people to always have the desire to do better, they must feel supported and helped in their initiatives, and their efforts must always be valued. Thus, there is no challenge possible without respect for people.

Customer

The word *customer* is used in this book to identify the end user and/or payer for your product. There may be different customers for the same product (e.g., for a toy, we can identify a child and their parents), and all these customers may have rather different motivations. In all cases, neither the end user nor the intermediate customers should be forgotten.

Flow

Flow represents the steady and continuous movement of elements (e.g., physical and non-material parts for a product) through successive stages in the direction of the value stream (such as design, development, production, and service) in a size that can be handled easily. We can then say that successive processes have become a product's flow when the various factors that inhibit or disturb the movement of information and items have been reduced, even eliminated.

Genba

Genba[10] and *genchi genbutsu* (often translated as *go and see*) are the subjects of much discussion. *Genba* is the place where things happen or work is done. It can thus refer to a lab, design office, shop floor, or the place where the customer uses products. *Genchi genbutsu* is related to problem-solving. *Genchi* is the exact location where the problem occurred, and where you can learn about the *genbutsu* (specific item or component) and any other 'real' elements that may have contributed to the occurrence of the problem.[11]

Genba Walk describes going to the 'actual' place where things happen to observe, question, and understand. This is one of the most fundamental and powerful concepts of Lean because many things follow on from this. It is also probably the easiest to explain, but among the most difficult to apply. Management through *genba* thus consists of systematically and regularly 'stepping out into the field (*on site*), seeing for yourself (*hands on*) and grasping what is happening to render sound business judgements and to adapt your approach and decisions to real-world circumstances (*in touch*)'.[12]

---

[10] The sound '*m*' does not exist in Japanese. Since the Kanji *Gen*, meaning 'real', 'actual' is in front of a *b*, Westerners replaced the *n* with an *m* in *gemba*.

[11] https://michelbaudin.com/2015/09/19/gemba-and-genchi-genbutsu/#more-1152684.

[12] Philosophy / Vision | About Us | Toyota Tsusho (toyota-tsusho.com).

Jidoka

Jidoka is often summed up as 'stopping at the first defect'. Indeed, the later a defect is detected, the more expensive it will be to fix. So you need to detect and fix anomalies as early as possible. However, as you might guess, *jidoka* is a little more sophisticated than that! Let's take a look at its *Kanji*.

JI - all alone, automatically   **DO** - move   KA - action of making something

FIGURE 3.2
Kanji of the word *jidoka*

'*Ji*' means 'all alone, automatically' and '*Do*' means 'move'. The simplest translation is therefore 'something that moves by itself'. Toyota has changed the second *kanji* from 'move' (動) to 'work' (働), by adding the radical 人 (in red in the figure) representing the 'human'. It changes its meaning to 'transformation into something that *works* by itself'.[13] The term *jidoka* therefore refers not simply to 'supervised automation', but has more a sense of 'automation with a human touch'. This meaning is sometimes translated by the neologism 'autonomation', a mixture of autonomy and automation. In concrete terms, each time the machine detects an anomaly, it stops and alerts an operator who is now available to analyse the causes of this stop. *With jidoka, the human–machine interaction is at the service of the human–product interaction.* It is a kind of 'smart automation'.

Achieving *jidoka* requires people working by hand to continuously improve a machine's mechanism to make it simpler, more flexible, and cheaper to maintain. As Toyota explains,[14] 'The work done by hand in this process is the bedrock of engineering skill. Machines and robots do not

---

[13] http://michelbaudin.com/2011/11/17/lets-talk-about-automationautonomation/ and https://www.linkedin.com/pulse/re-translating-lean-from-its-origin-jun-nakamuro?trk=hp-feed-article-title-comment.

[14] https://global.toyota/en/company/vision-and-philosophy/production-system/.

think for themselves or evolve on their own. Rather, they evolve as we transfer our skills and craftsmanship to them'.

However, anomaly detection should not rely exclusively on machines. People must be also able to detect anomalies, namely anything they judge as a deviation between the current situation and the expected situation. *Jidoka*, in the same way as it applies to machines, can also apply to people who can stop the line each time they suspect an anomaly, and signal it with the *andon* (signal which notifies abnormalities and highlights where action is required).

In both cases, the alert must be raised, either through a decision integrated within the machine, or through a decision made by the individual, as soon as an anomaly is detected, leading to a possible interruption to the flow.

What does *jidoka* mean for engineering?

In engineering, we find these two modes of application of *jidoka* according to the nature of the manipulated artefacts: intangible like data, information or knowledge, or tangible like software.

Upstream, artefacts are rather intangible. Indeed, you have to set out everything you need to know about your customers, competitors, and markets before you can set about defining an optimum solution. And you also need to know your own capacities: will you be able to design, develop, produce, install, maintain, and distribute the envisaged solution at the target cost? Doing this will help establish the 'known knowns' and 'known unknowns': in other words, identifying 'knowledge gaps' and closing them as needed.

A knowledge gap is thus the distance between the knowledge you already have, and the knowledge you need to secure your engineering decision-making. Without such knowledge, you cannot make decisions with confidence – or put a different way, without risk.

Let's call having this necessary knowledge an 'OK' situation. We can then describe 'not having the necessary knowledge' as 'not OK' ('NOK'). So here's how *jidoka* can apply to engineering: every engineer[15] has the criteria to autonomously detect a NOK situation – and stop the flow if necessary.

---

[15] This is the 'manual' version of the *jidoka*, since detection and alerting are originally performed by the machine to free up supervision time ('mechanical' *jidoka*).

Since it is information, rather than knowledge, that circulates, *jidoka* aims to detect the point where the information available is insufficient (or erroneous) to make risk-free decisions. Once alerted, the engineer considers if they can decide on the spot, or if they need additional or better quality information. Having a visual representation, showing the exact information requirements at any given point in time, helps to ensure this mechanism will work. We go into the details of such visuals in Part Two.

On more tangible artefacts, such as software, engineers can automate the integration and detection of anomalies with each modification in code, in effect creating an NOK integration test.[16] This detection can be combined with an *andon* type of light signal.

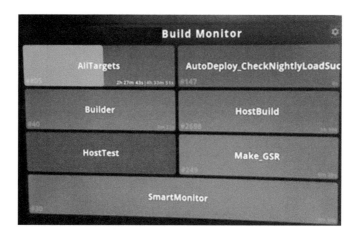

FIGURE 3.3
Continuous software integration andon

The same goes for code quality control, for example, with SonarQube,[17] provided that this automatic quality measurement immediately leads to an improvement action, and not just to an increase in technical debt! Many teams practising continuous integration find that they have set up *jidoka* without knowing it.

---

[16] For example, Jenkins is a tool for continuous software integration.
[17] SonarQube (formerly Sonar) is an open source software for continuous source code quality measurement.

Just-in-Time

If we were talking about road traffic, rather than product development, then we could think of Just-in-Time as relying on a set of practices aimed at eliminating everything that creates congestion. What causes congestion during peak hours?

- Firstly, more cars than usual are trying to take the same road, which is saturated. In this case, the best way to avoid the traffic jam is to limit the number of cars to the road capacity by delaying departure: initiatives such as congestion charging which encourage drivers to use the roads at off-peak hours.
- Secondly, anything that stops traffic can cause traffic jams, whether predictable (e.g., tolls) or not (e.g., accidents), which will create and amplify delays. Non-stop payment systems on toll roads help mitigate predictable stoppages.
- And thirdly, the irregularity of the distance between cars plays a crucial role. Simply put, a line of cars on a highway does not behave like a train. Instead, the gaps between each vehicle compress and expand like an accordion. Experiments[18] have shown how cars running in a single file at almost constant speed end up desynchronising – and cause traffic jams. To reduce this factor, we have to get cars more in sync with each other, over shorter stretches of road.

Just-in-Time is therefore about putting an end to these disturbances in the production process. First of all by smoothing, which means analysing the process's capacity and controlling the number of parts joining the process. Then, getting parts to circulate in the most fluid way possible, without unnecessary movements and without stopping. Next, use 'pull-flow' to synchronise the relative movements of all parts, starting with those leaving the process (i.e., those closest to the customer). So, Just-in-Time includes all the practices needed to eliminate flow disturbances and ensure smooth traffic.

---

[18] Traffic Jam without bottleneck – experimental evidence – YouTube.

A Clarification of the 'Pull' Principle

In Lean, 'Pull' commonly means that everyone responds directly to the demands of one's immediate downstream recipient in the flow, producing as required by the *final* recipient, i.e., the customer. Thus, the entire flow is pulled by the customer's requests. However, a key requirement for doing this effectively is to limit the Work in Progress (WIP). Contrast this with a 'Push' principle, where everyone produces 'what they have to do' as soon as they can and without any explicit limit, creating large amounts of inventory, congestion, and waiting time.

Did You Know That?

As early as the 1910s, Henri Ford introduced a number of elements of Just-in-Time that would partly inspire Toyota's managers.

We have found in buying materials that it is not worthwhile to buy for other than immediate needs. We buy only enough to fit into the plan of production, taking into consideration the state of transportation at the time. If transportation were perfect and an even flow of materials could be assured, it would not be necessary to carry any stock whatsoever. The carloads of raw materials would arrive on schedule and in the planned order and amounts, and go from the railway cars into production. That would save a great deal of money, for it would give a very rapid turnover and thus decrease the amount of money tied up in materials. With bad transportation one has to carry larger stocks.[19]

Jidoka, Just-in-Time, Two Sides of the Same Coin

Just-in-Time and *jidoka* are inseparable, which is why they are presented as the two pillars of the 'house' that represents the Toyota Production System (TPS). Just-in-Time establishes the flow, and *jidoka* stops it in case of anomalies. While these principles seem like opposites, they are complementary to each other, producing more and better elements.[20]

---

[19] Extract from H. Ford. (1922). *My Life and Work*. Book Jungle.
[20] https://www.allaboutlean.com/jidoka-2/.

Kaizen

Kaizen represents the essence of Lean, though its meaning is often misinterpreted. Again, let's start by looking at how the word is formed. *Kaizen* is represented by two *kanji* often translated as 'change' (*Kai*) for the 'better' (*Zen*), and adapted into 'continuous improvement'.

改善

FIGURE 3.4
*Kanji*s of the word *kaizen*

However, translations of the word have introduced some damaging misinterpretations of effective implementation. The idea of 'continuous improvement' emphasises what Jun Nakamuro[21] calls 'the physical improvement of processes, machines and technologies', for which he uses the term *kairyo* instead. According to him, '*Kaizen* is more personal, and it occurs within your own mind. *Kaizen* could be better translated as *continuous self-development*'. In other words, everyone develops and changes the way they think and do things by continuously challenging it – a concept that goes far beyond our usual understanding of the term. To achieve this *continuous self-development*, these conditions are necessary:

- *Kaizen* deals with problems that need to be solved by those who create these new gaps in order to improve the situation, because it is those who do the work who are best placed to improve it;
- Therefore, *kaizen* is practised by everyone, every day;
- To do this, *kaizen* does not require large investments by privileging the rapid testing of simple ideas (rapid PDCA loops).

Kaizen can be seen as a training (in the sporting sense) for everyone to boost their problem-solving skills and develop more critical thinking. Managers must thus be taught that their role is also to train their employees. Therefore, the greatest benefit of *kaizen* is not in the

---

[21] *Kaizen*: Lost in translation – Re-Translating Lean from Its Origin (https://www.linkedin.com/pulse/re-translating-lean-from-its-origin-jun-nakamuro).

short-term efficiency gains by implementing one-off improvements, but in having more critical thinkers ready to challenge today's situation to make it better tomorrow. In this sense, continuous improvement is rather the result of *kaizen*.

From Zen to Kaizen: Something to Meditate on

The *Zen* of *kaizen* has nothing to do with the *Zen* of meditation. The character for *Zen* in *Kaizen* is 善 (which can also be written 譱) and was originally written with the character 羊 (sheep) and the character 誩 (or 譱).

- The sheep 羊 was viewed positively and could represent justice.
- The character 誩 combines the character 言 (word, speak) twice, meaning debate or argument between two persons.

The resulting 善 for *Zen* can thus be interpreted as the ability to distinguish truth from falsehood in an argument between two people. This is seen as a virtue (see Keekok Lee. *Warp and Weft, Chinese Language and Culture*) and helps us to understand why *Kaizen* is seen as a human quality rather than something to do with a process.

There is another explanation of this Kanji *Zen* given in various writings. *Zen* is described as consisting of two characters, the sheep (which we agree with) and the altar of sacrifice. They conclude that *Zen* refers to the necessity of sacrifice to become good.

We think this is incorrect, because of a confusion of 善 with 禅, which is also pronounced Zen, but which has the other *Zen* meaning: meditation. The Kanji for the *Zen* of meditation contains 示 (means altar), but is not connected with the *Zen* of *Kaizen*.

Lean

The word *Lean* was first used by John Krafcik[22] in 1988 to describe the Toyota Production System (TPS) in contrast to a 'buffered' production system. Although the TPS has been constantly evolving to improve its efficiency since its creation in 1947, Lean is supposed to be its generalisation to other contexts than car manufacturing at Toyota. Besides, the word *Lean* is seldom used at Toyota!

---

[22] MITSloan.pdf (lean.org).

Never translated into any other language than English, *Lean* is a truly international concept. In its literal sense, we could think of the words 'slim' or 'slender'. However, the image of the athlete who trains hard to get in shape for competitions is perhaps a better image, whether they are 'slim' distance runners or 'bulky' weight lifters or shot-putters.

We can represent the Lean system as follows (2).

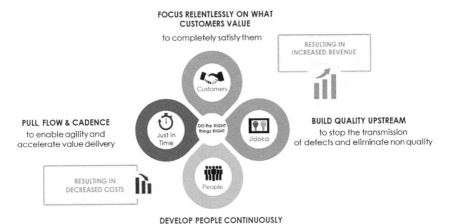

FIGURE 3.5
The Lean system

1. *Make the right product* to fully satisfy customers and increase revenue:

   The company must allow everyone to understand what creates real value for customers and more generally, for stakeholders. The objective is to build customer loyalty through a constantly updated understanding of the problems that customers want to solve by using your products, and the factors that will create the famous 'wow' effect that will bring them back.

2. *Do it right* to continuously eliminate wastes and decrease costs.

   The combined application of Just-in-Time and *jidoka* exerts a tension on the flow to reveal the problems to be solved which slow it down and, day after day, degrade the company's performance.

3. *Make it happen and sustain it* by continuously developing people. This is made possible by respecting people's thinking, training each of them to deal with the problems revealed within the flow and challenge the current situation to propose continuous improvements. Thus, each problem is seen as an opportunity to learn, develop critical thinking, and teach each other. The result is greater agility, allowing the company to cope better with an uncertain, complex, and ambiguous environment.

Lean represents a complete system, and it really is impossible to choose one element over all the others. Customer value is the 'magnetic north' of the Lean compass, and the development of people is the foundation of its sustainability. Just-in-Time establishes the flow, while *jidoka* can interrupt it, visually signalling problems to solve.

Levelling

Levelling out activities, and thus combatting unevenness in the volume of activity (*mura*), consists in limiting fluctuations and their effects between underutilising and overburdening resources (*muri*). For that, you need to work on two aspects:

1. Capacity levelling: by knowing and accurately characterising the available team's capacity, limit WIP (Work In Progress) so as not to go beyond that capacity.
2. Workload levelling: by constantly updating analysis of workload, balancing uneven workloads over time among people, and smoothing them as much as possible.

Muda, mura, muri

Muda[23] means waste, which is any activity you can stop doing without reducing your performance in any way. Taiichi Ohno has listed seven types of waste to help recognise them on the shop floor. *Muda* can be viewed as a set of symptoms of other phenomena known as *mura* and *muri*.

Mura means irregular, uneven. *Mura* exists when there are load variations over time and/or between team members at the same time. These variations

---

[23] More musings on 'Muda' (Waste) – Michel Baudin's Blog.

create oscillations between overload (*muri*) and underload. In engineering, the nature of activities is highly variable and their duration is quite unpredictable. For example, misjudging knowledge gaps or waiting for information creates *mura*. Another usual source of *mura* is the uneven customer demands. However, processes, organisations, or management styles are quite often the largest providers of *mura*: deciding too early, imposing the same processes whatever the nature of knowledge gaps, working in batch mode, assigning the same person to several tasks, adding or removing resources to a project, promoting incompatible tools, multiplying control points, rushing people to deliver, etc.

Muri Meaning from Kanji

Muri is represented by 無理. Mu (無) means 'empty', 'does not exist'. Ri (理) represents science or logic, and means 'correct way as a human.' Based on these symbols, the meaning of *muri* should be the following:

- No science or logic;
- Ignoring the correct way as human

(From Hide Oba, Five Ri 理 | https://www.linkedin.com/pulse/five-ri-%E7%90%86-hide-oba/).

Muri means overburdened, unreasonable, and unsustainable. Having *muri* in a process means that people and/or machines are overloaded. The consequences for individuals are expressed as fatigue, stress, and even accidents or burnout. In engineering, work overload is an evil too widespread. This is mainly the result of this widely shared misconception: high resource utilisation should increase performance. This excessive use of resources gets worse with a lack of multi-skilling, knowledge, and co-engineering. By overloading resources, the slightest variation quickly leads to unbearable overload.

Obeya

Strictly speaking, *obeya* is a Japanese word that means 'big room'.[24] The *obeya* is the virtual or physical place where all the representatives involved in the development of a new product come together to visually share what matters to move their project forward and act accordingly during collaborative sessions. The *obeya* acts as a visual hub facilitating exchanges, transparency, and multidisciplinary collaboration. Making work visible

---

[24] The word *obeya* is associated with three Kanji (大部屋) that signify big room.

allows everyone to orient themselves independently and all to move in the right direction, at all times. To do this, these visuals are updated regularly according to the team's progress. The *obeya* is indeed the right place where the managers go to understand engineering problems and observe how people collaborate (see *Genba Walk*).

PDCA: Plan Do Check Act

The American physicist, engineer, and statistician Walter Shewhart was a pioneer in statistical quality control, writing a ground-breaking book on the subject in 1939 in which he defined – in the form of an iterative cycle – the three steps '*specification, production* and *inspection* (which) correspond respectively to making a hypothesis, carrying out an experiment and testing the hypothesis. The three steps constitute a dynamic scientific process of acquiring knowledge'.[25]

Edward Deming, influenced by Walter Shewhart,[26] refined this cycle during his teaching in Japan as part of the Training Within Industry[27] programme in the 1950s.[28]

1. Plan a change;
2. Carry out the change, preferable on a small scale;
3. Observe the effects of the change;
4. Study the results – what did we learn? what can we predict?
5. Repeat 1. With accumulated knowledge;
6. Repeat 2.

It was later adapted by the Japanese into its current form of PDCA or *Plan Do Check Act* (PDCA is sometimes jokingly referred to as *Please Don't Change Anything!*), while Deming himself, in 1993, has a slightly different formulation: PDSA (*Plan Do Study Act*).

PDCA is applied in an iterative and recursive way, whether on caused or created problems. Thus, depending on whether the problem concerns

---

[25] Ronald Moen and Clifford Norman. (2009). *Evolution of the PDCA Cycle.*

[26] E. Deming became interested in Shewhart's work while working as an intern at the Western Electric Co. plant in Hawthorne, IL, during the summers of 1925 and 1926.

[27] TWI (Training Within Industry) was introduced to Japan by the Americans to help rebuild its industrial infrastructure after the Second World War.

[28] W.E. Deming. (2000). *Out the Crisis.* The MIT press, reprint edition.

a process or a product, a deviation caused or created, the PDCA loops should be adjusted accordingly.

For a process, the problem is usually determined in relation to a standard. If this standard does not exist, another loop, SDCA (*Standardise Do Check Act*), can precede PDCA to set it. SDCA is sometimes used to establish a standard when one is not yet established. The objective is to set the first baseline from which the problems caused and created can be characterised. This becomes the reference for improvement. Once done, PDCA loops are run to close the gap, either to get back to the standard or to improve it.

For a product, gaps are more likely to be expressed in terms of performance. As long as performance is not achieved, PDCA loops aim to close the gap by acting on the right design variables. In cases where performance is to be improved, PDCA loops aim to extend the design domain accessible to the right variables (refer to *CID*).

Here we present an overview of the steps well adapted to problems caused to products (refer to *A3 Problem Report* for more details).

- **PLAN** – there are three key perspectives:
  - The What:
    - State the problem in one sentence.
    - Define the current state and specify the target state to characterise the gap. Go to the *genba*, observe the facts, particularly the most surprising ones, and collect data (*genchi genbutsu*) to get a common understanding of the situation.
    - What additional data could be useful for you to better understand the current situation? Where and how could you obtain them?
    - Once you better understand the situation or need, challenge your problem statement. Do you need to reword it?
  - The Why and The How:
    - Formulate the root cause hypotheses in the form of an '*if-then*' statement. Each hypothesis is tested in short PDCA loops. It is important to master the test conditions and parameters for each new loop in order to remove any ambiguity about what works and what does not (see the ACT step hereafter).
    - Reject disproved hypotheses and keep those that explain the problem.

– After discussion and deliberation, choose the countermeasure that will fix the problem at the root.

FIGURE 3.6
Small PDCA loops in PLAN to test hypotheses

- **DO** – implement the countermeasure to fix the root cause. How long will it take to reach the target? Track your success and keep score.

    In the same spirit as the PLAN step, this DO step can include rapid PDCA loops, as it is often better to operate in small successive changes than in one larger one.

FIGURE 3.7
Small PDCA loops in DO to break the action into small steps

- **CHECK** – look at the effects of the countermeasure to see that it has worked as expected. Analyse the actual results and compare them to the prediction as a basis for learning. Capture reusable knowledge.

    In the context of a *Genba Walk*, CHECK might even come first since it is about checking the current situation on the *genba* to grasp the situation. So, first CHECK on the floor to identify gaps with respect to what you desired, and then ADJUST your approach using what you just learned. Use it to establish the right PLAN for the next PDCA loop.

- **ACT** – act upon what has been learned from the outcome of the previous steps. You have three options:
  1. *Adopt* when no significant value is anticipated through the execution of additional PDCA loops.
  2. *Adjust* when there are still things to accomplish via additional PDCA loops. Adjustment means changing what is just necessary to control the representativeness of the next PDCA loop.
  3. *Abandon* when you have taken a wrong turn. Look for the reason – go back to the root causes. Abandon means 'stop maintaining the current hypothesis and choose another one', not abandon PDCA as such.

Whatever the adjustments, the PDCA framework reflects the fact that learning occurs by moving between the domains of thinking and doing. The PDCA loops are the basis of learning cycles. They fill the gaps between what is known and what needs to be known to design the right product.

Dewey's Pattern of Inquiry

In *How We Think* (1910), John Dewey describes five phases looped of inquiry.

Phase 1: feeling difficulty. The difficulty is produced by the gap between the conditions at hand and the desired result.

Phase 2: locating and defining this difficulty. Through careful exploration and inspection of the indeterminate situation, this phase leads to a suspension of judgement, a condition for determining the real nature of the problem and thus preventing rushing to a conclusion.

Phase 3: suggesting a possible solution. The inquirer transforms mere inference into more testable inference from a thorough observation of the original problem. Inferring alternative suggestions encourages further search for more evidence. It is a factor of good thinking.

Phase 4: refining the suggestions through reasoning. Once the suggestions have been stated, the inquirer traces out all the consequences and derives specific experimental tests.

Phase 5: testing the suggestion for acceptance or rejection. Once the most likely solution has been adopted after reasoning, the tests should verify whether these theoretically predicted results actually occur. If it is found that the experimental results agree with the theoretical results and reasoning, the solution is confirmed at least until contrary facts require its revision

---

Problem

Problem is a generic word used to characterise a situation where there is a gap between reality and expectation. To put it another way, there is a gap between what we have – undesired state, and what we want – desired state. We can identify two ways of seeing this gap:

1. The undesired state is caused by a deviation from what we want.
2. The desired state is created by an improvement from what we have.

In the first case, the solution to the problem is to get back to the desired state by removing the causes of the deviation. In the second case, it is to go beyond the current state by creating the causes of an improvement – the reference from which to establish deviations or improvements deserves to be standardised.

Let us take the analogy of the high jump to illustrate these two cases. The regular level a jumper achieves is 2.00 m (see Figure 3.8). The series of actions she follows to systematically succeed in jumping at this height are combined to create her standard. Thus, every time she drops the bar, it is a deviation from her standard, either because she does not meet it (sub-optimal run-up, wrong body positioning, etc.) or because she faces a new problem. In the latter case, each new countermeasure she brings in will enrich the standard to make her jump more repeatable and thus more reliable at 2.00 m. It is then time to raise the bar a few centimetres, to challenge the current situation and to draw out further improvements. The jumper must therefore change her standard. At 2.05 m, she will have to correct new problems that she did not have at 2.00 m, and thus improve the standard accordingly. By changing the standard, she has thus created new gaps to be filled.

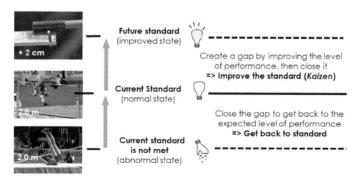

FIGURE 3.8
Caused problem versus created problem

The previous example illustrates process-related gaps. The standard is used to describe the best sequence of actions known today to achieve a given performance. Setting a new level of performance therefore requires the application of a new sequence, i.e., an improvement of the process standard.

When it comes to products, performance is the result of a sequence of design decisions. This sequence deserves to be standardised (see design checklist), as well as the information needed to make the right decisions (see trade-off curves). Thus, whether it is a matter of solving a problem to get back to the desired product performance or of closing a gap to obtain a better product performance, it amounts to rectifying design decisions, i.e., acting on the right design variables (see *CID*). In both cases, solving through PDCA loops is quite similar. It is about identifying variables, whether they cause a degradation or an improvement in product performance. Similarly, the skills expected in both cases are very similar because even to get back to the desired product performance, sometimes you have to propose something new.

Is every problem a gap from a standard? Not really. Not everything that is desired can be standardised. For example, the user experience of a product can be disappointing despite the product's compliance with requirements. In this case, there is a gap between reality and user expectation although no standard is directly concerned. Nevertheless, a problem always remains a deviation from a reference, whether it is formalised by a standard or simply corresponds to a performance or an expectation.

Whenever there is a problem, it is about getting to its root and asking the questions '*how ...?*' and '*why ...?*' rather than '*who did this?*' So go to the scene (*genchi*) to observe the facts and examine the real elements (*genbutsu*), not to find the culprit! Besides, this *hunt* for a culprit has two major drawbacks. First, it pushes people to hide their problems (to avoid getting caught) which prevent them from getting to the root. Secondly, it is all too easy for managers to pin the blame on a colleague (hence dodging any sense of responsibility themselves), and in total opposition to the concept of respect!

Respect

Here is a word that is not Japanese – but it is not without controversy over its meaning. In Lean, respect for people is a significant principle, going well beyond mere consideration for others. Here are some key points.

The first mark of *respect* is to consider that each of us has our own intelligence, and that the company will be better off if everyone has the opportunity to use this asset for further improvement. In other words, it is more profitable in the long term *not* to confine employees solely to an execution role, but to benefit from their ideas and intelligence. In the same vein, respecting people also means considering that everyone is well placed to improve their own work, better placed, in fact, than managers.

The second mark of respect is to stop looking for the guilty. If we combine the time spent looking for the guilty and the time spent by people justifying themselves, we can easily see the ineffectiveness of a punitive approach. If a company wants people to reveal problems and then learn how to solve them, the hunt for the guilty must be avoided. When there is no room for mistakes, there is no room for learning.

Respect for people also means working alongside them to do everything possible to simplify their daily work. What kind of work environment leads them to make mistakes? On the contrary, how can all the ambiguities that will inevitably lead people to make mistakes be removed? Beyond that, *respecting people means giving them the means to succeed every working day. Success is a right, not a duty!* Everyone has the right to do good work and to get good results; this lies at the heart of motivation. To allow everyone to have the pleasure of creating and contributing is *to respect everyone's humanity.*

Respect for humanity is the exact translation of the term used by Toyota. This means respecting the diverse capabilities and potential that each person inherently possesses. This is very different from being just polite![29]

---

[29] https://michelbaudin.com/2014/04/12/more-on-toyotas-respect-for-humanity/.

SBCE (Set-Based Concurrent Engineering)

SBCE is at the core of Lean Engineering. The objective is to define the accessible solutions space upfront and then continuously eliminate the weakest options until the best solution is found. In contrast, *Point-Based Concurrent Engineering* aims to select the solution as early as possible with the risk of having to rework it later.

Slow Build

As the name suggests, this expression means 'to build slowly' and covers the practice of assembling a prototype or pre-production equipment to observe all the manufacturing difficulties related to design decisions.

Standard

The word *standard* in Lean presents a minefield of misunderstandings, and we could devote an entire book to discussing standardised work, work standards, and all the ideas related to these concepts. Here, we will shed light on standards as they are understood within the framework of engineering.

The meaning of the word *standard* in Lean differs significantly from the typical dictionary definitions. It is not about being common and unoriginal (as in a standard piece of furniture), nor is it a norm (such as the ISO 9001 standard), nor a rule applicable to everyone (standards of decency), nor is it an example that everyone wants to copy (a jazz 'standard' played in a bar).

Standardisation, in Lean, is about making explicit, reliable and reusable what is already known, proven and often repeated, to guide actions and decisions while minimising waste, and thus producing more predictable outcomes. Therefore, deviations from a standard can prevent the achievement of expected performance, for example in terms of quality or cost. In this case, problem-solving aims to close the gap and get back to the standard. Conversely, to achieve a higher level of performance, the standard must be raised. And raising the bar also creates a gap that, this time, must be closed with new solutions. Thus, standards help to make a gap more explicit.

A standard needs to be established at the right level of the organisation, such as in a team or department. Hence, common sense is needed to know what should remain a local standard, which can then be managed flexibly, and which standards should be implemented more broadly. And while standards are not intended to be used beyond their area of application, it can be useful to share the learning that led to their establishment. In the TPS, this sharing of learning is called *yokoten* (meaning horizontal deployment), while the direct roll-out of standards via the Quality Management System (QMS) could be described as 'vertical deployment'. In addition, since a standard must be continually updated with each improvement, beware the red tape imposed by the QMS. Finally, a standard that is written in great detail can make it more difficult to apply properly.

Three types of engineering standards guide workers in performing a task or process (process standards), making design decisions (design standards), and developing new skills (engineering skill-set standards). They help avoid wasting energy 'reinventing the wheel' and maintain performance levels within defined limits (flexibility), while freeing up time to invent new solutions and respond to unpredictable changes (agility). However, not everything is standardised or standardisable in engineering. It is up to the experts and the functional management to identify which methods, practices, knowledge, and know-how are worth standardising.

Product Takt

Product Takt is the pace at which new products or new features are introduced to the market. In contrast, *Takt Time* is a time.

Teamwork

Teamwork can be seen as the foundation stone of the Lean system. The paradox of teamwork is that Lean is a development process for individuals. The challenge, therefore, focuses on the development of leadership as a condition for effective collaboration between individuals. Working with others is evidenced by defining, sharing, and applying standards.

Teamwork consists of developing individuals both in their 'business' expertise as well as in their ability to solve problems with people who are not necessarily from the same field of expertise. Marco Iansiti[30] represented this combination of competencies for an individual by the letter T. The vertical bar of the T is a representation of the individual's expertise in their specialty, while the horizontal bar shows their ability to interact with other fields of expertise, to foster the integration of diverse knowledge.

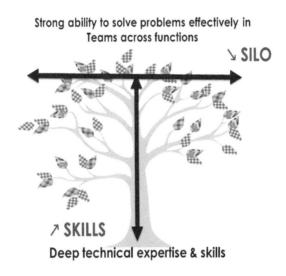

FIGURE 3.9
The T-shape

In this vision, the performance of a group – in other words, the quality of its *teamwork* – depends on the level of expertise of each member, as well as on their individual ability to combine this knowledge with that of others. If we consider that the development of versatility (i.e., having a second field of expertise) is also an important issue for successful teams, two letters 'TT' would probably be more suitable now than only one!

Teardown

Teardown is the practice of disassembling any object to observe and analyse its physical and functional architecture, technology, and manufacturing processes.

---

[30] Marco Iansiti. (May–June 1993). 'Real World R&D: Jumping the Product Generation Gap.' *Harvard Business Review*, 71, no. 3.

The Toyota Way

The Toyota Way defines the fundamental Toyota's values, expressed as guiding principles people should apply in every aspect of their day-to-day work. Some famous maxims illustrate the spirit embedded in the Toyota Way, whether the words of chairman Fujio Cho – 'first we build people, then we build cars', or the Toyota slogan – 'good thinking, good products'[31].

Trade-Off

Trade-off refers to a situation where two parameters are apparently in contradiction, and where favouring one is to the detriment of the other. Although closely related, the word 'compromise' refers rather to 'mutual concessions'. Rather than seeking a soft compromise, we prefer to take advantage of interactions between several antagonistic parameters: how much to relax on A to gain on B?

Exploring trade-offs also means identifying the limits of feasibility and understanding where to innovate. A battery, for example, can hardly be both powerful and small in volume, so the challenge of the electric car is to improve both parameters at the same time. The exploration of trade-offs, particularly in the form of trade-off curves, should enable you to respond to your challenge with innovative solutions – rather than with a failed compromise.

Visuals

The use of visuals is essential in Lean. Indeed, it is indispensable for the practical and concrete implementation of *kaizen* and teamwork. It is through visuals that each person knows in real time what is good (OK) or not good (NOK), and can react immediately accordingly. Visuals help remove the ambiguities at the source of errors and non-quality, and what's more, they even provide a source of thought and reflection for those who are compiling and creating them. We will return in more detail to this topic when we discuss the *obeya*.

---

[31] (TOYOTA MOTOR CORPORATION GLOBAL WEBSITE | 75 Years of TOYOTA | Current Conditions | Toyota Way 2001 (toyota-global.com)).

LOCAL CUSTOMS AND CULTURE

> *Several Lean principles widely applicable to any business have been defined to guide its implementation. However, applying them, like Toyota, with scientific thinking and the right toolkit, is no guarantee of success.*

Having run through these few words of vocabulary, you can get a strong sense that Lean has its own quite specific language. And alongside the language, it also has its own culture. Let's take a look at that next.

Is Lean a Philosophy?

Lean is an approach centred on the competitiveness of companies, so it seems difficult to think of it as a philosophy: the quest for competitiveness and profit is not generally thought about as some kind of path to wisdom and *eudemonia*.

Lean is based on a *human* vision of the company which places people's development at its core. But the focus is on developing people's critical thinking to solve practical problems and create knowledge about the challenges at hand – rather than questioning what it all means. Lean, unlike speculative philosophy, does not stray from the limits of what can be known and does not seek to understand all things by their ultimate causes.

And while Lean practitioners will be aiming to achieve a kind of personal perfection in their thinking and actions,[32] the purpose of Lean is to increase the company's profitability, rather than maximising one's own pleasure, or living in accordance with nature or some higher ideal.

Despite all this, Lean thinking still holds a singular place vis-à-vis other theories about labour and management in our industrial society. Over the centuries, industrialisation across the world has forced farmers and craftspeople, an already disciplined workforce, to work many hours a day

---

[32] Philosophers, especially those who have developed deep views in epistemology and logic, can be of great help to reason and learn more effectively day-to-day practice of Lean. We quote some of them: C.S. Peirce, J. Dewey, G. Bachelard, or K. Popper.

at monotonous and repetitive tasks. In absolute contrast to the concept of craftsmanship, mass industrialisation led to a dehumanisation of the act of producing: it became highly efficient in terms of productivity, but very costly in human terms. These repetitive factory jobs effectively dulled the minds of the workers engaged in them.

The Toyota Production System (TPS) can be seen as a truly radical departure from this apparently ineluctable trend. By turning its back on this division of labour, the TPS has contributed to the re-humanisation of work. It has allowed workers to re-appropriate craft skills and specialist tools, and to exercise their imagination. Rather than a philosophy, the TPS and its 'derivative', Lean, thus produced an alternative way of thinking and practising product development and industrial production.

Is Lean Scientific?

In the Lean community, it is a common belief that the TPS is founded on scientific thinking, and that PDCA is linked to the scientific method. It seems obvious enough: the TPS emerged from continuously solving practical problems observed on the *genba*, and it kept on evolving through many years of trials and errors, in effect, applying what common sense calls scientific method. However, while the TPS appears 'scientific', its aim was not to explain natural phenomena and establish theories about them, but to build cars in the most efficient way.

As we will see in the chapter *Sakichi and Kiichiro Toyoda: the continuous innovation*, the company's founder and his successors were engineers rather than scientists, using their intelligence and know-how to solve practical problems. When they closed knowledge gaps they did so with the intention of building looms, then cars, more efficiently, rather than pursuing knowledge for its own sake. They were looking not at theory, but at practical applications.

In this sense, the TPS feels closer to technical skills and engineering than it does to science. In other words, it is about the tools, methods, and know-how that are used to achieve a given purpose. Like science, it is based on empirically acquired knowledge though this knowledge is not necessarily scientific – in the sense that it is not experimentally tested to scientific standards.

It is appealing to think about Lean as a science, making it seem somehow more serious and rigorous. Yet the risk is then to see Lean as a theory with its own body of knowledge. Like many theories, it may seem elegant, but could turn out to be difficult to apply in the real world. Thinking about a Lean project as applying a theoretical approach to your company is the wrong way to go about it – and can come doomed to failure.

The vast body of Toyota's accumulated knowledge would seem to provide a head start for people starting a Lean journey. Yet of itself, all this is not enough. You also need to understand which parts of this existing knowledge apply to your own challenges, what specific knowledge is lacking, and how to use what you have learned to change the nature of our system (see below: Is *Lean* a One-Size-Fits-All Model?).

As the author of *The Toyota Way*, Jeffrey Liker puts it: 'Lean community should be more interested in using a scientific approach for improvement of actual systems, and less interested in building a body of knowledge of generalisations about which solutions solve which problems'.[33]

Lean, then, is not a scientific theory that you just have to apply to be successful. Its scientific dimension lies in the practice of Lean, with its constant back-and-forth between questioning facts and testing hypotheses to solve practical problems. This same 'scientific dimension' is found in any technique-based activity and is especially true of engineering.

Is Lean a One-Size-Fits-All Model?

Lean originates from the TPS, considered to be the best system to produce cars. However, it is a generalisation of the TPS, and as such, is not a system developed by a single company. But if Lean contains all the nuggets that make the TPS unique, how could other companies in other industries also benefit from Lean with the same success?

Lean takes strong and effective ideas from one industry and turns them into universal principles – but this does not mean the resulting Lean model is some kind of a 'one-size-fits-all' solution. It is thus down to each company to figure out how Lean thinking can help solve its own problems, and work towards continuously improving its system. In other words, to make the qualitative leap from the general to the specific.

---

[33] https://theleadershipnetwork.com/article/what-is-the-science-in-lean.

Is Lean Asking Questions or Giving Answers?

Questioning is the most powerful way to develop new knowledge,[34] and learning how to ask questions is the best way to develop critical thinking. Richard W. Paul,[35] a world reference in the study of critical thinking, proposes 'intellectual standards' to evaluate, by questioning, the quality of reasoning, and thus the presence or not of cognitive bias. We drew on his questions to produce our own list of questions and develop a deck of cards.

- *Clarity*: How could you clarify this point? How could you make this point more explicit?
- *Accuracy*: How could you check that? How could you test that? How do you know this is true?
- *Precision*: What precisely is the problem? What are the variables that could affect the problem? What details would make this point more precise?
- *Depth*: What factors make this a difficult problem? What are some of the complexities of this question? What are some of the difficulties you need to deal with?
- *Relevance*: How does this relate to the problem? What implication is there for the issue? How is this point connected to the question?
- *Perspective*: What would this look like from another angle? What objection could you make to your own point of view? What would someone who disagrees with your perspective say?
- *Logic*: How do these things make sense together? How does your thinking follow the evidence? What evidence do you have for that?
- *Importance*: What is the most significant information you need to address this issue? How is that point important in this context?
- *Honesty*: To what extent do you have any vested interest in this issue? How do you know that you are sympathetically representing the viewpoints of others? Why are you looking at this point this way?

Too often, the way a question is asked induces the answer. 'What's stopping you from doing your job properly?' obviously doesn't get the same reaction as 'Why are you doing this?', especially if the tone of the question is ironic

---

[34] 'All (scientific) knowledge is in response to a question' from the book: Gaston Bachelard. (2002). *The Formation of the Scientific Mind*. Clinamen Press Ltd.

[35] Richard Paul and Linda Edler. (2002). *Critical Thinking: Tools for Taking Charge of Your Professional and Personal Life*. FT Press.

or aggressive. So the sound of your voice and your non-verbal language have as strong an influence on the response as the words themselves. Your attitude is as important as your questions.

FIGURE 3.10
Critical thinking cards

As the French philosopher of science G. Bachelard wrote: 'Irrespective of what one might assume, (...), problems do not arise by themselves'.[36] So, the manager's mission (5) is to develop a sense of autonomy and critical thinking among their team members, and to do this, the manager needs to learn the art of questioning – (6) is a perfect illustration. It is not always easy, when working under pressure, to ask questions rather than give answers. *However, the learning is widely different in each case: potentially rich when you ask questions, and certainly poor when you just provide answers.*

---

[36] Ibid.

Is Lean a Toolbox?

This question is the subject of endless debate, and in fact we can say that it both is and it isn't!

It's not a toolbox: Lean uses a certain number of tools (and methods), which have been developed at different times and by different people. Their use depends on the type of industry, the type of function (such as production, engineering, or services), and, above all, the type of problems that need solving. Some of these 'tools', such as 5S, *kanban*, and Value Stream Mapping, are well known, so much so that their use is often equated with the implementation of Lean. This, however, is not the case. Just as using a hammer does not make you a carpenter, so using 'Lean tools' does not make your company a Lean company. It is not so much the tool itself, but learning how to use it (and practising to master it) that gives you a competitive edge in the long term.

It is a toolbox: If you are constructing a building, whether it is a detached house or an ultra-modern concert hall, you need something to support the work as it progresses: basically, you need scaffolding. However, if the scaffolding is not strong enough or does not match the building plans, the building won't happen. And if all your energy and know-how are used just to build the scaffolding, the building won't happen either. Scaffolding, as we can imagine, is never identical from one building to another, but even so, there are rules for scaffolding construction that are well known to contractors and architects.

The same reasoning applies when you want to use Lean methods and tools to design, develop, and manufacture great products: if the energy and creativity of your teams are being spent obsessing over the 'scaffolding' (the various Lean tools), then they are not being used to create or improve the product. So, yes, you need to respect Lean methods and tools which aim to develop everyone's learning. Talking about them, which in reality is a kind of procrastination – masking a refusal to learn or change.

Is Lean a Directive or Participatory Model?

It's both directive *and* participatory.

Lean encourages everyone to think and act on their own, rather than just a few experts and managers. In this sense, it is very much a participatory mode. However, this does not mean letting everyone go off in all directions.

In a piece of metal, there are electrons moving at all times, but as long as there is no difference in applied potential, there is no electric current, so there is no orderly movement. Similarly, teams must be given a vision and objectives so that the movement of each individual goes in the direction requested by the company. From this point of view, Lean *is* directive because it is asking managers to give this kind of direction.

So teams and individual autonomy can absolutely run alongside a rigorous and disciplined approach. But things only start to go wrong when one of these two dimensions is missing.

Is Lean a Visual Management?

In Lean, the visual is a privileged means of communication. It is also an easy way to share information, provided it is easy to read, easy to comment on, and not a source of stress. By stress (whether for an engineering team member or the customer), we mean anything that can lead people to avoid – or hate – using the information displayed. Above all else though, visuals must be meaningful, fact-based, and unambiguous. Irrelevant visuals can lead to errors and therefore non-quality, and may have negative effects on learning.

Respect and trust are closely linked. However, trust needs to be earned. Transparency is essential for trust, and the visual is the easiest way to instil transparency – because information is made visible and accessible to everyone at the same time. Visual management, then, is a simple way for managers to show respect for their teams, for example by highlighting problems, rather than acting as a means of exerting control. The visual is there to help people's learning and development – not to reassure managers that they are on top.

Setting up visual management means putting a wide range of visuals that everyone can see – or in other words 'making the walls speak'. Information displayed in this way should first get people thinking, and then (and only then) acting on it. So it's a matter of thinking first, then acting. This is what economist and psychologist D. Kahneman[37] calls *slow thinking*, which he contrasts with *fast thinking* (e.g., rule-of-thumb or intuitive thinking) which is strongly influenced by cognitive biases (when heuristics lead to inaccurate judgements).

---

[37] Daniel Kahneman. (2012). *Thinking, Fast and Slow*. Penguin.

With this in mind, you need to think about the initial effect that any visual will trigger on those who see it. If the visual display simply makes people want to work faster (acting without reflection), then it is missing the point.

A successful visual, then, is not just about taking data from your computer, creating a print-out, and sticking it on the wall. Rather, it is about considering which information will help people make decisions at the right time. This means having team discussions to separate out genuine information from opinions: the wheat from the chaff, as it were. It also means both managers and teams staying focused on analysing and understanding information to make the best decisions – without getting side-tracked by endless action plans or finger-pointing. You have to remember that Lean is not a management system, it's a learning system: so content, rather than management, is the key.

The preferred 'tool' for implementing visuals in engineering is the *obeya*. The *obeya* will be the starting point for Part Two of this guide.

DEBUNKING THE MYTHS

> *There are a lot of myths and misconceptions about what Lean really is, which we'd like to debunk as swiftly as possible. Here are the most common, in no particular order.*

Myth: Lean Is All Just Common Sense

Common sense is used to solve frequently occurring day-to-day problems based on past experience. But this collection of 'works best' – that's what we already do! – and heuristics is no longer sufficient when new problems or situations need to be faced and understood. However, it is quite difficult to suspend our judgement (e.g., by rejecting intuitive answers suggested by *System 1* or *fast thinking*[38]) and re-examine what we already know! Lean principles, methods, and practices aim to question our common sense and, in so doing, develop our critical thinking.

---

[38] Ibid.

Myth: Lean Is First and Foremost Made for the Japanese

You only have to observe Japanese companies to realise that Lean is no more natural or easy to achieve in Japan than it is anywhere else. Of course, the benchmark company in this field is the Japanese automaker Toyota. But it is striking to note that outside of the Toyota ecosystem (which includes sub-contractors and former Toyota employees) misunderstandings about Lean are as prevalent as in any other country. The authors' experience of working in a large international group has shown us that beyond Japan, there is, in reality, no country or culture that is 'naturally' Lean. When you compare the extent of Lean implementation between teams and sites around the world, the differences are mainly down to the commitment of managers and the demands of customers. So for any given country, we can observe some quite outstanding Lean experiences on one site, while on a neighbouring site, there could be a total absence of Lean – or a half-hearted or grossly distorted version of some of its concepts.

Myth: Lean Is Just about Cost-Cutting

This is a commonly held myth based on the belief that Lean is 'a hunt for waste'. From the equation '*Expected Margin = Target Selling Price – Cost*', cutting costs obviously improves margin. But focusing on the cost side alone is risky (see Target Costing). If you cut costs at the expense of customer satisfaction, customers will look elsewhere and revenues will fall, cancelling out the expected margin.

Cost-cutting must obviously not endanger employees, for example, by exposing them to the risk of accidents, or physical or psychological illness as a result of poor working conditions. Nor should it jeopardise the company's ability to respond to customers on time and with the expected quality level. It is simple enough to cut costs, but much more difficult to improve profitability in the long term. This is essentially why Lean is emphatically *not* a cost-cutting approach. The elimination of waste, which is part of Lean thinking, only makes sense if Customer Value is clearly understood and constantly developed.[39]

---

[39] See Jean E. Cunningham and Orest J. Fiume. (2003). *Real Numbers Management Accounting in a Lean Organization*. Emily Adams.

In Lean companies, it is striking how far everything is done to ensure that the people who create and provide value are working under optimal conditions. This is a major change in the way of thinking. Paradoxically, it also gives meaning and value back to so many of the functions often considered as a 'necessary evil' (such as 'unproductive' support functions) and which are often the first to be targeted in cost-cutting (7).

Myth: Lean Is for Factories

We have mentioned elsewhere how Lean in engineering is not just a simple 'copy-and-paste' job to transfer the production approach of Lean and apply it to engineering. However, when we think for a moment about the underlying principles of Lean, it seems clear they are applicable everywhere. 'Challenge, Respect, *Kaizen*, Teamwork, *Genchi Genbutsu*' are not solely relevant to production. The same goes for Just-in-Time and *jidoka*. Moreover, seeking total customer satisfaction through the value of your products is not something to worry about on an assembly line, because by then it is too late: it must have already been designed into the product at the engineering stage. And, as for sustainable people development and the agility that goes with this, why should it be the prerogative only of factories?

Myth: Lean Is Another Form of Taylorism

'Scientific Management' was an early attempt to apply scientific principles to industrial processes in the USA towards the end of the 19th century, and is often called 'Taylorism' after its founder Frederick Winslow Taylor (1856–1915). A century later, we still hear the term used in a disparaging way to criticise bad working conditions that often have nothing to do with Taylor or his thinking. Lean expert and writer Michel Baudin[40] notes that the treatment reserved for Taylor after his death had him marked out as a 'convenient villain' for all the ills of 20th-century industrialisation. Later, the term 'Toyotism' was coined to serve a similar purpose, referring to all the industrial practices developed by Toyota in its most (imagined)

---

[40] For example, Taylor had nothing to do with the implementation of the production chain immortalised in Charlie Chaplin's film *Modern Times*.

harmful form for workers. But amid what looks like a certain amount of mud-slinging, let's just pause for a moment to look at what makes Taylor's scientific management fundamentally different from the TPS, and therefore different from Lean.

Taylor's methodology involved measuring the time it took different workers to perform the same task, and from this, he came up with the minimum time needed to do that particular task. By imposing this time on all workers as a requirement, he thereby prevented them from colluding to work less quickly. The resulting increases in performance were rewarded by salary increases. Taylor concluded that workers were, above all else, motivated by money. In the language of Lean, we could conclude that he had a far too simplistic vision of human potential, and was insensitive to the notion of respect,[41] two key aspects of Lean thinking.

Another aspect – standardisation – also had a different logic to that of Lean. By simply timing a job rather than analysing its content he then felt he had discovered the 'one best way', irrespective of who was doing it. Taylor-style standardisation is based on the idea that work can be optimised by eliminating any initiative on the part of operators through a kind of 'dissociation' between their brains and their hands. All manual actions and interventions are therefore simplified to make them reproducible in an almost automatic way by the greatest number of workers. For Taylor, standardisation is achieved through the 'de-skilling' of workers, and this standardisation was determined by experts and management, not by those who conduct the work.

By contrast, Lean sees each person as an expert, a craftsman, ideally placed to continuously improve their work along with their team colleagues. To reach this level of expertise and autonomy, each individual is constantly developing their skills and being trained with the support of managers and experts. In Lean, everyone's intelligence is brought into play. In Taylor's system, individual intelligence was pretty much ruled out.

---

[41] http://michelbaudin.com/2015/02/03/fairness-to-frederick-taylor/.

Myth: Lean Prevents Innovation

Innovation is about developing a new idea that brings value to customers by solving their problems. It requires creativity and conditions conducive to generating new ideas. The myth is that Lean somehow gets in the way of this. Yet nothing could be further from the truth.

The myth draws on the idea that creativity can only emerge where structure, organisation, and process are absent. While certain structures can obviously hinder creativity, at the other extreme, confusion and permanent disorder also do nothing to help their development. Methods such as Design Thinking and *Lean Startup* (4) aim to structure innovation through cycles rather similar to those of PDCA. The same is true for SBCE, the Lean Engineering process that promotes innovation.

The best ideas come from repeated interactions between multidisciplinary teams, which can stimulate new ways of thinking and create new knowledge. Such meetings need to be facilitated, and Lean has an ideal structure for this: the collaborative visual hub, i.e., the *obeya*. It promotes a creative flow of ideas, driven by the knowledge gaps that need to be closed, and which are identified in plain sight on the walls.

However, *obeya* is not the only place where innovation can happen. More broadly, the work environment must provide conditions to stimulate ideas and test them quickly: namely, a FabLab[42] or something similar should exist in every engineering workplace. In the authors' projects, we regularly request the creation of these creative spaces with free access, equipped with rapid prototyping tools, 3D printers, Raspberry® or Arduino® cards, PCB design software, telecom devices, interactive whiteboards and more. When space permits, we place the *obeya* near the FabLab, sometimes co-located in the same room.

This vision is supported by the concept of the *ba* developed by the Japanese philosopher Kitarō Nishida, and adapted by Ikujiro Nonaka.[43] The *ba* is a shared space where knowledge is created and shared through positive and dynamic interactions. It is the same *ba* as found in the word *genba* (literally 'the real place'), the scene of the action, the place you need to go to observe the facts and understand the situation. While the *genba* in

---

[42] FabLab: *Fabrication Laboratory*.
[43] Ikujiro Nonaka and Hirotaka Takeuchi. (1995). *The Knowledge Creating Company: How Japanese Companies Create the Dynamics of Innovation*. Oxford University Press.

production terms is the shop floor, the scene of the action – in engineering terms –is first the *obeya*.

Once new ideas emerge, Lean helps accelerate their development into products and their path to market. Lean is built around the concept of one continuous flow from ideas to products, driven by customers (and other stakeholders). The *obeya* makes this flow visible to teams, whose objective is to accelerate it by eliminating unnecessary activities. Thus, from the generation of new ideas to their materialisation in the form of new products, Lean, particularly through *obeya*, is an accelerator of innovations.

Another recurring objection sees the concept of *standardisation* acting as a brake on creativity. In fact, it is quite the opposite. The standard allows everyone to avoid reinventing what is already known and seen as important for process or product-related activity. It thus makes innovation *more likely* by freeing people's brain power to seek out genuinely new ideas where they are most needed.

Last but not least, Lean thinking sees failure not as a source of blame[44] but as an apprenticeship and a condition for greater success. This is a way of thinking that fosters creativity and makes innovation possible.

Myth: Lean Engineering Means Obeya Everywhere

Let's not forget that implementing visual management is never an outcome, but the starting point. O*beya* is a framework to support co-engineering, and it will be pointless if nothing changes in the way you work. Worse still, *obeya*, like any visual management, can become a tool of command and control if all it is doing is displaying Key Performance Indicators (KPIs) which are of use only to the manager.

Myth: Lean Is Basically Value Stream Mapping (VSM)

There is an enduring myth that Lean is little more than VSM. VSM is a diagram that maps a process, focusing on the added value of activities, and is itself the subject of countless books.[45] It is a tool that fascinates managers, to the point that some believe that without VSM there is no Lean. We suggest, however, that VSM be used sparingly and wisely.

---

[44] Henry Petroski. (2018). *Success Through Failure*. Princeton University Press.

[45] One the most famous books – Mike Rother. (1999). *Learning to See: Value Stream Mapping to Add Value and Eliminate Muda*. Productivity Press.

There are several problems with VSM. Having a diagnostic tool that allows you to have a shared vision of a situation is of course a good thing. However, thinking that all you need to do is draw the process on a diagram, identify problems, and then solve them will lead only to dead ends and disappointment. In engineering, if you believe that things always happen the same way each time then you are kidding yourselves. You would have to draw dozens of VSM to characterise activity, and even this would be completely unrealistic and would tell you nothing of real interest. As a result, VSM often presents a very theoretical and generalised view, leading to a conceptual schema that is inadequate for making any real progress.

VSM also gives rise to long and complex action plans which can sometimes seem endless – quite the opposite of what the PDCA framework proposes. And finally, to have any relevance at all, VSM needs to be conducted with large numbers of people, who may be already working at full capacity. As a result, work on VSM is left out of the daily routine, and most often, at the end of the exercise, everything returns to its original place as if the VSM project had never happened.

There is, however, one form of VSM that really does deserve to be used in engineering, and this is the mapping of the customer's consumption process. By visually characterising the successive basic interactions of the customer with the product, you can identify those bringing satisfaction and those generating waste.

Myth: Lean Is a Management System

To say that Lean is not a management system may sound a little provocative. What do we mean by this? Well, let's define 'management system' here as *the way in which an organisation manages the interrelated parts of its business to achieve its objectives*. In that sense, then, a management system (along with the various structures put in place) are both key elements of *any* company's operations. But here's the crux: whatever the processes and structures that are part of 'the system', the company must still learn to use them in the constantly changing uncertainty of the real world. Organisations are made of human beings, reality is never exactly what you expect, and customers, markets, and contexts are fluctuating and uncertain: you have to learn to navigate in the fog. Lean, then, is not a management system, but a *learning* system.

Myth: Lean, Just Apply It and Everything Will Be Fine

Experience teaches us that this is just wishful thinking. Companies have been selecting 'methods' and laying down processes for decades, yet still manage to create products that are not what customers want, with development costs that are almost always higher than anticipated. In engineering, two things should never be forgotten: first, a bad engineer will never design good products; and second, a good engineer is not one who knows everything, but rather one that knows what they need to learn. Engineers, like good craftsmen, must master the techniques, technologies, algorithms, physical laws, and everything else they need to design and develop high-quality products. The method – any method – will never replace that.

So having picked apart many of the myths about Lean, we'd like to leave you with three thoughts before you set off on this journey:

1. Think of Lean as a different way of doing your existing engineering activities, rather than as a method you apply alongside or in addition to these activities.
2. It is much easier to teach Lean to an engineer who knows their subject and is open-minded than to train a Lean expert in product design.
3. Being the best in Lean Engineering is not an objective. The objective is to get better engineering every day. Lean can effectively contribute to this.

4

Practical Tips for the Journey Ahead

Maybe you are now starting to think that Lean in Engineering could be a good journey for you, and you might also have a clearer idea about what you may find there. But, as with any journey, there are practicalities to take care of: where will you start your journey, who will you take with you, and do you have any kind of 'travel insurance' – in other words, what if things don't work out as you expect?

There is one rock-solid insurance against the downside risk of an enterprise like this: whatever happens on the way, you will learn from it. For any engineer or technician, this is still reassuring. Not only will you learn; you will also *learn to learn*. You will discover how to identify knowledge gaps and then close them. And you will learn how to take advantage of all your mistakes and you may learn to improve the way you work.

This may be a slightly daunting thought, but it is an important one nonetheless: Lean is an endless journey.

DOI: 10.4324/9781003381945-5

THE LEAN JOURNEY HAS NO END

> *Lean is a continuous improvement approach, and by its very nature, improvement is endless.*

There is no final destination because it is driven by the endless desire to do better.

- Do better for your customers, who will be quick to look elsewhere if you do not manage to bring them the solutions that they need.
- Do better for all the other stakeholders, your collaborators, and your colleagues, so they continue to engage with you and give you the benefit of their skills, knowledge, and questions.
- Do better for the wider community by driving your growth in tandem with positive social and environmental outcomes.
- Do better to solve your own problems, which will constantly reappear in different forms.
- Do better than your competitors, who never stop trying to do better themselves.

Lean asks you to establish a sustainable and long-term approach based on continuous learning, and then use this to face up to and adapt quickly to an environment of rapid change. So your Lean journey is not about reaching a final destination: rather, it is about constantly questioning the way you see things and how you learn and work, so that continuous improvement becomes part of your daily working life, as a *second nature*.

So if the Lean journey needs a one-way ticket, you might also wonder how fast that journey ought to be: express service or local path? Direct flight or stopover? To answer this, consider the learning capability of your organisation, the involvement and enthusiasm of management, where you are starting from, the challenges you will face, and much more.

If you go too fast, you risk neglecting the progressive and individual nature of the learning process, which could leave people feeling demotivated. Or they may simply pretend to go along with the process before quickly reverting to old ways. Conversely, if the pace of learning is not sufficiently sustained, you risk staying too close to your starting point without having made any real improvements: while the initial improvement initiatives may seem promising enough, getting learning to take root requires it to be repeated and sustained in daily work. Without this, it can remain superficial and eventually fizzle out.

WHEN AND WITH WHOM TO GO?

> *There is no 'best time to start'. The situation is never ideal, managers and teams are never convinced enough, work pressure is never light enough. But there are some obvious mistakes you can avoid.*

It is best not to set out on a journey into Lean if your company is facing some kind of crisis. When order books are full, we see many companies happy to continue as they have always done in the past. But when orders suddenly dry up, they decide to implement Lean. Bad move: Lean is not a magic formula that suddenly allows you to solve all your problems at a stroke. And proposing Lean in the middle of a desperate situation could be the best way to *bury* any desire for change. With so many fires to fight, there will be little appetite to start implementing deep-running change in daily work practices. And then it will be easy to say 'You see? It doesn't work!' As John F. Kennedy declared: 'the best time to repair the roof is when the sun is shining'.

Model Cases

Your approach needs to take into account the nature of your engineering projects. Where you start will depend on where you are in the life cycle of a project, the skills and experience of the team, how well you know your customers' needs, the existence (or not) of a product line, and many other considerations. But the ideal is to start Lean as far upstream as possible. The further downstream Lean applies in a project, the greater the temptation will be to look at the symptoms (reworks, delays, and extra costs already incurred) rather than to look at the root of the problems in the upfront design phase.

Once you have identified the engineering project you will use to start your Lean journey, the next set of questions will always come up in the same order:

1. Have you identified what creates value for the customer and the other stakeholders?
2. Have you identified what creates value for your business?
3. Have you identified the knowledge you have and the knowledge you need to create this value?

The answers to these questions will help you choose the path you need to follow.

To emphasise that this first engineering project is above all a *learning* case, we use the term 'model project' or 'model case', by analogy with a 'model plant' – which is a term from Lean manufacturing. This is not the same thing as a successful 'pilot project' that will need only to be copied in the course of a subsequent roll-out. Rather, it is a project where the development of learning is just as important as success: the idea is to take advantage of this learning to disseminate the Lean approach throughout the company. As long as your Lean deployment remains at this project level, you will be using the term 'model cases' until Lean has been propagated throughout the entire company. Choosing your 'model case' is a key part of planning your Lean journey. So who are you going to take with you?

Managers

When deploying Lean in Engineering, as anywhere else, the role of managers is crucial. As a manager, you must 'be the change you want to see' in your company. You cannot be a mere spectator or sponsor, delegating the implementation of Lean to others. This well-known graphic shows how the role of management is inextricably linked to improvement.

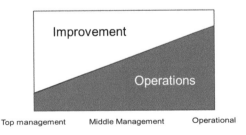

FIGURE 4.1
Degree of involvement in the improvement

> *In one of Toyota's sites, we even saw an application of this curve by measuring the time spent coaching at each management level, with this time being 'calibrated' at each level in order to ensure that managers are playing their role in facilitating improvement.*

Let's say that improving means 'doing better tomorrow than today'. It is quite logical to think that the higher a manager is placed in the organisation, the more their job is to prepare for a better future for the company. The Lean journey, in engineering as elsewhere, begins with a manager. But if your business is a large one with hundreds or even thousands of staff, at what level should you start? Do you need to convince the CEO? Should the whole management team not only buy into the ideas but also become personally involved? This could turn out to be very ambitious, and possibly unrealistic.

Engineering activities are highly creative and usually follow a project-based development approach, so there is at least one manager who must be involved from the very start in the Lean journey: the project manager, or their equivalent in your organisation – along with their team, of course. Dissemination of ideas and knowledge from here to other levels of management may then occur, or they may not. In any case, if you want to get the most out of your Lean approach by improving engineering across the board rather than just across one project, you will need the support of other managers – and quickly. As well as your project managers, you will also need support from functional department's managers. They are also fundamental, as they are developing usable knowledge for future projects. It is thus important that they quickly embark on the Lean journey too.

Collaborators

The challenge is to develop for all individuals not only their craft skills but also their ability to work and solve problems with others (see Teamwork).

Think about who has the power to make things happen or, on the contrary, who has the power to block them. It is then a question of how best to involve them in your Lean journey. You have to go with people who want to move with you: at the very least, this is a project manager and a team who are convinced and ready to learn. Lean Engineering is about learning. But no one can be forced to learn.

Partners: Staff Representatives

Lean does not always have good press, though it is seen more positively by those with a better understanding of this thinking. When applied in a partial or restrictive way, e.g., with the focus simply on removing waste, cutting costs, and eliminating 'dead time', the very essence of Lean – which is continuous people development – can be totally absent, giving such 'Lean' organisations a bad name that then tarnishing the image of Lean thinking in its entirety.

Fortunately, this negative vision is changing significantly, as shown by Michel Sailly's 2017 (8). Sailly is a French ergonomist who has worked for many years in Japan. As a member of the FGMM-CFDT (a major trades union federation in France), he has worked with a group presenting Lean Management as a set of practices that employees can use to improve the quality of their working lives and help re-shape the industry of the future.

Unfavourable prejudices about Lean will not go away completely however, and some of them are based on very real negative cases. So some people will avoid using the word Lean. It's up to you how you go about it, but don't let misconceptions get in the way of your goals. So what's the best way to deal with them? Certainly by starting with a model case and communicating the results. Most often people will be won over quite quickly once they see the real benefits to their own daily work. They will then become your best supporters.

USEFUL AND CREDIBLE SOURCES

The following books and links might prove useful in helping to understand the main principles.

Websites

- www.lppde.org: Lean Product and Process Development Exchange.
- https://www.lean.org/: The Lean Enterprise Institute publishes expert articles from the likes of Durward Sobek, Jeffrey Liker, and James Morgan.

- https://rapidlearningcycles.com/: Rapid Learning Cycles Institute (K. Radeka).
- www.institut-lean-france.fr offers training courses through the Lean Engineering Academy, as well as dedicated masterclasses and books.

Books

Here are some key works on Lean Engineering which we feel are either seminal foundation texts or which illustrate particularly well one of the concepts of Lean in product design and development.

- Allen C. Ward. (2007). *Lean Product and Process Development.* Boston, MA: Lean Enterprise Institute (completed in 2014 by Durward K. Sobek).
  A. C. Ward was a professor at the University of Michigan. This book remains for us the absolute reference for Lean Engineering. It deserves to be read and re-read, bringing new reflections and discoveries each time.
- Jim M. Morgan and Jeffrey Liker. (2006). *The Toyota Product Development System.* New York: Productivity Press.
  J. Morgan and J. Liker describe the product development principles and practices as applied by Toyota. They were either students or professors (even now for J. Liker) at the University of Michigan.
- Michael N. Kennedy. (2003). *Product Development for the Lean Enterprise.* Richmond, VA: Oaklea Press.
  M. Kennedy is the author of several books. The book *Ready, Set, Dominate: Implement Toyota's Set-Based Learning for Developing Products and Nobody Can Catch You* (Oaklea Press, 2008) focuses on the concepts of Toyota's set-based and knowledge-based product development.
- Dantar P. Oosterwal. (2010). *The Lean Machine.* New York: Amacom.
  D. P. Oosterwal describes his experience at Harley Davidson, which began with the support of Allen Ward.
- Katherine Radeka. (2017). *The Shortest Distance Between You and Your New Product.* Chesapeake Research Press.
  K. Radeka, who was coached by Allen Ward, presents her approach she calls 'Rapid Learning Cycles'.

- Michael N. Kennedy, Brian M. Kennedy, and Penny W. Cloft. (2018). *Success is Assured*. New York: Productivity Press.
  This is the first book that describes Set-Based Design in an easy-to-apply way. It provides a set of powerful tools and methods developed by the authors and shows how to apply them through many examples.

5

A Bit of History

To fully understand and apply certains principles, it's also useful to know where they come from. A better knowledge of the past is more likely to open the right doors for the future.

LEAN ENGINEERING ROOTS

If you have been wondering about the roots of Lean and specifically Lean Engineering, and who the 'inventors' were, this chapter may prove to be enlightening. Among the inventors who inspired us, we have chosen first, Sakichi Toyoda, the founder of Toyota, and then the Wright brothers who made the first sustained, powered, controlled flight.

The roots of Lean in Engineering go back more than a hundred years, even though the term 'Lean' itself only dates back to the final decades of the last century. To fully understand how this approach is now so well adapted to the digital age, it is worth looking back to see how it has *always* been about a learning approach. And that is what makes it feel so modern.

Lean: From Just-in-Case to Just-in-Time

In 1988, John Krafcik, a young researcher at MIT, proposed the word *Lean*[1] to describe the *Just-in-Time* system of the Toyota Production

---

[1] J. Krafcik. (1988). 'Triumph of the Lean Production System'. *MIT Sloan Management Review.*

System (TPS). His choice brought out the contrast between the TPS and traditional production systems, which tended to favour a high level of inventory. This *Just-in-Case* approach, as it was known, was supposed to make firms more robust with respect to uncertainties, and therefore more efficient. The paradox was that the more frugal *Lean* system, *a priori* more fragile and risky, actually surpassed the inventory-rich firms in both quality and productivity.

Toyota solved this apparent paradox by transferring the robustness of the system to each employee in the plant. By developing the individual capacity to solve problems that *lean* stocks no longer masked, it was able to make the system robust to uncertainties while gaining agility. In this system, each employee is thus able to limit the effects of disturbances, whereas, in a *Just-in-Case* system, these are simply buffered by the size of inventory.

The book *Lean Thinking*[2] dedicated the word *Lean* as the generic and exclusive label to reference the TPS. Later, in 2004, and thanks to *The Toyota Way*,[3] Toyota's approach began to be seen as a way of thinking rather than strictly a production system. More generally, everything that comes from or claims to come from Toyota is labelled *Lean*. So when Allen Ward discovered that Toyota also distinguished itself by its specific way of developing its products, he also awarded it the label *Lean Product Development*.

So is Lean Engineering also *Lean* in the sense defined by J. Krafcik? In terms of Lean thinking and principles, it definitely is. However, we have seen that there are many differences between production and engineering. So, was it really relevant to affix *Lean* to *Engineering*, given the risk of creating confusion with the specific meaning of *Lean* as originally described? To avoid this risk, Brian M. Kennedy preferred to speak of *Knowledge-Based Development* to refer to the key role of knowledge in Toyota's engineering.

For this book, we preferred to keep the word *Lean*, on the one hand, to remind us all what engineering owes to Toyota, and on the other, to insist on the continuity and consistency of principles and thinking between

---

[2] James P. Womack and Daniel T. Jones. (1996). *Lean Thinking: Banish Waste and Create Wealth in Your Corporation*. Productivity Press.

[3] Jeffrey K. Liker. (2004). *The Toyota Way: 14 Management Principles from the World's Greatest Manufacturer*. McGraw-Hill Professional.

engineering and production, and more generally along the whole value stream.

Engineering: Engines and Genius

The words *engineering* and *engineer* originate from the Latin *ingeniare*, which designates a machine used in war (then, by extension complex machines) and know-how (ingenuity).

The word *genius* is a convergence of two Latin words *genius* and *ingenium*. The meaning has evolved, moving from the sense of the 'genie' emerging from Aladdin's lamp, to individuals with an innate intelligence beyond the norm (genius, as an attribute, can be regarded as a gift of nature, while talent can be acquired and learned).

In the 18th century, the word *genius* was used to relate to a corps of *engineers* in the army, and their technical expertise to direct the machinery, or *engines* of war in the attack and defence of fortifications. The *engine* is a mechanical object (contrivance, machine, tool, instrument, etc.) to produce an effect. *Engineery* is a collection of *engines* for a specific purpose.[4]

The *engineer* is thus the *genius* who drives the *engine*. To do so, they need to acquire, use, and develop knowledge. In a modern sense, the engineer is also the engine maker. Thus, the word *engineering* covers accumulated knowledge (which may be scientific or not), and technical means and know-how used intentionally to find novel and ingenious solutions to practical problems in the field of design, development, and implementation of complex systems.[5]

---

[4] David Booth. (2017). *An Analytical Dictionary of the English Language, in Which the Words Are Explained in the Order of Their Natural Affinity, Independent of Alphabetical Arrangement.* Andesite Press.

[5] https://www.adeli.org/document/41-l76p05pdf.

It is exciting, then, to see that Lean in Engineering has its origins in part in principles and practices adopted by *genius* inventors of *engines* who were to dramatically change industry and mobility through the 20th century. We will be looking at four members of two illustrious families:

- Sakichi Toyoda, inventor and designer of a motorised automatic loom machine, whose success helped his son Kiichiro finance the start-up of Toyota Motor Company, an automotive production company that would revolutionise the automotive industry and beyond;
- The Wright brothers, inventors and designers of the first powered controlled flying machine, an invention that contributed to the rapid development of aviation and more broadly of the aeronautical industry.

Sakichi and Kiichiro Toyoda: The Continuous Innovation[6]

FIGURE 5.1
Sakichi Toyoda

Sakichi Toyoda, the founder of Toyota Industries Corporation, was born in 1867 on the outskirts of Nagoya into a farming family. By the age of 18, he had become a skilled carpenter with a desire to do service to his community.

---

[6] Some elements are from William Mass and Andrew Robertson. (1996). 'From Textile to Automobiles: Mechanical and Organizational Innovation in the Toyota Enterprises, 1895–1933'. *Business and Economy History*, 25, 2.

The year of his birth, the Meiji Restoration took place, marking the end of Japan's isolationist policy in favour of opening up to modernity.

When S. Toyoda watched the women of his village struggling daily with their weaving looms, he began to wonder whether, if the looms were designed a bit differently, the task of weaving could be made easier and more efficient.[7]

FIGURE 5.2
Toyota Commemorative Museum of Industry and Technology – weaver

With no previous knowledge of weaving nor of looms, he disassembled and then reassembled a large number of looms to better understand their mechanisms. His carpentry skills allowed him to quickly prototype his improvement ideas, which he tested directly with the weavers themselves. In other words, following an empirical approach, he validated the relevance of his hypotheses to solve the observed problems.

Hungry for new knowledge, he left his home town in 1890 to visit the Third National Machinery Exposition in Tokyo. For a month he spent time each day learning the operation of each machine, and developing what would become a lifelong passion for machines and engines.

In 1891, aged just 24, he filed a patent for his first major invention: 'linking the flying shuttle of the loom to the movement of the reed when beating

---

[7] David Magee. (2008). *How Toyota Became #1: Leadership Lessons from the World's Greatest Car Company*. Portfolio; Reprint edition.

down the weft'.[8] The weaver's comfort was improved, and the work required was halved. In addition, the machine reduced irregularities in the fabric.

Weaving, however, still involved many manual operations which reduced productivity, and S. Toyoda's attention turned naturally to power looms. To finance his research, in 1894, he invented and marketed a yarn winding machine twice as efficient as existing machines at the time. These machines improved productivity so much that a single weaver could then operate two to three steam-powered looms,[9] a factor which ensured their success throughout Japan. He released his first steam-powered loom in 1896.

At the same time, he tested his looms in operational conditions in a pilot plant with 36 active looms, and regularly went and observed them in action. It is probably during his *Genba Walks* that he developed the famous methods of root cause analysis – the 5 Whys.[10] Solving problems enabled him to improve the design of the looms and gain manufacturing experience.

FIGURE 5.3
Toyota Commemorative Museum of Industry and Technology – wooden loom

---

[8] Ibid.
[9] Ibid.
[10] Five whys – Wikipedia for definition.

In 1903, Type T made it possible to change the shuttle to replenish the weft yarn without stopping the machine – a huge breakthrough which thus eliminated stopping times.[11] Unlike competitors who had to change the spool, the shuttle-changing mechanism was less sensitive to the fragility of the yarn and required a less precise adjustment of the structure. In 1909, he further improved this mechanism, which became much more flexible and faster to implement for team members. These continuous improvements aimed at reducing shuttle changeover time.

However, these looms were not very robust and their high variability limited the possibility of having real interchangeable parts. In addition, the enlargement of the looms made them more vulnerable to vibrations. An early improvement was to switch to an iron chassis. To further improve the manufacturability and robustness of these looms, Toyoda called on the skills of Charles A. Francis[12] a mechanical engineering teacher at Tokyo University. This American 'machinist' had acquired his industrial skills at Pratt & Whitney in Hartford, Connecticut, a pioneering firm in the industrial implementation of the interchangeable parts concept.

From 1905 to 1907, Francis designed new industrial tools, improved the precision of machines, aligned the production sequence of machines, and established gauge systems, all of which together allowed the use of interchangeable parts.[13] He also trained employees in new industrial practices.

In 1908 and 1909, the first all-iron frame models (the model H) were mass produced in Japan's most modern factory. Productivity was doubled. The success of these new looms allowed Toyoda to finance new industrial experiments on an even larger scale and solve new problems.

In 1910, eager to broaden his knowledge, he went to the United States and then to England to visit loom factories. It was not so much the machines that impressed him as the discovery of the book *Self-Help*[14] by the Scottish humanist author Samuel Smiles. In this book on personal development and positive thinking, Smiles celebrated the virtues of individual effort,

---

[11] https://www.toyota-industries.com/company/history/toyoda_sakichi/.

[12] https://www.lean.org/LeanPost/Posting.cfm?LeanPostId=61.

[13] Fred Stahl and Joel Cutcher-Gershenfeld. (2013). *Worker Leadership: America's Secret Weapon in the Battle for Industrial*. The MIT Press.

[14] *Saigoku risshi-hen* translated in Japanese in 1870 by Nakamura Keiu.

perseverance, discipline, enthusiasm, field experience, and acceptance of one's mistakes – illustrating the ideas through the lives of famous inventors who changed the course of society by combining ingenuity with humanism.[15] S. Toyoda made these virtues his own, later passing them on to his son Kiichiro,[16] who then joined him in the company in 1921.

In 1924 Sakichi and Kiichiro Toyoda invented Type G, a non-stop shuttle-change automatic loom, which was the result of more than 30 years of continuous improvement. This Type G brought together numerous innovations (24 patents in all), of which one in particular would remain the most famous: the stop of the machine on detection of abnormal functions. As Taiichi Ohno described[17]: 'The loom stopped instantly if any one of the warp or weft threads broke. Because a device that could distinguish between normal and abnormal conditions was built into the machine, defective products were not produced'.

What Ohno was describing there was in fact the first application of *jidoka*, which later became a key principle of the TPS: 'Stopping the machine when there is trouble forces awareness on everyone'. By eliminating the unnecessary supervisory tasks, it became possible for a single operator to operate 25 machines. By simultaneously eliminating the production of defective products, unnecessary handling, and downtime, the Toyoda father and son were incredibly successful in improving labour productivity.

Kiichiro oversaw the construction and implementation of a plant to produce this loom, and installed 520 of them in an experimental textiles plant. In 1927, he introduced flow production in an assembly line capable of producing 300 units per month. He showed the potential of what would become the Just-in-Time principle. The sale of Type G would begin, and it proved to be an immediate success.

---

[15] See the David Magee's book already cited.

[16] Jeffrey Liker. (2004). *The Toyota Way: 14 Management Principles from the World's Greatest Manufacturer*. McGraw-Hill Professional.

[17] Taiichi Ohno. (1988). *Toyota Production System: Beyond Large Scale Production*. Productivity Press.

FIGURE 5.4
Toyota Commemorative Museum of Industry and Technology – machine stops when there is a trouble

In 1929, S. Toyoda concluded a patent rights transfer agreement with Platt Brothers and provided European, Canadian, and Indian[18] licences. K. Toyoda used the money from this transfer to create an automotive department within Toyoda Automatic Loom Works on 1 September 1933.[19] His goal was to produce the first all-Japanese car.

His study at the prestigious Imperial University of Tokyo did not distract him from his father's core principles: quickly testing his ideas and learning by doing. Accordingly, before designing and producing a car engine, he tested his hypotheses on a small engine. He also procured a Chevrolet car that he began disassembling, to study each part,[20] as his father did earlier with looms (refer to Teardown).

A first pilot automobile plant dedicated to prototyping was built in 1934, equipped with machine tools brought back from Europe and the USA. Toyoda was producing its first G1 trucks on a production line

---

[18] https://www.toyota-industries.com/company/history/toyoda_sakichi/.
[19] http://www.fundinguniverse.com/company-histories/toyoda-automatic-loom-works-ltd-history/.
[20] Ibid.

in 1935. A year later, the first Model AA passenger car rolled off the production line.[21]

FIGURE 5.5
Toyota Commemorative Museum of Industry and Technology – the first Model AA

In 1936, the Toyota name was adopted and the logo finalised. Toyota Motor Corporation (TMC) was officially founded on 28 August 1937.

The transfer of knowledge from the textile industry to the automobile industry was carried over by Toyoda and then, after the war, by Ohno, an industrial expert from *Toyoda Spinning & Weaving*.

We generally think of the Toyota Production System as being the sole legacy of the teachings of Sakichi and Kiichiro Toyoda. But these two men also had a lasting impact on engineering, notably through their entrepreneurial vision, and through a set of principles and practices that they developed over nearly 30 years: observing users actually using a product in order to understand their needs and problems; going to the *genba* to

From Toyoda to Toyota

Several explanations are proposed for the change from Toyoda to Toyota. In Katakana, which is one of the four possible scripts in Japanese, the word Toyota requires only eight strokes instead of ten, which is simpler, and differs from a name reminiscent of rice fields (*da*) that did not suit the group's international ambitions, and uses a lucky number, the eight. It is also a name that has the advantage of being totally symmetrical when written in Roman characters, allowing the use of vertical signs that can be read from both sides! (http://japantravelcafe .com/japanese-language-nihongo /learn-japanese-from-car-names -toyota-part-2-toyota-logo).

---

[21] Ibid.

observe facts and collect data; quickly testing hypotheses; developing and sharing knowledge; automating the detection of abnormal situations, and developing autonomy in decision making; solving problems where they arise; and last but not least, the enduring practice of doing everything possible to innovate and continuously improve.

The Wright Brothers: Learning Then Designing[22]

The year 1867 saw not only the birth in Japan of Sakichi Toyoda, but also, on the other side of the world, the birth of Wilbur Wright in Indiana, USA. Four years later, Wilbur's brother Orville was born, and 36 years later, in 1903, the Wright brothers completed the first controlled powered flight that marked one of the greatest human adventures of all time: the conquest of the sky.

FIGURE 5.6
Orville and Wilbur Wright

Growing up in Dayton, Ohio, the Wright brothers received an education that fostered their curiosity and developed their ingenuity. Wilbur was a studious and brilliant student. However, he did not pursue higher

---

[22] Refer to David McCullough. (2016). *The Wright Brothers*. Simon & Schuster, https://wright.nasa .gov/index.htm and https://airandspace.si.edu/exhibitions/wright-brothers/online/index.cfm.

education because recovery from a serious hockey injury had plunged him into severe depression. He then returned to his family home and divided his time between books and family, notably by taking care of his sick mother. Orville was less studious but seemed to have a talent for mechanics.[23] He was passionate about bicycles (at the time seen as highly complex mechanical devices), and soon began to build his own. Later, he built a printing press with recycled materials to print his own newspaper – the *West Side News*.

At the end of 1892, the brothers opened a bicycle rental and repair shop, 'the Wright Cycle Exchange'. They gained formidable skills in mechanical design and manufacturing, and four years later began marketing their own models. The commercial success of their bicycle business later allowed them to finance their other major passion: sustained human flight.

Their interest in flight may have originated from childhood, when in 1878 their father offered them a toy helicopter based on a design by Alphonse Pénaud.[24] It rose under the effect of rotation, and the two brothers tried very quickly to build their own version.

About 15 years later, they closely followed the methodology and discoveries of Otto Lilienthal, a German engineer who was developing 'heavier than air' flying machines that looked a little like today's hang gliders. Lilienthal thought he should first learn how to fly, experimenting continuously, and perfecting his gliders before than going on to motorise them. Like earlier pioneers of aviation such as George Cayley and Étienne-Jules Marey, he observed the flight of birds and was able to work out the parameters that favoured better lift.[25] He then confirmed his observations by measuring the components of aerodynamic force (lift and drag) acting on the wings of kites, with the help of a large rotating arm device.

In 1891, he made the first gliding flight in history, covering a distance of about 25 m. Over five years, he made more than 2,000 gliding flights of up to 250 m in length, allowing him to adjust the profile of the wings,

---

[23] Tom Crouch. (1991). *The Bishop's Boys: A Life of Wilbur and Orville Wright*. W. W. Norton & Company.

[24] Alphonse Pénaud was a 19th-century French pioneer of aviation.

[25] He publishes in 1889 the result of his observations in a reference book, explaining, among other things, the importance of cambered airfoil wings: *Der Vogelflug als Grundlage der Fliegekunst* (*Bird Flight as the Basis of Aviation*).

refine his calculations, and improve his piloting skills. However, his glider was not well prepared to fly in windy conditions, and the wind on 9 August 1896 was too strong to control it. His pioneering work ended abruptly that day when his glider pitched forward and crashed. He died the following day.

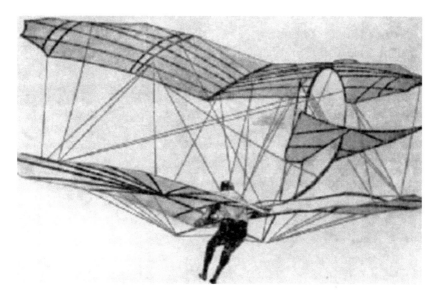

FIGURE 5.7
Otto Lilienthal and his glider

Lilienthal's fatal accident fuelled the Wright brothers' desire to prove that flying did not have to be dangerous: humans, they believed, could fly on machines heavier than air without endangering their lives.

To identify the problems to be solved, they studied everything that had already been learned about human flight. They immersed themselves in the reference[26] documents written by Lilienthal, as well as those by

---

[26] In 1899, Wilbur asked for all available information relating to aeronautics to the Smithsonian Institute.

Octave Chanute[27] and Samuel Langley.[28] They concluded that three major problems needed to be solved to design a flying machine:

1. **The lift problem**: basically, this was about the trade-off between the aerofoil of the wing, its mass, and the robustness of the structure: how to produce maximum lift with light but robust wings? Since Lilienthal and later Chanute had addressed this problem by testing gliders, the Wright brothers believed that the problem had been more or less resolved.

2. **The propulsion problem**: this concerned the trade-off between the power, mass, and robustness of the engine: how to develop enough power with a lightweight but also robust engine? In the 1890s, Augustus Moore Herring equipped his glider with an engine, while others such as Clément Ader, Hiram Maxim, and Samuel Langley powered more sophisticated flying machines. High-performance engines had been developed, then, but without the realisation of successful, controlled flights. Various test flights using engines did not give much in the way of learning opportunities

3. **The control problem**: Lilienthal's understanding of the causes of lift allowed him to greatly increase the number of flights, giving him a better idea of the problem of balance and control of the glider in real-life flying conditions.[29] Although he succeeded in modifying his trajectory by using the transfer of his body weight, his accident in 1896 fatally illustrated that he had only partially solved the problem of control. As with the two other challenges of lift and propulsion, this ultimate problem was also accompanied by a trade-off between two opposing concepts: stability and control. An aircraft can be designed to be very stable, in the sense that it returns to equilibrium after a disturbance without any pilot intervention. But the price of this stability is that the aircraft is then rather difficult to control. In other words, to be able to control an aircraft, you have to somehow overcome its built-in stability.

---

[27] Octave Chanute published in 1894 the *Progress in Flying Machines*, a compilation of the best articles published on the topic of 'flying machines heavier than air'.

[28] Samuel Langley – Wikipedia.

[29] It confirms G. Cayley's intuitions. He was the first to define lift and drag forces and to introduce the concept of the fixed-wing airplane, separating lift from propulsion. He strongly inspired O. Lilienthal and the Wright brothers.

So the brothers had to find a way to characterise the knowledge gap that separated them from the solution to this ultimate problem: how do you control all the phases of flight?

As keen cyclists and with quite a bit of expertise in the physics of cycle design, the Wright brothers were well aware that control of a bicycle cannot be achieved without a certain amount of built-in instability. A bike without a rider is extremely unstable when moving forwards and will simply fall on its side – demonstrating instability on its longitudinal axis (roll axis). To stay upright, the bike relies essentially on the dexterity of the rider. The Wright brothers believed that this model was applicable to piloting an aeroplane, and that a plane might be controllable, like a bike, along its roll axis. Experts like Chanute hadn't understood this. Indeed, the prevailing theories at the time saw aeroplanes rather as boats floating on the water, which automatically regained their stability after tossing and turning.[30]

Wilbur wrote[31]: 'my observation of the flight of buzzards leads me to believe that they regain their lateral balance when partly overturned by a gust of wind, by a torsion of the tips of the wings'. Louis-Pierre Mouillard, a French artist and aviation innovator who was also studying the gliding flight of birds, had already understood this principle, and in 1897 a US patent was granted jointly to Chanute and Mouillard that clearly covered this 'warping' of wings.[32] From this observation, the Wright brothers applied a process of inductive reasoning that led them to hypothesise that it may be necessary to warp the tips of the wings to better control the movement of the aeroplane on its longitudinal axis.

In 1899, they designed a biplane kite, around 1.5 m in length, to confirm the effect of wing warping. They attached a line to each corner of the four wings, and controlled the kite by deforming the wings using a pair of control sticks.[33] They validated their hypothesis and carried out the first steering command to control the roll. *They had completed the first in a long series of learning cycles.*

---

[30] D. L. Slusser. (2001). 'Learning to Fly: The Untold Story of How the Wright Brothers Learned to be the World's first Aeronautical Engineers'. *Thesis*.

[31] http://www.lettersofnote.com/2009_11_16_archive.html.

[32] Bruce D. Callander. (September 1989). 'The Critical Twist'. *AIR FORCE Magazine*.

[33] https://airandspace.si.edu/exhibitions/wright-brothers/online/fly/1899/kite.cfm.

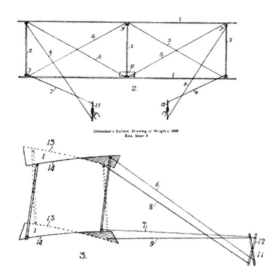

FIGURE 5.8
Kite – 1899

The next step was to validate this wing warping mechanism on a glider big enough to carry a man. Indeed, in their model, since the pilot controls the aeroplane during flight (as a cyclist controls his bicycle during a race), this kind of 'manned flight' experimentation became the norm. Lilienthal, in five years of intense development work, had accumulated just five hours of flight time. The Wright brothers wanted to accumulate this in just one day.

Based on the best aerodynamic data of the time, they built a glider small enough to be piloted like a kite (with a wingspan of 5.2 m), but which was large enough to carry a pilot. They positioned a fixed stabiliser to add weight at the front, to better control climb and descent while avoiding tilt and stalling while the pilot could control wing warping using a foot pedal.

FIGURE 5.9
Glider – 1900

They addressed the trade-offs on lift (shape versus mass versus strength) by using a spruce frame covered with satin for the wing structure, which limited its mass while offering a certain amount of rigidity. And the glider could then be easily modified and repaired in the case of breakages.

The first tests took place on the sandy hills south of Kitty Hawk in North Carolina, and the Wrights made several tests in kite mode, weighing down the structure to simulate a pilot's mass, and measuring the tension in the wires and the angle of flight. These measurements allowed them to confirm the effect of warping on larger wings. But the many measurements of lift and drag were far from the desired values. The kite did not seem to have the expected performance: it could fly on its own, but could hardly support the weight of a pilot without a strong wind. Knowledge gaps remained to be closed.

In 1901, they embarked on a new test campaign with a modified glider, which is designed with widened and thicker wings to increase lift sufficiently to take the weight of a pilot. Wilbur made over 50 flights, lying flat on the lower wing to reduce drag. The deformation of the wing was still controlled with a pedal, but this time, the front stabiliser was made adjustable to add pitch control and validate new learning. This location at the front had the advantage of making it visible to the pilot, allowing him a faster reaction in the event of pitching, and offering him a greater margin of safety[34] (Figure 5.10).

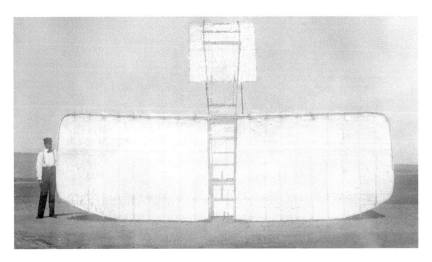

FIGURE 5.10
Glider – 1901

But once again, the glider generated only one third of the expected lift. They tried to compensate for this lack of lift by accentuating the curvature of the lower wing, but without much effect, and worryingly, their results seemed to contradict all their calculations based on Lilienthal's tables of coefficients of lift and drag for single-wing aerofoil shapes. The brothers began to doubt if the data in those tables was accurate.

Back home in Dayton, they felt the whole enterprise was doomed to fail. After several tests, they had finally flown very little and faced an unexpected problem: the potential inaccuracy of the data they were using. 'Not within a thousand years will man ever fly', wrote Wilbur despondently in August 1901. They were ready to give up, but it was Chanute who encouraged them to keep going. After further analysis, they made the assumption

---

[34] In contradiction with the work of Cayley in 1799 and then Pénaud in 1872 which showed the longitudinally stable character of an airplane with an empennage placed at the rear.

that there were errors in the Smeaton[35] pressure coefficient and perhaps even in the Lilienthal tables. The question then was what to do about this. Once again, the Wright brothers engaged in a new learning cycle with rapid prototyping to test their hypothesis and eventually close this new knowledge gap.

They conducted a simple experiment with a rotating arm mechanism, mounting a wheel on the front of their bicycle to test two wing profiles: a flat plate and an aerofoil shape. But the measurement of the angle of the wheel facing the wind once the balance of forces had been reached did not correspond to the expected value, which meant their hypothesis seemed validated: something was wrong with the coefficient, or with Lilienthal data, or both. They now had to find out where the mistakes were.

To counter possible errors in the Lilienthal tables, they were using their own measurements in the drag and lift equations to find the value of the Smeaton coefficient.[36] Their experiments showed the value as 0.0033, while the 'official' Smeaton value was set at 0.005, some 50% higher! This anomaly would explain why the size of their wings was *always* too small for the lift they were expecting – and their piloted aeroplane, quite literally, never got off the ground.

However, the new calculations with the corrected Smeaton coefficient still failed to deliver the values suggested by Lilienthal's tables. The brothers then decided to dispense with Lilienthal's data altogether and generate their own lift and drag coefficients – using a wind tunnel, a device developed in 1871 by Francis Herbert Wenham.[37] They built their own wind tunnel with spare parts, and then, using two sets of weighing scales inside the tunnel, set out to determine the coefficients of lift and drag.

---

[35] John Smeaton is an 18th-century English engineer who helped establish the lift equation used by the Wright Brothers and left his name to the air pressure coefficient.

[36] The correct value is 0.00327 but it is no longer used today. Lilienthal and Chanute used the value 0.005 in their work which influenced the Wright Brothers https://wright.nasa.gov/airplane/smeaton.html.

[37] F.H. Wenham is an engineer who established the importance of bird wing curvature in lift. His work was published in Chanute and largely influenced the Wright Brothers http://www.ctie.monash.edu.au/hargrave/wenham.html.

FIGURE 5.11
The wind tunnel built by the Wright Brothers

They implemented a Design of Experiment approach by varying one geometric variable of the wing at a time. They thus tested about 200 different wing shapes (squares, rectangles, ellipses), curvatures, profiles and sizes, and measured the effects produced, while controlling the most influential external factors, i.e., the angle of attack and the wind speed (see *CID*). They established new tables of lift and drag coefficients that could be used in the equations for design.

FIGURE 5.12
Tests results

The Wrights soon realised that the lift coefficients of one wing profile (say a fairly short and wide wing) could not simply be transposed to a differently shaped wing (such as a long and narrow wing).[38] Since the wing profiles of the Wrights' gliders were different from those drawn by Lilienthal, his tables could not be directly used to calculate lift in other wing shapes[39]: it was this *wrong application* of data that had led to errors in the calculation of lift during the brothers' experiments at Kitty Hawk in 1900 and 1901. Applying the coefficients found by the Wrights to the wing profiles used by Lilienthal, they found that Lilienthal's data were in fact validated.[40] As they wrote to Chanute in 1901: 'It would appear that Lilienthal is very much nearer the truth than we have heretofore been disposed to think'.

The Wright brothers had, in effect, completed a new learning cycle and established knowledge that would go on to define the domain of solutions to the lift problem. Within this domain, they could then select the best trade-off between the various parameters to design their next glider model. The new glider design was going to have longer and narrower wings with a thinner aerofoil and an aspect ratio (length-to-width) of 6:1, which was twice that of the previous glider. The wingspan was an impressive 9.6 m.

They returned to the sand hills at Kitty Hawk for the third time in late 1902 with the new glider. This time, they added a double vertical surface at the rear, acting as a vertical stabiliser to reduce the adverse yaw effects of the previous glider. The first tests led them to further improve their model by tying the wing warping to the movement of this stabiliser, which thus became a rudder.[41] The actions on the wings and rudder were no longer performed with levers, but via a mobile cradle positioned under the pilot's hips. Meanwhile, control on the pitch axis was affected by the pilot moving both hands forwards or backwards to lower or raise the front stabiliser (known as the canard plane).

---

[38] However, the value of lift coefficients (published in a table by O. Lilienthal in 1895) varies with the shape of the wing and takes into account the angle of attack.

[39] John David Anderson. (2010). *An History of Aerodynamics: And Its Impacts on Flying Machines*. Cambridge University Press.

[40] ehttps://wrightstories.com/lilienthal-data-not-in-error/.

[41] After 1905, the brothers removed this solidarity control between roll and yaw.

FIGURE 5.13
Glider test – 1902

The Wright brothers then went on to make hundreds of flights, breaking successive records for distance, time, and speed. They accumulated more flight experience than any other pilot had ever achieved, and learned how to fly by actuating control surfaces on each of the aircraft's three axes. The knowledge gaps relating to lift and control were thus closed!

The next stage was to address the propulsion problem, which would effectively conclude the next learning cycle. The Wrights envisaged a propulsion system comprising two propellers driven by an engine, which had to develop enough power to move the aeroplane without weighing it down too much. They needed an engine that would develop at least 8 hp for a mass lower than 90 kg. But having not found any manufacturer able to provide them with such a model, they decided to build it themselves. It would be a four-cylinder engine with internal combustion, developing 12 hp and weighing in at just 72 kg. It was built in only six weeks.

Developing this engine was not the most remarkable aspect, and rival engineer Samuel Langley had already developed a more efficient engine. Rather, it was their approach to the design itself that is most interesting. The Wright brothers wanted to validate the design of their aeroplane by powering it. For that, there was no need for a sophisticated engine. It just had to match the best trade-off in terms of its mass-to-power ratio. They decided to use aluminium to solve this trade-off. Beyond this, the engine needed to be simple to manufacture and repair and be sufficiently robust.

The other propulsion challenge came with the propellers. The efficiency of available propellers at the time was poor, at only around 50%, and the Wright brothers had to improve this to convert the maximum power developed by their rudimentary engine into thrust. Rather than starting from the propellers used by ships, they assumed instead that a propeller blade has some of the properties of a wing. They could thus reuse all the knowledge acquired on wing aerodynamics as captured in their models, and complete it with a new set of wind tunnel tests. Their hypothesis had been validated, and the result was a propeller design that was 66% efficient. This was seen as a major innovation to the credit of the Wright brothers.

They equipped their new 12-m wingspan glider, named Flyer, with their aluminium engine and high efficiency propellers. The Flyer weighed in at 274 kg, too heavy to fly two people,[42] and with its lack of wheels it was pushed on rails up to the launch site. Prior to the launch, they checked the validity of their calculations on the thrust by ballasting the Flyer with sandbags, allowing them to measure the force needed to keep the plane stationary once the engine had started. This measure confirmed that the thrust being generated was sufficient to get the plane airborne.

FIGURE 5.14
The first controlled flight in 1903

---

[42] They flipped a coin to pick the first pilot, and Wilbur won the toss.

On 17 December 1903, Wilbur took off in the Flyer, but the plane stalled and made a hard landing. Following repairs, it was finally Orville who carried out the world's first ever controlled motorised flight, which lasted for 12 seconds over 120 ft – around 36 m. The brothers made four flights during that same day for a cumulative duration of 98 seconds, with the longest flight lasting 59 seconds, and crossing 850 ft, or more than 259 m.

Nine days earlier, their rival Samuel Langley[43] attempted to take off with his *Aerodrome A* craft for the second time in two months. It was catapulted from a houseboat over – and unfortunately into – the Potomac River in which it finished the race without ever taking off.

That historic day of the first flight on 17 December 1903 was just another step in the continuous learning of the Wright brothers. The Flyer could only be flown in a straight line, and its control was laborious. However, it validated all the knowledge they generated during their many learning cycles. They also knew that there was still room for further improvements.

The 1904 model had less stability. The brothers also had to add ballast to shift the centre of gravity forward. On 20 September 1904, Wilbur took off in the new plane, succeeded in making two turns, and returned to land the aeroplane at the take-off point. He had just demonstrated that it was now feasible to control a powered aeroplane.

In 1905, their sixth model since 1900 improved on the stability of the previous models, and they could now fly over the surrounding woodland for 35 minutes, stopping only when the fuel ran out. With no flights in 1906, they resumed tests with a new model in 1907. They still had not completely resolved the stability issues, despite pushing the centre of gravity further and further forwards. The configuration with tail at the rear, already imagined by Cayley and later taken up by Pénaud, was finally adopted on the 'Model B' of 1910. For the first time, a motorised aeroplane was longitudinally stable and controllable on each of its three axes.

The Legacy of the Wright Brothers

The Wright brothers succeeded not only in designing and building the world's first controllable aircraft, but also by adopting a completely

---

[43] https://www.dailykos.com/stories/2014/1/29/1250870/-The-Langley-Aerodrome-A-The-Story-of -Almost.

new method of product development[44] inspired by the scientific method. While their approach may in some ways resemble the back-and-forth between inductive reasoning (in the generation of models from observations) and deductive reasoning (in the application of these models), it is primarily abductive and hypothetico-deductive reasoning that have allowed them to establish the framework from which they have been able to predict the designs that work. Its steps ran as follows (see PDCA (Plan Do Check Act)):

1. From the theoretical models, formulate the fundamental problems that must be solved to achieve powered flight (aerodynamics, control, and propulsion) along with the trade-offs associated with each of these challenges;
2. Formulate the theoretical framework and select the critical variables as to their contribution in explaining the expected effect (see *CID*);
3. Generate hypotheses explaining the effect, test them quickly through a series of short PDCA loops (e.g., with rapid prototyping) – close the knowledge gaps;
4. Analyse data, interpret the meaning of the results, and conclude (adopt, adjust, or refute the hypothesis);
5. Capture the new knowledge in reusable formats, update the model, and apply this knowledge in the new design stages.

Unlike Langley, the Wright brothers did not set out to try to design 'the best' aircraft. Instead, they developed the knowledge that would enable them to develop the right product. 'Product development isn't so much about developing products as it is about developing knowledge about the product', as Lean expert Kennedy puts it. This is in effect an illustration of the principles of the Set-Based Concurrent Engineering (SBCE).

The Wright brothers clearly did not wish to spend hundreds of expensive hours designing flying machines only to risk their lives on a test flight lasting just a few seconds. So they moved from *selecting, designing, and then testing* as applied by contemporaries like Langley, to *inferring, testing, learning, and then designing*, as had already been initiated by Lilienthal. Sadly, this paradigm shift in the development process had almost no effect

---

[44] http://planet-lean.com/before-developing-a-new-product-assess-your-idea.

on most 20th-century companies. Instead, they stuck stubbornly to *design then test*, to the point where it has become an irreplaceable reference in product development.

It was more than a century after the Wright brothers' experimental flights before the book *The Lean Startup* (4) was published. Inspired by the PDCA loop, the author, E. Ries, formalises product design and development in the form of a short 'learning loop'. First suggest *ideas*, *design* a *Minimum Viable Product* to test this idea, *measure* its relevance to produce *data*, and then *learn* from results – leading to a decision to adopt or pivot. The Wrights' use of kites, then gliders, and finally motor-powered aeroplanes is a convincing application of the experimental scientific method, revisited by Eric Ries a century later.

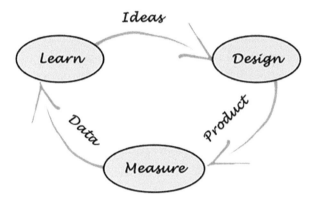

FIGURE 5.15
The Lean Startup learning cycle

Identifying knowledge gaps and formulating the right hypotheses[45] require you to be aware of the limits to your current knowledge: to identify the 'knowns' and then ask the right questions to find out what you don't know – but should know. Lilienthal, for example, lacked knowledge of materials. Such knowledge would have revealed that his design was not robust enough to withstand the forces acting on his glider. Ignoring this knowledge gap, he did not test the stress resistance of the glider's structures.

The Wright brothers had a broader domain of expertise. As designers and manufacturers of bicycles, they knew about the materials and structures needed to make them robust, without weighing them down. As experienced cyclists, they knew that balancing the bicycle is ensured by better control of the longitudinal axis. As well-informed readers of publications about aerodynamic data and flight experiences, they knew the rules for designing an efficient and lightweight aerodynamic surface. And as sons of an expert in mathematics (Susan Koerner Wright), they knew how to establish equations and analyse the results of

The Wright Family

The family environment also played a key role in the success of the Wright brothers. Their father Milton, a Baptist church bishop, was a cultured, book-loving man who sought to make his children constantly improve, pushing them to ask questions and encouraging them to solve problems. Their mother, Susan, was perhaps even more instrumental in their success, as a skilled mathematician with a strong mechanical aptitude. As a child, she spent many hours in her father's cart workshop learning how to use the various tools. Then she studied literature, a rare opportunity for a young woman of her time. She made toys for her children and mechanical devices, and both she and her husband had long discussions with their children and shared with them in reading the many books in their rich library.

The Wright brothers had two other brothers and one sister, Katharine. Although less famous than Orville and Wilbur, she distinguished herself by participating in the first Suffragette movement in the United States. A Latin teacher, she left her job to support her brothers in the development of their company after 1909, and held the honour of becoming the third woman in the world to fly!

---

[45] We prefer to use the word *hypothesis* rather than the word *idea* to recall the scientific origin of the learning cycle.

their experiments. Finally, as ingenious do-it-yourself types, they knew how to quickly build and repair their prototypes.

Thanks to these various and interlocking areas of expertise, they were able to identify the right problems to solve and generate new questions exposing their knowledge gaps. They were also able to capture their new knowledge in the form of reusable models, such as trade-off curves.[46] They thus accelerated the integration of what they already knew with what they had just learned, enabling them to seek out new knowledge gaps quickly.

Operating as an entrepreneurial family business with limited means, they also knew how to use all this knowledge to design exactly what they needed, with a minimum financial investment. This entrepreneurial approach has also been revisited by Ries.

From the Wright Brothers to Toyota

In 1907, after they had failed for two years to sell their aircraft in the United States and in Europe, the US Army Signal Corps placed an order for a single aircraft. Then, in 1908, it was the turn of a group of French businessmen to do the same. And the orders followed one after another. To satisfy demand, they built an aircraft manufacturing plant. All the manufactured models, civil or military, were evolutions of their original Flyer.

They also established flight training schools in the USA and Europe. Orville himself supervised training for several future pilots on the Huffman Prairie Flying Field in Dayton, Ohio. In six years, the school certified 119 pilots including the famous future Air Force General, Henry H. Arnold.

But the spreading of their know-how and their models allowed competitors to imitate them more easily.[47] In 1916, their main rival, Glenn Curtiss, founded the Curtiss Aeroplane and Motor Company, which became the largest aircraft manufacturer during the First World War.[48]

---

[46] See the curves drawn by the Wright Brothers preserved by the Franklin Institute https://www.fi .edu/history-resources/wright-notebooks.

[47] A long battle over property rights between the Wright Brothers, patent holders, and G. Curtiss, pilot and designer of competing airplanes.

[48] In 1929, the Curtiss–Wright Company was born from the merger of the companies founded, respectively, by G. Curtiss and the Wright Brothers. The 'Spirit of Saint Louis' engine was produced by this company.

Wilbur died in 1912. Three years later, Orville sold the Wright Company. He became a member of the board of the National Advisory Committee for Aeronautics (NACA) which was founded in 1915 (later renamed NASA). While research on aerodynamic theory remained unknown in the USA throughout the First World War,[49] he helped NACA catch up in the 1920s. He was also a consultant for aviation companies, and was honoured by some 15 prestigious universities (including Yale and Harvard).

After the First World War, Japan sent researchers to the USA and Europe. As early as the 1930s, many Japanese aeronautical engineers were graduating from MIT and Stanford University. The best of them served as apprentices at Curtiss Aeroplane and Motor Company, or at Douglas, Boeing, and Lockheed, and they learned the design and development methods of aircraft being practised in the United States: methods inspired by the Wright brothers.

To speed up this transfer of knowledge, Japan also invited leading scholars to present their work and advise the Japanese government. At the same time, the Japanese aeronautics industry was developing rapidly, under the impetus of the army in particular.[50] In 1938 Lockheed exported transport aircraft to Japan, and the Tachikawa Aircraft Company produced its first aircraft under licence. By the time the USA blocked the sale of aircraft to Japan in 1939 (including technology transfer and components), Japan had already acquired full autonomy to develop and produce domestically.

With the end of the Second World War, a large number of talented Japanese aeronautical engineers found jobs in the automotive industry – the most influential of these being the talented programme managers known as *shusa*. The crossover was not surprising: an aircraft is a complex system whose integrity and reliability objectives require a particularly coherent design approach between the various disciplines involved. Aircraft development programmes needed to be rigorously led to and the *shusa* were both powerful product managers and being expert programme managers.

Tatsuo Hasegawa, a young *shusa* at Tachikawa Aircraft[51] during the war was one of these. He joined Toyota and brought with him this rigorous product management system, the associated development methods, and

---

[49] Most of aerodynamics laws have been established by European scientists.

[50] Takashi Nishiyama. (2014). *Engineering War and Peace in Modern Japan, 1868–1964.* Johns Hopkins University Press.

[51] Takahiro Fujimoto. (2001). *Evolution of Manufacturing Systems at Toyota.* Productivity Press.

his own technical knowledge. He became the *shusa*[52] for the Toyota Corolla model in 1953 (see Chief Engineer). Toyota was for a long time the only car manufacturer to adopt this new role (Honda followed suit in the 1970s).

Thus, we can trace a kind of ancestry between the pioneering work of Wilbur and Orville Wright at the start of the 20th century and the development of Toyota Engineering some 50 years later. We can see how Toyota, by welcoming engineers and product managers from the aeronautics industry (many of whom had trained in the United States), was able to apply and build on their design methods and knowledge, which in turn had been directly inherited from the inventions and practices of the Wright brothers.

Sakichi Toyoda and the Wright Brothers: Multi-skilled Craftsmen, Inventors, and Entrepreneurs

Like many other great inventors (such as Thomas Edison or Nikola Tesla to name but two), neither Sakichi Toyoda nor the Wright brothers went to college. Instead, they were curious, experimental, analytical, and equipped with excellent 'DIY' craft and mechanical skills from a young age. They all started working on their future inventions before the age of 30. Their manual skills, coupled with great ingenuity, allowed them to prototype ideas and learn more quickly. Each of them thus engaged in a series of learning cycles, enabling them to continuously develop their products. They also took advantage of new technologies – the development of mechanisation and motorisation – to build new machines. *Developing and promoting this engineering craftsmanship should be at the heart of every company's concerns to develop better products.*

The Wright brothers, like Sakichi Toyoda, were born into a rapidly changing technological environment (Dayton was one of the cities with the most patents per inhabitant in 1890). They wanted their ideas to change society. They also had a strong desire to profit from their inventions and protect them by filing patents. They were true entrepreneurs. And all three have transformed both mobility and industry in the 20th century.

---

[52] In 1989, the term *shusa* was abandoned and replaced by the term Chief Engineer to better refer to its real position.

FROM TOYOTA: AND BACK TO THE WEST

While our discussion of the Wright brothers shows how the ancestral line of Toyota's engineering process traces some of its genes to the USA, we can also see how, later in the century, a process of cross-fertilisation saw many Western business process thinkers picking up and running with ideas that had been maturing in Japan.

Let's return briefly to the PDCA loop developed by Edward Deming in Japan in the 1950s.

This was 'rediscovered' in the USA 30 years later, and Deming's work on this lies at the heart of improvement initiatives as well as software development methods. For instance, Tom Gilb first proposed the EVO model (for *Evolutionary Value Delivery*) in the 1960s and defined it as an evolutionary development process that frequently delivers high value-added elements and adjusts quickly through regular feedback (substantiated the Iterative and Incremental Development). Indeed, Gilb saw EVO as a specialised variation of the PDSA cycle.

- PLAN: plan the EVO cycle;
- DO: implement the EVO cycle;
- STUDY: analyse the results according to the context;
- ACT: decide what to do in the next cycle.

More generally, several authors have been inspired or say they are inspired by the Toyota model, particularly in the field of software development. Among the most famous of these is Jeff Sutherland, inventor of Scrum, who said in an interview in 2014 that Scrum 'is based on Lean Product Development at Toyota'.[53] 'We opened up the first chapter of (Allen Ward's) book,' he recalls, 'and it described Scrum, perfectly!'.[54] Rather less overtly, Martin Fowler[55] acknowledges that 'Lean ideas can help us come up with better ideas for software development'.[56] As for Alistair Cockburn[57] he discovered, by reading *The Toyota Way Fieldbook* (2006) by Jeffrey Liker,

---

[53] https://www.stickyminds.com/interview/scrum-guide-interview-jeff-sutherland?page=0%2C1.
[54] https://www.youtube.com/watch?v=5vSc4WhkrMs (35'53").
[55] He helped create the 'Manifesto for Agile Software Development' in 2001.
[56] Martin Fowler's blog: https://martinfowler.com/bliki/ToyotaFailings.html.
[57] He helped create the 'Manifesto for Agile Software Development' in 2001.

that Toyota had already been implementing what he was suggesting (and beyond) for agile development.

In the same way, Eric Ries, author of the famous *The Lean Startup* (4), explains that the title of his book:

> takes its name from the lean manufacturing revolution that Taiichi Ohno and Shigeo Shingo are credited with developing at Toyota …. In the world of software, the agile development methodologies I had practised until that time had their origins in lean thinking.[58]

We could also mention the *Kanban Board*, supposedly inspired by the TPS *kanban*, as explained by David Anderson in his book.[59] However, it is less a *kanban* system than the application of the proven 'Constant Work-In-Progress'[60] method in software development.

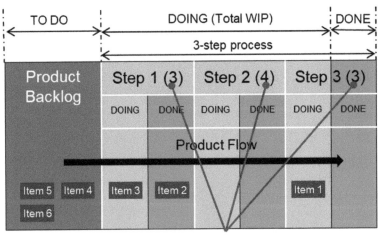

FIGURE 5.16
Example of a *Kanban Board*

---

[58] From the book *Lean Startup* (4), pp. 28 and 55.

[59] David J. Anderson. (2013). *Kanban: Successful Evolutionary Change for Your Technology Business.* Blue Hole Press Inc.

[60] CONWIP (CONstant Work-In-Progress) is a method used in production to regulate the pull flow by keeping the quantity of WIP constant.

Another waypoint in this cross-fertilisation of ideas can be seen in the work of Mary and Tom Poppendieck, authors of *Lean Software Development: an Agile Toolkit* (2003) (9). The clue is in the title, with the word *Lean* replacing the more commonly used term 'Agile'. They go on to formulate seven Lean principles for software development. This book and their following ones became so widely known that for many readers, Lean no longer refers to the Toyota Product System (TPS) but to Lean Software Development (LSD).

The First Kanban Board

The *Kanban Board* is often used by Scrum teams in the form of three columns to visualise the progress of tasks on a Sprint: TO DO, DOING, DONE. This board was not invented by a member of the Agile community, but by Lillian Gilbreth, a psychologist and industrial engineer who at the beginning of the 20th century was one of the first female engineers to earn a PhD. She and her husband Frank carried out numerous 'time and motion' studies to make operations in factories easier for workers and improve industrial processes. What is less known is her interest in visual management. In a speech to the National Federation of Business and Professional Women's Clubs in New York in 1930, she defined the three columns of the *Kanban Board* (Domesticating Efficiency: Lillian Gilbreth's Scientific Management of Homemakers, 1924–1930 by Laurel D. Graham).

The family of Lillian and Frank Gilbreth has been popularised by a humorous novel written by two of their 12 children (Frank Jr and Ernestine), *Cheaper by The Dozen*, which tells how modern management methods can be applied in the family context. This novel was a childhood delight for one of the authors of this guide.

A NOTE ON THE AGILE MOVEMENT

First, it is amusing to note a similarity of approach in the choice of the words *Agile* and *Lean*. While *Agile* replaced *Light*, *Lean* replaced *Fragile*.[61] These first choices, *Light* and *Fragile*, finally expressed the same idea: development or production processes deliberately made lighter or even more fragile, but whose performance and robustness would ultimately be

---

[61] Fragile was the first word chosen by J. Krafcik.

From Individual Agility to Agility at Scale

Before characterising a framework, agility is, first of all, an individual aptitude partly linked to *mental* or *cognitive flexibility*. It is one of the executive functions of the brain which enables us to appropriately adjust our behaviour according to a changing environment – the cost–benefit ratio between repetition and exploration is an equation that the brain is constantly trying to solve, especially when a person's environment changes.

For an individual, the more standard responses to predictable situations they have integrated, i.e., a repertoire of automatisms allowing to free up memory, the more their brain will be available to better react to unpredictable changes. Training is therefore important for developing agility. It can then become a skill.

The agility of an organisation first depends on the agility of the individuals within it. Agility at scale emerges from the coordinated application of individual agility to a collective, which in turn allows each individual to actualise their own agility a little more of in social contact.

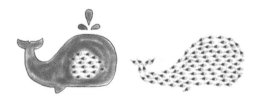

FIGURE 5.17

Agility at scale

The agility of a system is first the result of the agility of its constituents (credit T. Conter).

regained by greater involvement and autonomy of people: *because people, not processes, create value.*

In 2001, several inventors and practitioners of Iterative and Incremental software Development methods co-authored a document that summarised their learning in the form of values and principles common to all these methods. This document took the name of the Manifesto for Agile Software Development.[62] It thus definitively consecrated the term *Agile* as the unifying name for the movements that use it. It should be noted that the use of the word *Manifesto* fits this document well: it is a public statement intended to draw attention to values and principles, and not a single method.

Moreover, agility is the term used to characterise the need for more flexibility and responsiveness in a changing, complex, and ambiguous environment. To simplify, it is the ability to cope with change. One

---

[62] http://agilemanifesto.org/.

can, therefore, be agile without strictly applying the principles of the Manifesto.

Let's just summarise that the different methods of Agile software development and Lean Product Development share many common principles, but also differences due to their distinct historical contexts and their scope of application. Understanding them well makes it possible to exploit their complementariness. However, this is not the purpose of this guide.

6

On Site: Daily Life

Last point before leaving for your journey. Once there, it is important to know how to interpret some cultural differences. For example, some paradoxes can defy your common sense. Moreover, you will have to avoid some pitfalls so that your journey does not end too early.

LEAN ENGINEERING PARADOXES

> *The paradoxes of Lean are such that common sense alone will not be enough to guide you through.*

An expression sometimes used is 'ambidextrous' strategy, which means promoting both short-term results through a policy of cost control and long-term profitability by investing wisely. This places the acceptation of paradox, i.e., the acceptation of 'two seemingly contradictory forces or ideas at the same times',[1] at the highest level of the company. For example, accepting black and white at the same time is not about choosing either black or white, or blinding them into grey. It is accepting that black and white exist in duality, are interdependent, are complementary, and together form a mutual whole, like in the *tàijí tú*, the symbol representing *Yin* and *Yang*.[2]

---

[1] Paradox vs. Tradeoff (dalemeador.com).
[2] Jim Collins and Jerry I Porras. (2004). *Built to Last: Successful Habits of Visionary Companies.* Harper Business.

DOI: 10.4324/9781003381945-7

FIGURE 6.1
The tàijí tú, the symbol of Yin and Yang

A Lean company embraces both extremes across a number of dimensions at the same time:[3] short-term AND long-term, exploitation AND exploration, standard AND innovation, robust AND agile, *jidoka* AND Just-in-Time, etc. Here, we present four paradoxes that seem to us to be typical of Lean Engineering. The challenge is thus to bring out their positive potential.

Decision Paradox: Delay Decisions AND Deliver Faster

At first glance, this may seem like a shocking idea, as organisations are so keen on making firm decisions with minimal delay. On closer inspection, making decisions too early when information is lacking increases the likelihood of errors in judgement, which lead to revisited decisions and potential costly rework (blue curve as presented in figure 6.2).

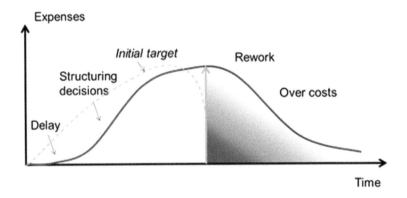

FIGURE 6.2
Typical project expense profile

---

[3] See 'genius of the AND' – Ibid.

Unfortunately, putting pressure to accelerate the decision-making process remains the favourite mode of project management. And this pressure is all the stronger when the project is delayed. While making structuring decisions as soon as possible may appear to be an expression of strong determination, we see it more as an expression of wishful thinking.

> *We often hear managers complain that decisions are never made. However, it is not so much the lack of decisions that penalise projects as the fact that they are made too early, and therefore often revisited. Thus, this continuous questioning gives the impression that decisions are never made. And teams spend time going back over decisions already made.*

Managing the decision paradox means that you seek to be effective at delaying the decision[4] so you can make it with confidence AND speeding up the decision so you can be on time. This paradox leads to solving the trade-off between the cost of rework caused by a bad decision and the cost of waiting to make the right decision.[5]

Frontloading resources to enable knowledge to develop more quickly and make better decisions later changes the expense curve. So, this requires trust from the management, but it pays off in the long run.

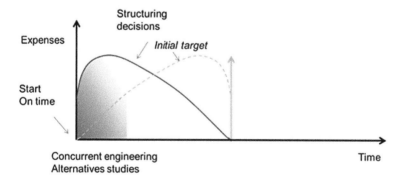

FIGURE 6.3
Expense profile for a Lean project

[4] Cost of Delay by Donald G. Reinerstsen. (2009). *The Principles of Product Development Flow.* Celeritas Pub.

[5] Mary Poppendieck: 'Don't make expensive-to-change decisions before their time – and don't make them after their time!' http://www.poppendieck.com/.

Predictability Paradox[6]: Short-Term Planning AND Long-Term Plan

Let's return to Allen Ward's (3) memorable quote 'Instead of learning to surf, conventional organisations try to control the waves. This almost never works'. For a project, wanting to control the waves means wanting to resist disturbances by erecting, like a dike, a protective plan for the project team to follow, whatever comes up ahead. Of course, building on a solid foundation is crucial to successful project management, because you can't build with confidence on a shifting foundation. However, in the face of turbulent and ever-changing conditions, robustness turns into rigidity and resistance into intolerance. The paradox is obvious: trying too hard to create predictability creates an opposite effect. Faced with the unexpected, the dike breaks.

> *As one of our bosses once said when speaking of our Quality Reference System: 'instead of the Ten Commandments, we wrote the Bible'.*

The challenge, therefore, is to define and commit to key shared objectives AND to adjust the resulting plan as needed based on local conditions. 'Learning to surf' means recognising the importance of implementing pull, flow, and cadence into your product development process. And it provides the conditions for everyone to learn and improve continuously in order to be able to adapt quickly to unpredictable situations (see *kaizen* definition).

Unfortunately, most of the time, this paradox is managed by prioritising wave control as close as possible from the workers on up, and through the implementation of micro-management. The principle is simple: reducing the margin of manoeuvre of each one, by a centralised control system which is, in theory, considered infallible. Plans and schedules are

Plan or Planning?

When President Eisenhower said in 1957, 'Plans are worthless, but planning is everything', he emphasised that it is the planning activity rather than the plan itself that is useful. In turbulent and ever-changing conditions, the initial plan quickly becomes obsolete: 'plans are good until the first bullet flies'. That is why it is useful for each team to learn how to adjust the plan as it goes along.

One planning meeting a week is almost 50 opportunities to learn how to plan in a year! It's not a question of controlling people or event 50 times, but rather of teaching the team to constantly improve their powers of predicting and reacting.

[6] Mary Poppendieck. (2003). 'Lean Development and the Predictability Paradox'. *Cutter Consortium*.

determined with minute detail, which makes them *de facto* permanently obsolete and reduces all initiative. You have probably already seen the kind of crisis situations where follow-up meetings are multiplied, leaving no chance for teams to solve problems because they are too busy preparing for the next meeting. This way of doing things only aggravates the crisis, giving rise to yet more meetings in a vicious circle that is very difficult to break. A paradox cannot be managed as a dilemma!

Problem Paradox: Say 'Welcome!' to Problems AND Accelerate the Flow

We have defined a *problem* as a gap between the current situation and the target situation, whether this is achievable or dreamed. Whichever it is, the idea behind seeing problems as gaps is simple: whenever you try to reduce such a gap, there is something to be learned. Saying 'welcome!' to problems means that every new problem is an opportunity to develop people's problem-solving skills, to learn new things, and thus to continuously improve the system and its quality.

Serendipity, What Is That?

The serendipity, a neologism invented on 28 January 1754 by Horace Walpole, coming from Serendip, the ancient name of Sri Lanka, and meaning 'the ability to grasp and interpret with sagacity what comes to us unexpectedly, is a good illustration of 'welcome to problems'. It is very close to abductive reasoning (C. S. Peirce). There are numerous examples of serendipity such as the discoveries of penicillin (A. Fleming), Viagra®, Post-its®, pulsars (J. Bell), radioactivity (H. Becquerel), and also the Tarte Tatin (Tatin Sisters). And many other things! However, serendipity is not just a matter of luck. It is above all the ability to recognise a new idea in an accident or an error.

At the other pole of the problem paradox is the desire to accelerate the flow. However, each new problem is a 'thrown forward'[7] obstacle slowing down the flow. Thus, accepting this paradox leads to both encouraging flow and stopping it. This is an illustration of the Just-in-Time – *jidoka* paradox where two opposite poles are managed in a complementary way.

Nevertheless, the goal is certainly not to solve a problem simply because it has to be done. 'Solving' the wrong problem surely makes learning

---

[7] Problem etymology from Greek *proballein*: '*pro*' forward + '*ballein*' to throw.

useless. The right problems to solve are the ones that come along the way to the next goal. So it is essential to define that next goal well. When there are no more problems to solve, that's a problem – it's time to set a new, more ambitious goal to outline the next gaps to fill.

Efficiency Paradox: Flow Efficiency AND Resource Efficiency

The word 'resource' is used here in its broadest sense (and includes human resources as well as computer resources, machines, benches, and so forth). It goes without saying that people are very specific resources, and in no way comparable to machines. But despite this, and all too often, human efficiency is measured only in terms of basic productivity, which unfortunately tends to put human beings in the same bracket as machines.

The tension between resource efficiency and flow efficiency is called *Efficiency Paradox* in (10) and is summarised in this matrix.

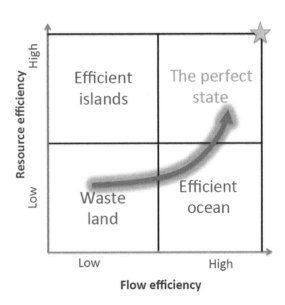

FIGURE 6.4
Resource efficiency and flow efficiency (from Niklas Modig and Pär Ahlström)

Resource efficiency is related to the capacity utilisation of each resource (i.e., real working time over available working time), while flow efficiency is related to the throughput time of each flow unit (information, product's item, etc.). Note that the term 'resource efficiency' does not consider productivity.

- In Wasteland, there is neither resource efficiency nor flow efficiency.
- In the Efficient islands, resource utilisation is made efficient at the expense of flow efficiency. Maximising resource utilisation per silo ('island') leads to an increase in WIP (Work in Progress) for the entire system. What is seen as an advantage by each engineering function turns out to be a disadvantage for the customers as the lead time increases.
- On the opposite side, in the Efficient ocean, flow efficiency is achieved at the expense of resource utilisation efficiency (resource is not utilised at full capacity). Here, priority is given to the flow (e.g., by limiting WIP) in order to better satisfy customer demands. To achieve this, the vision is then global ('ocean') and no longer local ('islands').
- The least intuitive, but most striking, aspect of this matrix is that it is not possible to target the Perfect state by first optimising resource utilisation. Local optimisation does not pave the way to a global optimum. You need an efficient flow first – flow efficiency produces resources efficiency – before you go on to improve value for money. This seems to go against the grain of what so many companies have been thinking for decades.
- Last but not least, the Star can never be reached due to the combined influence on the lead time of two factors: utilisation and variation.
  - The higher the resource utilisation, the longer the lead time (*muri* effect), except with no variation.
  - The higher the variation (arrival and process variation), the longer the lead time (*mura* effect).
    These two factors are multiplied by each other: at a given utilisation, the lead time gets even worse with a higher variation.

Thus, the upper right corner represents the *Efficiency frontier*, which emphasises the fact that it is impossible to optimise both high resource utilisation and high flow efficiency due to variation (refer to Just-in-Time). The challenge is to push the *Efficiency frontier* through *kaizen*.

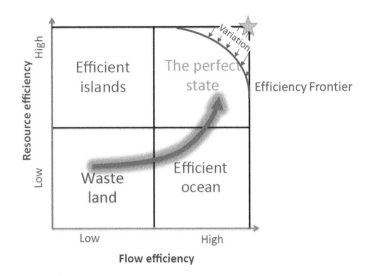

FIGURE 6.5
Efficiency frontier (from Niklas Modig and Pär Ahlström)

Let's take an example. Each individual strives to demonstrate their efficiency, while being occupied at 100% of the time – or even at 110%, given the 'presenteeism' tendency to spend long hours at work. However, if *flow efficiency* is not prioritised, there is zero chance that any individual will actually reveal problems that might be impinging on their own efficiency, as this could show them in a bad light – in other words, it could show them as being less than totally efficient. If bringing such aspects to light is not incentivised, then doing so could appear as a kind of pointless self-sacrifice.

A resource tracking indicator had long been used in one organisation to measure capacity utilisation. Managers refused to give it up, arguing that good management must rely on resources being utilised as near as possible to 100%. The products being developed were highly complex and expensive, and workers had become accustomed to a high defect rate. However, when the market became more competitive, the defect rate became costly and unsustainable. In the year with the worst financial results, the resource tracking indicator had never been so 'good' in terms of the highest levels of resource utilisation: both humans and machines were working full tilt in producing products, many of them defective!

PITFALLS

> Lean is a journey, and not always with an easy road to navigate; often our eyes are fixed on the road ahead rather than on the ultimate destination. In other words, we can get so fixated with the 'method' that we forget those two essentials: the product and the customer.

Impose Top-Down Lean Rollout

The transition from the early adopters to rolling out new processes across the board is often problematic. Deployment leads to disappointment. It is difficult, and rarely sustainable, to imagine that everyone will buy into the idea unless you take the time to install a new learning culture. And simply *imposing* good practices universally, even if they have already proved their worth on a smaller scale, almost never works.

Instead, you need to think about the rollout differently: it must be done horizontally, between teams, on the basis of local successes and that people want to see reproduced elsewhere. This is the principle of horizontal deployment or *yokoten*. It is not simply a matter of sharing good practices; *yokoten* requires going to see for oneself on the *genba*, sharing with one's peers what has been learned from both successes and failures and understanding what can be adopted as is and what needs to be adapted to one's own context. *Yokoten* is really a success multiplier! And this multiplication of good examples will accelerate as top managers engage in *Genba Walks*.

Falling in Love with Your System

Generally speaking, 'bureaucracy'[8] is perceived as a form of organisation. It has become necessary to ensure the functioning of increasingly important structures and did not originally carry the negative connotation of 'red tape' that is now associated with its excesses.

Bureaucracy is, therefore, also an important part of the functioning of any company which needs to be managed efficiently. And any system

---

[8] The word 'bureaucracy' was apparently coined in 1764 in France. The French academy accepted the word in 1798. It means the 'rule of desk'. Max Weber (1864–1920), was one of the most famous sociological writer's on bureaucracy.

of a certain size has a natural tendency to consume more energy in maintaining itself, and somewhat less in the exchange with systems outside. The well-meaning aim of bureaucracy is to take control of all this effort to maintain a company's internal functioning and make it more efficient. Unfortunately, bureaucracy itself often becomes yet another self-sustaining system. Put simply, there are two models of bureaucracy (note that these two models coexist in most companies with different intensities):

- Mechanistic bureaucracy: this imposes a series of detailed rules and regulations fixed in a kind of 'command and control' model and applied uniformly in all cases.
- Enabling bureaucracy: this proposes continuously improved guidelines and standards in a learning model. This way develops critical thinking, collaboration, and responsibility for everyone.

Lean, of course, aims to develop this enabling model. In this model, managers become critical to the success of such organisations. The 'command and control' mentality is no longer relevant. Unfortunately, a Lean structure with its deployment roadmaps and actions, certification paths, coaches, tools sheets, etc., always risk being reduced to a kind of mechanistic bureaucracy – one that shifts from reasoning to enforcement. This risk can be a consequence of falling in love with your creation and putting all your energy into it, while completely forgetting the initial goals. As the proverb puts it so aptly: 'When the wise man points to the moon, the fool looks at the finger'. Lean principles, practices, and tools (the finger) are not business' objectives linked to the customer (the moon), but only a way to reach them. So let's not install a Lean structure, and then fall in love with it to the point of forgetting what it was meant to be used for.

Part Two

Map, Territories, Pathways

Now, get ready to travel! We propose two paths linking three *territories*, offering places already known and others less visited that will make you want to go further. Several itineraries are possible. In the third part, we provide some guidelines to create your own itinerary.

- The path to *Growth and Profit* connects the *Territory of Customers* to the *Territory of Products*. You will discover how to quickly and efficiently convert the problems of customers into valuable solutions.
- The path to *Knowledge and Sustainability* travels the *Territory of People Development*. This 'continuous improvement' path provides the conditions for sustainable value creation for your company.
- The *Territory of Customers* is outside the company. This is where customers interact with the products and experience problems or satisfaction. Paying attention to these experiences is the basis of Voice of Customers (VoC).
- The *Territory of Products* covers the company and its partners. This is where solutions are designed and developed to solve problems and fit the needs identified in the Territory of Customers.
- The *Territory* of *People Development* is in the company. It represents the place to learn for all employees. Often missing in most companies, this territory gives Lean its unique identity.

Per *territory*, each place represents a practice, a tool, or a method rated from 0 to 3 stars. These stars are awarded on both their impact and their difficulty. The most powerful practices but requiring more experience are identified by three stars (***). The easiest to access is identified by one star (*).

All these *territories* and *pathways* should be displayed on a map to help you make better decisions as you navigate through and progress within them. And what could be a better map than an *obeya* (see the next figure)?

DOI: 10.4324/9781003381945-8

FIGURE 7.0A
The *obeya* map. Source: This map has been created by Johanna Guillaum

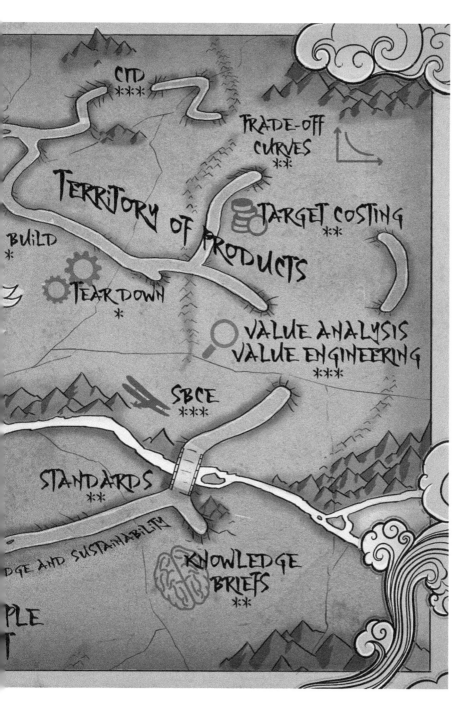

FIGURE 7.0B
Continued

7

Obeya*

Obeya is the visual place where people in charge of the development of a new product share their information and collaborate to review, analyse, and act upon.

OBEYA, THE MAP

Your *obeya*[1] must act as a map. Visuals are displayed on its walls; each wall is specific to a *territory*. They provide everyone with the necessary information to direct themselves autonomously. This information is updated as the team progresses on the itinerary.

THE VISUALS

The Customer Wall

The Customer Wall makes visible what has been learned from the exploration of the Territory of Customers. The teams progress as they answer the following questions:

- Who are the customers and other stakeholders?
- What are their preferences, expectations, needs, and problems?

---

[1] For the origin of *obeya* refer to http://leanpd.org/you-cant-manage-a-secret/.

DOI: 10.4324/9781003381945-9

- How to express customer value? Which Key Value Attributes (KVAs) are most important to customers (and other stakeholders)? Where are the key trade-offs?
- Which KVAs are most important to your company?
- How is the competition positioned in the marketplace?

Each new answer makes the Voice of Customers (VoC) ... much clearer!

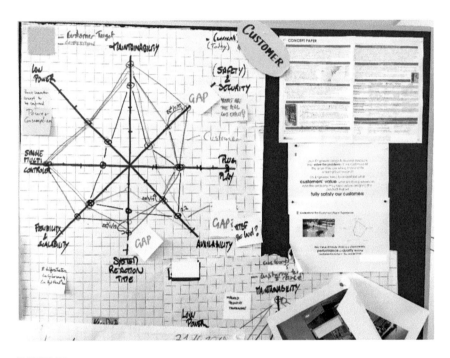

FIGURE 7.1
Example of KVA and Concept Paper visuals on the Customers Wall

The path to *Growth and Profit* starts and ends with this Customer Wall. It informs most future decisions. The quality of the posted information captured during the exploration of the *Territory of Customers* is therefore critical for the success of your product development.

The Product Wall

The Product Wall displays the engineering parameters translated from the Customer Wall information. The path between these two walls follows the path to Growth and Profit, as a metaphor for the product development flow. This path is outlined in the Concept Paper.

The teams progress as they answer the following questions:

- What are the key product performance requirements, parameters, and constraints? What are the target levels that define the region of interest for the customers? What is the Target Cost? Where are the key trade-offs between all this data?
- What might the product look like? What are the candidate concepts and architectures? What are the key features and key functions?
- What may be the differentiators?
- Where are the challenges and knowledge gaps from technical, technological, industrial, and business perspectives?

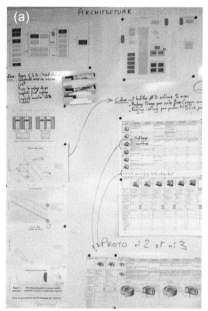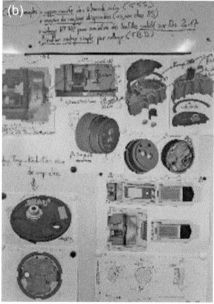

FIGURE 7.2

Example of visuals on the Product Wall

The Flow Wall

The Flow Wall visualises the progression of the flow units, i.e., all the artefacts defined, produced, exchanged, and integrated by the teams to form the expected product. This flow acts as the path to Growth and Profit.

A Pull-Scheduling Board, or a *Kanban Board*, can be used to visualise and manage this flow. In this way, each team member can see what to deliver to whom *Just-In-Time*, with the required level of quality.

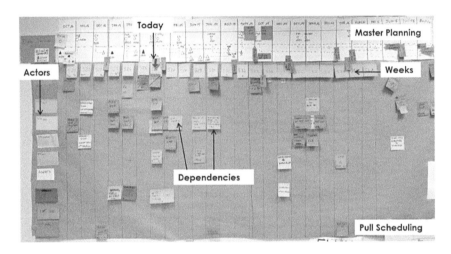

FIGURE 7.3
A Pull-Scheduling Board on the Flow Wall

The Problems Wall

This Problems Wall visualises the problems coming from any other wall. For example, if the quality of a unit flow prevents it from being processed by the recipient, or if the flow is slowed down, the information about the problem is displayed on the Problems Wall (refer to *jidoka*), thus avoiding future downstream disruptions. The problem is removed from the wall once solved. This way, no problems are left unreported and unfixed.

FIGURE 7.4
Example of Problem Wall

Four Walls, Is That All?

Not really! We suggest adding a sandbox to make an *obeya* an even more effective place for collaboration. At a minimum, this sandbox is a whiteboard used to draw ideas, formulate problems, and share information. The information that emerges can feed the other walls. Without this extra feature, the *obeya* can become a place of reporting, or worse, a place of control.

Our advice for building an effective *obeya* is to apply the following layout. However, feel free to adapt it to your specific case by including everything you think you need to facilitate collaboration and learning. Be careful to always keep a logical and coherent flow of information between all visuals.

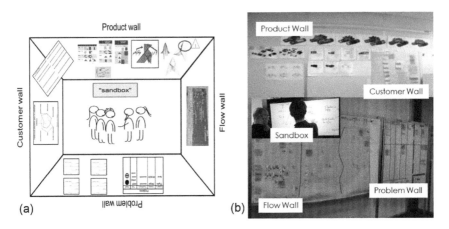

FIGURE 7.5
Obeya layout

Visuals are key! They make the *obeya* different from other collaborative workspaces. They get people to interact about what is important to customers and the product, and reflect their level of understanding. Short stand-up meetings in sync with the development flow energise these interactions and keep the visuals up-to-date.

Above all, be careful not to reproduce in your *obeya* what it was supposed to change, i.e., a management system, where the walls are covered with planning, action lists, and KPIs, where the team's issues overshadow those of the customers, where the process takes precedence over the product. These 'eye-catching visuals' have little impact on performance, since it is no longer about learning but only about monitoring and controlling!

To summarise, *obeya* is as much a map that displays what you need in order to make progress in the territories in a simple, visual way, as it is a collaborative working place for sharing, deciding, acting, and learning[2] together.

---

[2] Job = work + *Kaizen*.

8

Genba Walk***

The *Genba Walk* consists of going to a specific place to observe the situation and understand how to improve it. In the engineering field, the *genba* to focus on are the customers' premises and then the *obeya*.

GENBA WALK, WHAT IT IS

Genba Walk is a routine for managers which consists of systematically and regularly going to the field, i.e., on the *genba*, to observe the facts first-hand and act accordingly, rather than based on what others say.

For the manager, it is therefore a matter of observing, touching, feeling directly, and therefore testing their beliefs by questioning and communicating with the people who do the work. The Toyota Chairman Fujio Cho translated it this way, 'go see,[1] ask why, show respect'.

GENBA WALK, WHAT IT IS NOT

This is not a workplace visit that the top manager makes with the board of directors once a year.

---

[1] It is more about observing than seeing. By seeing, you are only capturing the view of the phenomena; by observing, you are analysing what you see. In this quote, the analysis is covered by 'why'.

DOI: 10.4324/9781003381945-10

This is not the opportunity to incriminate those who are being observed in their work. This is also not the time to pick up indicators that were not transmitted the previous week or to enforce micromanagement.

This is not the time to solve problems either. Identifying them is good enough.

THE PURPOSE

So why go to the *genba*? There are essentially two reasons:

1. To understand how customers use your products.
2. To understand what prevents your teams from doing their job. So you must go and observe them at work. As managers, you need to understand the difficulties they face and how they interact with the products.

Genba Walks are also aimed at top managers, not just operational and frontline managers. One of our executives once admitted, 'We're kind of in our ivory tower here in our offices. We make decisions, but we don't have time to see what the consequences are'. The more important the decisions (e.g., strategic decisions), the greater the risk of scattering in their execution on the ground – as knowledge and power span multiple organisational levels. Indeed, while corporate executives make decisions, frontline managers can either weaken or strengthen them depending on the actions they first take based on their own daily operations.

Becoming aware of the consequences of one's decisions can only be done by going to the place of their execution, i.e., to the *genba*! While *hoshin kanri*[2] helps ensure that frontline activities are aligned with tactics and strategy, only *Genba Walks* provides an accurate, real-time understanding of a given situation. In this way, the company can react quickly and adjust decisions accordingly. This series of micro-adaptations is an opportunity to change direction on a small scale, while enabling larger-scale changes such as redefining strategic objectives before it is too late.

---

[2] 'A management process that aligns – both vertically and horizontally – an organization's functions and activities with its strategic objectives. A specific plan – typically annual – is developed with precise goals, actions, timelines, responsibilities, and measures', from the *Lean Lexicon* 5th Edition by Lean Enterprise Institute, Inc – January 21, 2014.

We accompanied a software department manager for his first Genba Walk. Intrigued by a screen that seemed to indicate a queue, he asked a developer what it meant. After a few exchanges, he understood that the software integration process (compilation, testing, qualimetry), while fully tooling up, took nearly four hours. While waiting for his turn, each developer continued to develop new code, increasing the stock of untested code and the risk of generating non-quality later on. This waste gave the manager the opportunity to explain that improvement should be part of the job. The decision was made to drastically reduce the build time and to accompany this reduction with the necessary resources. With this message, the team felt encouraged to invest time today to save time tomorrow.

HOW TO

Tips

While the *Genba Walk* can be seen as a managerial method that helps reconcile strategy with execution and top-down decisions with *genba* reality, there is no true method to succeed in *Genba Walks*. Nevertheless, we can propose some tips:

- Be ready to face your ignorance, to challenge your beliefs, and to review your opinions. There is no need to show off on the *genba*!
- Show respect and interest for people and their work. Be attentive to their difficulties;
- Make good use of questioning and judgement;
- Be curious to see what others do not see – or do not want to see;
- Come back regularly to observe and encourage progress. It is less a question of checking if the teams are doing well than of focusing on what they are doing better.

The place where a manager puts their feet informs the employees about what is important to them. Taking a close interest in the work of each team is seen as a sign of respect. This has a positive effect on everyone's commitment. A manager who has the humility to learn on the *genba*, who sees their role as much in training teams to solve problems as in training themselves, is considered an exceptional leader.

Where to Go?

In engineering, it seems a bit tricky. Imagine the scene in an engineering office, with a team hunched over their computers, typing, moving the mouse: the *genba* is not telling you very much. Engineers are essentially handling intangibles that are more difficult to observe, so it is critical to make visual some of this information. This is the role of *obeya*. *Obeya* can be viewed as the main *genba* for engineering activities. You could also consider labs, technical meetings or software code as forms of *genba*. Do not hesitate to sit next to an engineer to observe and understand how they interact with information displayed by their workstation (refer also to *Dojo*).

> A manager sitting at the workstation of a customer support team member was surprised that red-flagged complaints in the complaint management software were staying in the backlog waiting to be processed. He was so surprised when the engineer told him that the claims missing the deadline were only being processed at best. He felt that once the contractual date passed, it was better to focus on those that were still on schedule. After explaining that all claims should be handled, particularly the late ones, it was time for the manager to question the management's communication and the context that had led the team to behave this way!

Beyond the engineering premises, there are other *genba* that may be of interest to heads of engineering: those where the impact of engineering decisions can be observed. Remember, *design and development decisions create operational value streams!* In this case, the *genba* are the shop floor, production line, assembly line, or any place where service happens.

Beyond management, every engineer has to learn from these *genba*, to understand how their design decisions can cause problems for operators (e.g., problems related to components, workflow steps and sequence, testing facilities). In the same way, problems related to product installation or maintenance may originate from design decisions.

Whatever the *genba*, remember that a key element to focus on is people! Are they able to succeed? Does the office layout help engineers develop better products (comfort, visual management, etc.)? Are they often interrupted or disturbed? How many of them are actually working on a product and creating value for the customer? Are there engineers who wait several long minutes in front of their workstations for the results of the software integration?

It is also an opportunity to lead engineers who have their noses to the grindstone back to the root causes of their problems.

How to Proceed?

To be effective, a *Genba Walk* process requires preparation, practice, and debriefing. Good questions are what make it work.

> **Before** – A *Genba Walk* begins with developing a goal and hypotheses. A set of questions can help define them: why are you going here rather than there? What information are you looking for? What opinions do you seek to test against the facts? Be prepared to be surprised or even disconcerted!

> **During** – once in the *genba*, start by questioning yourself:
> - Do I understand what I see?
> - Am I puzzled by what I see?
> - Am I not seeing what I should have seen (and vice versa)?
> - How can I confirm my understanding?
> - Can I relate my past decisions to what I see?
> - Is it getting better than before? At the right pace?

Feel free to write down some of your observations. You can also ask the team questions if you need to, but be careful how you phrase them.

> - Are they open-ended or closed-ended questions?
>   - Open-ended questions begin with an interrogative word (why, where, how, what, which, etc.). They allow people to give free-form answers. In this way, you can get deeper and new insights and minimise misunderstandings;
>   - Closed-ended questions begin with a verb (Do you …, Does that …, etc.). They have a limited set of possible answers: 'yes', 'no', or 'I don't know', which limits the discussion.

- Are they biased or trick? These questions can hinder communication efforts and damage your relationships with others:
  - Loaded questions contain presupposition that the respondents might disagree with – e.g., Are you still generating technical debt?
  - Suggestive questions suggest that a certain answer should be given in response – e.g., Don't you agree that the problem is quite evident?

For newbies, in addition to a *sensei* or a Lean coach, it may be helpful to be accompanied by a peer observer. The observer's role will be to provide you with feedback based on objective, observable evidence of the impact of your behaviour, and actions on the desired outcome of the *Genba Walk*. You should agree on the purpose of the observation and the evidence to be observed. This evidence can be the number and type of questions you ask and the number of answers you get, the type of interactions with people (monologue, dialogue, open discussion), non-verbal communication, etc. The observer notes their observations to share with you during feedback.

After – A common mistake is to leave the *genba* with a stack of actions to be closed by the team for the next *Genba Walk*. *Genba Walk* is not a new way to increase your control! Moreover, your teams probably already have enough actions to complete. However, you know that some actions are necessary to improve the situation. Choose a topic with the team to initiate a tangible improvement. Make sure that it is not extra work, but less waste. You have to respect people, their time, their work, and their opinions.

After the *Genba Walk*, perform a debrief with the *sensei* (and the observers if any). Ask what worked and what didn't work, what thing you can do better next time. Each *Genba Walk* should be a new learning experience for you.

THE DIFFICULTIES

> *A Vice President told us that 'one of the most difficult exercises for management is the* Genba Walk. *The first time is a big slap in the face, the second time is ownership, and the third time is the beginning of continuous improvement'.*

Why is it so difficult?

- Lack of leadership.
  - 'I regularly visit the *obeya* to check the indicators and as soon as something goes wrong, I ask for an action plan. My teams are there to find solutions, not to talk to me about their problems'. It is a common attitude, which consists of not changing anything about the usual command and control mode while using visual management to do it. 'When the manager comes into our *obeya*, it's to control us even more, not to help us!' In this case, the teams prefer that the manager stays in their office.
  - 'I come every day to see my teams. I know perfectly what is happening'. Really? Saying *hello* is a highly commendable practice, certainly, but largely insufficient to ensure that things are going in the right direction and that teams are making progress.
- Lack of time: 'I have so many meetings that I don't have time to go and see what's going on. I request a summary report, and so I am perfectly aware'. As a result, teams spend more time reporting and less time-solving problems, which is even more important. *The time supposedly saved by the manager is really lost by the team.*
- Lack of confidence: 'I am not able to help my team when they have problems'. You must overcome your fear of not answering the questions your employees will ask you. You learn at least as much as your teams when you go to the *genba* because you cannot know everything the experts know. Continuous improvements come from combining the knowledge of the engineers with your own. And confess when you don't know.

- Lack of objectivity: During *Genba Walks* you are bombarded with signals and can quickly become saturated with much visual data, especially for untrained eyes. Fortunately, your attention selects only the data to be submitted for analysis. Conversely, paying attention to some events or facts to the detriment of others can cause you to miss weak yet useful signals.[3] This happens in particular when the stimulus does not fit into the idea of what the observed situation is supposed to look like. You more easily detect the information that matters to you. These effects induced by selective attention can be amplified by other biases of observation. Among the best known is the *streetlight effect* that occurs when people are only looking for something where it is easiest to look at, for example, under the lamppost because that is where the light is! Becoming aware of the limits imposed by your mental patterns is the first step towards conscious, focused, and active observation. Then, with the experience, your vision will be refined, the questioning will become more relevant and the problems will become more visible, 'beyond the lamppost'!

You have to go to the *genba* with the open mind of those who want to learn.

- Compare the observed situation with your mental models: do you observe unexpected situations that are out of step with your conception of what should have been?
- Question the possible causes of the observed anomalies: why is this happening? What potential hypotheses can you formulate?
- Question your hypotheses: what confidence do you have in them? What evidence refutes them? What are the other options?

Facts don't have the power to change minds, critical thinking does. So *Genba Walks* give you a great opportunity to practice and develop your critical thinking.

---

[3] Christopher Chabris and Daniel Simons. (2011). *The Invisible Gorilla: How Our Intuitions Deceive Us*. Harmony.

The Top-Down Attention Process

Top-down attention, or goal-directed attention, refers to the voluntary control of attention to select the most relevant information for a given objective. An area of the prefrontal cortex is specialised in maintaining this objective, i.e., our intention of the moment, in memory. It is therefore better to have one clear intention at a time in order to make action plans immediately available (aka *task set*) capable of selecting the right subset of the input and ignoring the rest.

It is therefore the intention that guides the attention, which then filters incoming sensory information that is relevant to the goal at hand. It creates zones of light in our perceptive field (the streetlight effect).

This top-down processing also allows us to make sense of the information that has already been brought in by the senses, working downward from initial impressions to specific details. It learns from past experiences and prior knowledge.

Thus, the more often you go to *genba*, the more you develop automatisms and patterns, and the more efficiently you act with a minimum of attention. This gives you more space to process new visual information, as we say, beyond the lamppost!

9

The Path to Growth and Profit

This path travels from the Territory of Customers to the Territory of Products. It connects the problem (the customer's need) to the solution (the product) via different itineraries.

People don't primarily buy products as such, but rather solutions that solve their problems, i.e., that bridge the gaps between the situation they are experiencing and the situation they want. Applying this principle, Michelin® has moved a part of its core business from selling tyres towards selling kilometres. And from most Software as a Service (SaaS) companies, people do not merely buy software but rather solutions.

It is essential to understand what problems need to be solved to propose the best solution. This is why the journey begins with the exploration of the Territory of Customers, aimed at characterising the Voice of Customers (VoC) and then establishing the Key Specification ranges. The data collected during this exploration is synthesised in the Concept Paper, the entry document for the exploration of the Territory of Products. This exploration is first of all that of the solutions space. The objective is to identify which region is hosting the best solution, i.e., the one providing the best trade-offs.

DOI: 10.4324/9781003381945-11

EXPLORING THE TERRITORY OF CUSTOMERS

This exploration aims to gain insight into the problems, needs, desires, perceptions, preferences, and expectations of your customers. Once this VoC is characterised, it will guide your decision-making. That's why identifying problems that penalise the user experience comes first.

Analysing Customer Complaints*

The analysis of customer complaints is the main source of information on how your customers use your products and perceive value. So consider customer feedback as your golden ticket to improve your products and therefore the customer experience!

The first problems to solve are those directly reported by the users themselves. Through this action, they bring problems to your attention and expect you to solve them as soon as possible.

These complaints should not be seen as a disavowal but rather as a learning opportunity. Bill Gates said it in a stronger way: 'your most unhappy customers are your greatest source of learning'. By complaining, the users take the time to educate you on what is important to them. You should be wary of the opposite reactions that would aim to educate the users or even blame them for their misuse of the product. If they express their frustration, it is primarily to improve their experience, instead of switching immediately.

Thus, when the user pulls the electric heater on caster wheels by the electric wire and breaks it, uses the wrong buttons among the ten proposed to programme the TV, etc., it is pretentious and damaging to consider that it is because the user is stupid. It is more profitable to learn how to design a product that will not require more effort to use than to insist on creating value.

> *A team had delivered populated cabinets to its customers. In case of blocked processes, a standard troubleshooting procedure had been provided to restart them correctly. A few days after installation, the customer called the support team to complain about a bad response from the servers. After investigation, the diagnosis was clear: this customer had not applied the procedure. Faced with a blocked process, he had powered off the whole cabinet. At the restart, some servers were not responding as expected. In response, the support service then chose to blame him for not having applied the supposedly great procedure. Misjudgement and refusal to learn! During operations, it was simply not possible for the customer to take the time to analyse why a process is blocked and what procedure to apply. Logically, his reflex was to power off the servers and wait for a return to nominal mode. He thus pointed out the uselessness of the procedure, better, the lack of robustness of the system. The engineering team eventually implemented an automatic restart after an untimely shutdown. The initial procedure was therefore probably never used.*

This example illustrates that satisfying each customer requires precise knowledge of the uses of products and services. Users' complaints are a source of this learning. Through each complaint, each customer should be considered a partner to whom attention must be paid. It is important to clearly demonstrate that you care about what the users experience as value and waste. *This mutual consideration makes your customers more loyal and your business more sustainable.*

Once complaints are recorded, they must be dealt with quickly by engineers. Unfortunately, engineers rarely receive these complaints directly and, in any event, rarely ask for them. Even if they had the good idea to do so, they still need to know where to get them! This can quickly turn into a real treasure hunt. They are often told that it is not their business, even though it is a mine of information for them. If they access these complaints, they can post them on the Customer Wall in their *obeya*. These posts are a good opportunity to start new learning cycles.

The First HP® Computer

In his excellent book, *Little Bets* (2011), Peter Sims tells the story of Bill Hewlett and Dave Packard, the creators of HP®. Until the 1980s, HP® never did marketing studies. Instead, its engineers were in contact with and listening to its customers. For example, the first HP® computer is the response to users of HP® voltmeter who complained that they could not record the measurement values over time.

Walk on the User's Premises***

A good way to understand users' problems is to go, observe, and question how they happen at the user's premises.

Only a portion of users report problems encountered while using a product. For those who don't, a large proportion switches to a competing product. To really grasp most of problems faced by users, go and observe for yourself on the user's *genba*, specifically where the customer interacts with the product.

'There are no acts inside your building, so get outside' to quote Steve Blank, author of *Four Steps to the Epiphany*. Taiichi Ohno said nothing else when he asked his directors to go to the production workshop on the *genba* to understand the situation for themselves.

The recurring image of the shortcut caused by the wear and tear of the grass under the repeated footsteps of passers-by, a few metres from the concrete path that has become useless, is symptomatic of the lack of knowledge of the problems that users face with current solutions. The campus where we work is composed of buildings scattered in a green area, quite pleasant. A path has been laid out in the lawn to access a rest area from the buildings. When entering the site, it is tempting to join this path, provided you first cross a few dozen metres of lawn. Over time, this shortcut has become the preferred path. After trying to prohibit access without success, the site management decided to make it an alternative access path to the buildings.

FIGURE 9.1
Go and see to understand the problems experienced by users

Once the product is out into the marketplace, designers should go to the user's *genba* to gain valuable insights into how people use the products they design and understand how their past design decisions affect the user experience – like a senior manager going to the *genba* to see how their past decisions impact the current employee experience. Unfortunately, designers rarely put themselves in the position of observing users interacting with products. There is a common belief that they should stay in their lab and rely solely on their inspiration and previous knowledge! Yet alternatives do exist, for example, by accompanying installation teams or recreating operational conditions.

Passive observation is not enough. It is the quality of the question raised by the product–user interaction that will make the observation fertile, especially if it is problematic. Is the message conveyed by the product received by users as intended or transformed for other uses? Designers may discover that the product has not been used in the field in the way they had imagined. This feedback from the User's *genba* was called backball by Donald Schön, 'because the designers were not just being told *'You're steering slightly to the left when you should be moving to the right'*. They were being told, *'This product is not what you think it is'*. Consumers were projecting onto the product meanings different from the intentions of the product designers.[…] For example, users did bizarre things with 3M® Scotch Tape. The designers, in turn, picked up the new messages that users were sending to them through consumer behaviour, reframed the meanings of the product that they had designed, and incorporated those meanings in new variations of the product'.[1]

In this sense, the analogy with the experimental method is instructive. 'Devising an experiment is like asking a question'[2] said Claude Bernard. User–product interactions can thus be seen as so many experiments whose observation would allow *a posteriori* confirmation or refutation of design decisions, these decisions being seen as hypotheses. Like in any experimentation, the observation should not be naïve at the risk of being insufficient to provide useful evidence. It is not the mere observation of a fact that can directly inform the observer. It is a reflection that gives meaning to the observed fact by suggesting how it relates to past design decisions, i.e., the causes, and by suggesting new experimentation, i.e., new design decisions (see *CID*). This reflection must be stimulated by questioning. Why is this happening? Why is this effect occurring? What possible causes can be established?

Each experiment, i.e., each new user experience, provides the opportunity to learn how to improve the product. This knowledge, in turn, takes the form of new design decisions and thus new user experiences, and so on. These learning cycles must be rapid. If they're too long, the customers will flee!

Accelerating learning can be facilitated by using digital technology to craft user's experiences. For example, through usability testing, user's behaviours can be tested, measured, and analysed almost continuously during product design and development, without going to the user's *genba*. The collected data is used to determine which solution is supposed to solve which user's problem. This mix of data and hypothesis-based design helps product designers better understand how users interact with their products, what problems they encounter, what works, and what doesn't.[3]

---

[1] *Bringing Design to Software* Ch 9 – Schon (stanford.edu).
[2] Claude Bernard. (1957). *An Introduction to the Study of Experimental Medicine*. Dover Publications.
[3] See *The Lean Startup* (4) or the Lean UX – the build-measure-learn loop.

Remote access to user's behaviour and acquisition of large databases is not limited to digital applications. The deployment of *IoT* (Internet of Things) makes data collection possible even for more traditional hardware products. However, in this case, it is less the rapid testing of design hypotheses that is accessible than a more global evaluation of already deployed solutions. The knowledge produced is then used to guide the evolution of the product.

Regardless of the process used to capture the data, the key is not so much about getting the maximum amount of data, but about accessing high-quality data useful for improving the user's experience. Understanding why problems occur and what causes lie under the observables is essential. Useful metrics for this purpose are those that can be linked to design variables to guide future design decisions. *Thus, be careful not to turn walking on the user's premise into drowning in a data lake!*

Unfortunately, most digital metrics tend to be market-driven (e.g., quantitative data collected for market research) and focus less on user experience. Paradoxically, the more digital data there is, the less likely it is to reveal each user's experience. Indeed, the mathematical correlations established between data mask the original relationship between the user's act and the effect produced. Correlation is not causation! The data, in its digital nature, is cut off from its causal and factual origin. What data says about the world is arbitrary and is established by mathematical correlations and then interpreted independently of the context from which it is extracted. Too much data loses the humanity of the facts it studies. Finally, it tells us very little about the reality from which it is derived.[4]

Only the *Genba Walk* allows us to observe the facts *in situ*. This is in essence what Taiichi Ohno's famous quote says 'Data is of course important in manufacturing, but I place the greatest emphasis on facts', which can be applied to any *genba*.

Without denying the often decisive contribution of data, this should not replace the *Genba Walk*. These two learning methods, one based on data and the other based on facts, must be seen as complementary!

---

[4] https://www.unilim.fr/interfaces-numeriques/386.

Walk in the User's Shoes**

> *'Walk in the customer's shoes' consists of putting ourselves in the customer's position when interacting with the product. It is about experiencing the experience!*

Walking in the user's *genba*, of course, but also walking in the user's shoes! That is to say immersing ourselves more intensely amongst potential users[5] and observing how they solve their daily problems. So, rather than seeing ourselves as an add-on, we begin to see ourselves as part of the same tribe. We begin to think like our customers and to use products as they do.

In this respect, the story of the Chief Engineer of the Toyota Sienna is famous. In order to identify the evolutions of the Sienna required to please American drivers, he decided to drive across more than 50 states, from Mexico to Canada, in a rented Sienna.

Even more emblematic is the story of Muhammad Yunus. In the 1970s, this Bangladeshi-born economics professor decided he could help farmers in his region out of extreme poverty. To better understand their situation, he did not conduct an extensive analytical study or engage in advanced research. He shared the daily life of these farmers and their families. Whether during the day in the rice fields or in the evening in the homes, he observed, listened, debated, and learned a lot. This complete immersion made him discover that poverty was not the consequence of a lack of skills, courage, or will. These villagers worked hard, more than ten hours a day. The little money they received was barely enough to support them and kept them irreparably in poverty. Any desire for emancipation through entrepreneurship was hampered by the impossibility of borrowing what little money was needed. On the strength of this learning, Mr. Yunus imagined an original solution to solve this problem: to lend very small sums of money by betting that they would be fully reimbursed. Microcredit was born. He tested it locally first. He guaranteed the loans, the banks having refused to take the risk of lending to the poor farmers. So, to develop his

---

[5] See ethnographic and empathic design as practiced in Design Thinking Methods.

idea, he created his own bank in 1983, the Grameen Bank. From success to success, microcredit has become a global phenomenon, copied by the biggest banks, the very ones that rejected it in its early days. Muhammad Yunus received the Nobel Peace Prize in 2006.

Therefore, walking in the user's shoes is a good way to experience what users see, hear, and feel. It is no longer a question of imagining the user's experience in a meeting room, but of living it in representative operational conditions! Good and bad experiences are then shared and analysed, creating new knowledge leading to better design decisions. This sharing can be done visually through an empathy map.[6]

The Jinba Ittai

Mazda engineers have also embraced the user's experience. Preparing the third-generation Mazda Roadster (MX-5), the 42 members of the team in charge of its design tested all types of sports cars of similar and superior categories (Honda, Porsche, Fiat, BMW ... including the first two generations of Mazda). Every engineer could ride a whole day with different models. In the evening, they shared their experiences and driving sensations. Getting in the customer's seat allowed them to have a common understanding of the characteristics of a good Roadster and especially to feel the *Jinba Ittai* ('*Jinba-Ittai* reflects the feeling that the sense of oneness between a rider and his beloved horse is the ultimate bond'). To achieve oneness between car and driver, the Chief Engineer Takeo Kijima explains that Mazda must recreate in its Roadster the same tactile sensations experienced by the rider communicating with his horse. For example, the activation of certain arm muscles depends on the position of the gear lever. To apply the *Jinba Ittai* is to find the position that ensures the best trade-off between the force of the movement and the comfort of the driver (http://insidemazda.mazdausa.com/the-mazda-way /mazda-spirit/jinba-ittai/).

---

[6] https://medium.com/the-xplane-collection/updated-empathy-map-canvas-46df22df3c8a.

User Value Stream Mapping (VSM)**

> *To better understand the customer experience, you can map how a user interacts with your product.*

VSM, one of the tools most used by newbies and Lean consultants, could be advantageously diverted from its traditional use to visualise user–product interactions. By mapping each step, the user VSM helps distinguish value-added experiences from wasteful ones.[7]

Consider the VSM of a vacuum cleaner user's experience. The key problem to be solved, also called the 'job to be done', is to suck up as much dust as possible while minimising handling for the user. A user VSM should exhibit these main steps for a corded and bagged vacuum cleaner (in this example, only the touchpoints representing every physical interaction between the user and the vacuum cleaner are mapped):

1. Pick the vacuum cleaner up out of the closet;
2. Plug the vacuum cleaner in and turn it on;
3. Move the vacuum cleaner back and forth across the floor;
4. Turn off the vacuum cleaner and unplug it;
5. Check the dust bag regularly, change it, and replace it with a new one when it is the right time to do so;
6. Store the vacuum cleaner.

The primary basic function is formalised in step 3. Maximising the added value of this step while making the other functions waste free for the user is obviously the goal of vacuum cleaner designers. That means:

- Improving manoeuvrability in step 3. A cordless vacuum cleaner with more ergonomic wheels for better comfort;
- Reducing handling in step 5: 'say goodbye to the bag' (Dyson®️ value proposition) and use a better mechanism to empty the bin. In addition, this solution improves suction performance (step 3) and prevents you from getting dirty after cleaning.

What could be the next improvement to further reduce waste and thus make the user experience even better? For example, by making the

---

[7] *Design Thinking* methods propose an equivalent, the *Journey Map*.

vacuum cleaner autonomous, e.g., a vacuum cleaner robot that returns to the charging station when cleaning is finished, so that the user no longer has to perform this boring chore (step 3), and by removing the filter for easier handling (step 5). The user VSM could be updated as follows:

1. Schedule cleaning;
2. Empty the bin.

Time spent on cleaning can be now used for other things!

Beware of Direct Questions!

> *Surveys submitted directly to users may produce responses that are misleading or that we don't know what to do with.*

Whether dealing with user complaints, walking in the user's *genba* or in their shoes, or mapping the user's experience, all of these practices contribute to better characterising the VoC.

Other techniques[8] can be used to complete or refine this VoC. On the other hand, those that directly ask for the customer's opinion on their product experience are often less informative (e.g., satisfaction surveys, market tests, interviews, focus groups).

- Customers don't know what they really need (Henry Ford or Steve Jobs said it so well!). A company that simply offered exactly what the customers were asking for would not learn anything about their problems and therefore would not have the knowledge to answer them in a better way. Theodore Levitt adds:[9] 'focusing on what existing customers are asking for is exactly what leads companies to ignore new, disruptive technologies until it's too late';
- What we can learn from satisfaction surveys shouldn't just be a differentiator from competitors who can do it just as well without more effort.

---

[8] Design Thinking, Lean Startup, Lean UX, Blue Ocean/Red Ocean, Radical Innovation Design®, etc.

[9] T. Levitt. (July–August 1960). 'Marketing Myopia'. *Harvard Business Review.*

And the Competitors?

> *Better knowledge of your current or future customers can also come from your competitors.*

The products developed by your competitors tell you how they solve customers' problems. There is always something to learn from your competitors (refer to *Teardown*). However, be careful not to wait until a competitor establishes its product on the market to discover it has already solved the problem very well.

Model and Make Visible the Voice of Customers (VoC)*

> *Now you need to capture and categorise what you've learned from your customers in a simple and effective way, especially regarding the product attributes they pay the most attention to.*

Although the value perceived by the customer is partly subjective, they naturally compare the products with each other to determine which one best meets their expectations. This comparison between products is based on the evaluation of their different attributes. These product attributes are the properties that make the products what they are. It is therefore essential to understand which attributes lead to a specific value in order to characterise the VoC and therefore design the right product.

Customer Key Value Attributes

We call Key Value Attributes (KVA) the attributes that matter the most for the customers. These KVA are thus the 'determinant attributes on which customers will make choices about which products or services to purchase'.[10]

---

[10] Alan Zimmerman and Jim Blythe. (2013). *Business to Business Marketing Management: A Global Perspective*. Routledge.

We consider three types of KVA. This classification is inspired by the functional analysis:

- *The functional attributes*[11] relate to the operational characteristics of the product: does it work as expected? These attributes are objective and measurable and are generally associated with the primary basic functions of a product. They are the 'functional jobs to be done' customers are trying to achieve;
- *The quality attributes* represent the non-functional attributes, mainly the constraints, generally expressed by *Ilities*[12] such as reliability, availability, and maintainability, as well as cybersecurity or safety. They ensure the usability and performance of the complete product: how well does this product work, how well does it install, how well is it protected against cyber-attacks, etc.? Like the functional attributes, they are objective and measurable;
- *The emotional attributes* consist in making a product attractive to consumers by first playing on its initial perception: how do people feel about this product? These attributes are subjective and non-quantifiable.

While all of these attributes are important since the customers evaluate and select a product on the basis of this set, they first want to make sure that the product performs the functions it was created for (i.e. the functional attributes). Thus, while it is possible that the aesthetics of a product triggers the desire to own it, when considered further, it still needs to demonstrate its utility to make the experience possible.

Indeed, each customer bases their purchasing decision by comparing the benefits with the sacrifices brought by a combination of product attributes. Since a product never fully meets their expectations, there is always a gap between what they want and what they are willing to accept … and then to pay for it. For example, the benefits brought by all the attributes of a desired product may be outweighed by the delivery time, which is considered too costly a sacrifice! The value perceived by the customer thus results from this trade-off[13] between what they perceive as a benefit of the product and

---

[11] D.A Garvin. (1987). 'Competing on the Eight Dimensions of Quality'. *HBR.*
[12] See ISO/IEC FDIS 25010 or Bart Huthwaite. (2012). *The Lean Design Solution.* Huthwaite Innovation Institute.
[13] See also Conjoint Analysis.

what they perceive as a sacrifice to acquire it.[14] It can be expressed by this 'Value Equation':

$$Perceived\ Value = \frac{Benefits}{Sacrifices} = \frac{Key\ Value\ Attributes}{Waste + Indirect\ Costs}$$

Here, the key perceived sacrifices correspond to indirect costs that the customer estimates they have to spend throughout the process of consumption (e.g., immediate expenses for transport, installation, or training as well as life cycle costs such as using, servicing, disposing).

Other less quantifiable issues, like unnecessary activities, stress, frustration, waiting, risks, add to the above sacrifices. They are waste which further deteriorates the value perceived by the customer and, ultimately, the overall cost of ownership of the product. Most of this waste is due to poor design decisions that make the product complex, fragile, unpredictable, dangerous, not green friendly, etc. (see *Target Costing*).

The purchase price does not first determine the product value perceived by customers. Each customer incorporates the purchase price into their evaluation to decide whether they are getting their money's worth (value for money).

While this equation is satisfactory from the customer's perspective, it would be incomplete if, at the same time, it did not also take into account, on the one hand, the share of the value that goes to the company and, on the other hand, the waste that this company generates internally. That means that the benefits your company expects from the product should also be expressed in the form of KVA.

Thus completed, this equation simply expresses the goal of Lean Engineering, i.e. maximising value creation while minimising waste throughout the whole product's lifecycle.

An easy way to model the relative value of each of the KVA is ratings! A Radar Chart makes it easy to achieve this relative ranking between the KVA. Each KVA is rated on a 5-point scale with '5' being 'extremely important'. One Radar Chart is plotted by product type, by user

---

[14] Note that Dr Alexander Osterwalder, the author of the Value Proposition Canvas, prefers to use *Gain* and *Pain* rather than benefit and sacrifice.

segment, or by type of business model (e.g., intermediate buyer and final consumer).

Customer Radar Chart

A Customer Radar Chart shows all customer KVA concurrently. In addition, this chart allows existing products to be compared to expectations and competition. In this sense, it exhibits the gap to close in order to fully satisfy the VoC – what the Kano model[15] does not do. Using this comparison, the chart enables engineers to see which KVA are most in need of improvement or those that differentiate the product from the competition. Figures 9.2 and 9.3 represent this comparison.

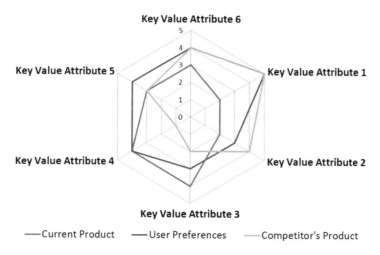

FIGURE 9.2
Radar Charts overlap

---

[15] Kano Model: Characteristics – Part 1 of the SEEBURGER series.

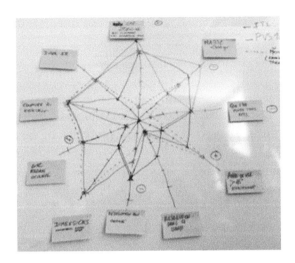

FIGURE 9.3
Radar Charts in an *obeya*

Let's take an example of an astronomical telescope. Two segments are identified: the beginners and the experts.

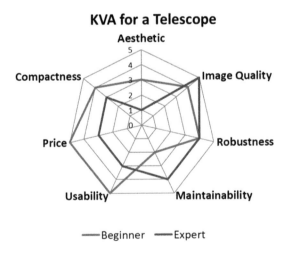

FIGURE 9.4
Customer Radar Chart for an astronomical telescope

A judgement matrix performing pairwise comparisons between each pair of KVA avoids overestimating one KVA at the expense of another.[16] The results are transcribed onto the Radar Chart. This matrix evaluates a subset of KVA for experts: quality prevails over maintainability and robustness.

	Image Quality	Robustness	Maintainability	Result
Image Quality	X	1	1	2
Robustness	-1	X	0	-1
Maintainability	-1	0	X	-1

FIGURE 9.5
Judgement matrix

Relative evaluation is not enough. It is essential to understand the type of interrelationship between KVA: independent or correlated? Which ones are involved in conjoint analysis, i.e., those for which the customer is led to make a trade-off? A component interaction matrix can be used to model the type of correlations between KVA: 0 no correlation; (–) antagonist correlation (a trade-off exists); (+) synergetic correlation. For example, the increase in image quality is likely to be paid for by additional clutter (negative impact on compactness) and higher price.

	Image Quality	Compactness	Ease of use	Price
Image Quality		-	0	+
Compactness			+	+
Ease of use				+
Price				

FIGURE 9.6
Correlation matrix

The House of Quality[17] also allows the prioritisation of product attributes from the customer's perspective and provides a competitive evaluation. However, the Radar Chart is easier to use and more visually explicit.

---

[16] Many other methods exist, such as Analytic Hierarchy Process (AHP).
[17] The HoQ is a key component of the Quality Functional Deployment (QFD).

Whatever modelling is used,[18] the evaluation must be collective, in the same spirit as a *Planning Poker*[19] session. Ideally, the customer should be present. This evaluation is preferably done in the *obeya*, using what has been learned from complaints or users' *genba*, in the presence of the Chief Engineer. Several sessions may be necessary before converging towards a common vision. The model is thus refined at the speed of learning.

The simple visual comparison fosters debates and reveals disagreements. The controversial values become evident. Indeed, what is more risky than starting a product development without being aware that people do not all share the same vision of customer preferences?

The Radar Charts are posted on the Customer Wall and reported in the Concept Paper.

> On one project, once the KVA had been identified, the first comparative assessments highlighted the disagreements between team members (engineering, purchasing, marketing, project management). Some participants argued that the product recurring cost was the most important attribute, while others placed innovation at the top. This divergence, while not totally contradictory, could not lead to the same product. An exchange with the client helped to resolve this issue and share a common vision.

Company Radar Chart

In the same way, a Company Radar Chart enables engineers to see at a glance which KVA the company seeks from the new product, given the customer's KVA. The objective is thus to make the best trade-offs among customer KVA and company KVA.

---

[18] See the George Box's aphorism 'all models are wrong, but some are useful'.

[19] A consensus-based estimating technique used to estimate the relative effort needed to complete each User Story on a software product backlog.

Set and Visualise the Key Specifications*

> ***In the same way as the Customer Radar Chart, the Product Radar Chart visualises how well your product covers the target product attributes.***

KVA represents the VoC as expressed by customers. To provide clear guidance, each KVA is translated into Key Specifications. A specification (or a requirement) describes what the product has to do and under what conditions and constraints[20] it has to do it effectively. It typically consists of a metric and its value. A specification is key when its impact on the user's experience is significant, i.e., expressing a highly rated KVA. For example, a high-rated KVA for a folding beach chair is *Easy to fold*. One of the corresponding Key Specifications may be written as 'the time to fold the chair shall be less than 3 seconds'. Another Key Specification could specify the maximum mass of the chair, etc.

Traditionally, the team sets one single value by Key Specification early in the product development. The risk of precisely (and arbitrarily?) setting values too early is to fail to design a product that meets all of them simultaneously. As a result, these overconstrained specifications will then have to be reworked to make the product feasible. This way of setting one single value by specification is called 'hard specification' or 'Point-Based Specification'.

Setting Key Specifications on a range of values – at least X; no more than Y; between X and Y; among X, Y, or Z – rather than on hard goals is more efficient (aka 'soft specification' or 'Set-Based Specification'). By combining the values expressed as ranges, teams establish the boundaries of the solutions space, and *de facto*, the boundaries of the design space to be explored (see SBCE). This shift from one point to a set makes it possible to convert the impossibility of simultaneously respecting two values into a trade-off. Rather than being forced to say: 'I can't give you A and B at the same time', it becomes possible to propose: 'Tell me how much A are you willing to give up to get more B?'

---

[20] The conditions can be operational, environmental, legal, logistical, etc. The constraints can be physical (e.g., SWaP, form), interface-related, cost-related, etc.

To be able to set the boundaries of this solutions space and explore the right trade-offs, you must characterise the evolution of customer satisfaction as a function of the specification value over the range. Utility curve allows modeling this sensitivity to values. It is normalised between 0 (no satisfaction) and 1 (full satisfaction). This example shows how customer satisfaction increases as the fuel consumption for a car decreases.

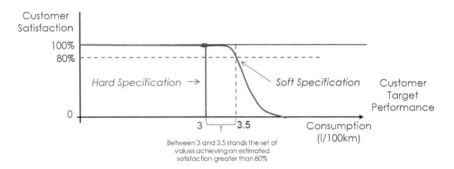

FIGURE 9.7
Example of utility curve

It is possible to visualise the two levels between which customer satisfaction is considered assured:

- The level beyond which the satisfaction is not assured because the product performance is no longer acceptable to the customer (on the figure, the limit is set at 80% satisfaction). This is the veto level (11);
- The level of complete satisfaction beyond which further improvements are of no interest to customers. This is the target level (keep in mind the opportunity of a potential *Wow* effect beyond this level!).

These two levels delimit the region of interest for the customers, which, when applied to all specifications, represents the target solutions space. This is where trade-offs between conflicting specifications must be identified[21] and resolved (see Trade-off curves).

It may be also useful to visualise how cost changes as satisfaction increases[22] (see *Target Costing*).

---

[21] The roof of the house of quality shows this interrelationship.

[22] For further explanations, see James N. Siddall. (1982). *Optimal Engineering Design: Principles and Applications*. B01FJ0FG72. Chapters 2 and 4.

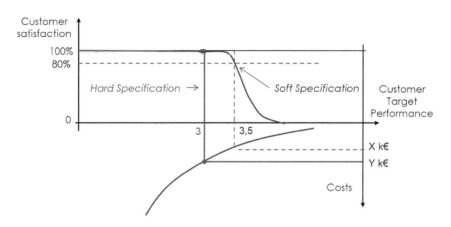

FIGURE 9.8
Relationship between utility and cost curves

The Utility Curves can be posted on the Customer Wall. However, the interest of these curves lies mainly in their elaboration, when the Chief Engineer and the teams exchange and then converge on the profile of each curve.

A Product Radar Chart, established from the Customer Radar Chart, is well suited to visualise the target region of the solutions space. It also highlights the gap between the current product and the target product. In Figure 9.9, the KVA 1 is translated into five Key Specifications, one per axis.

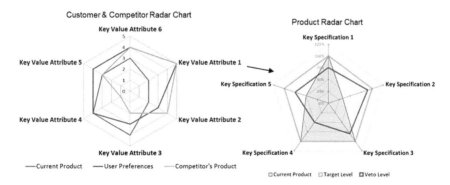

FIGURE 9.9
From KVA to key specifications

On the Product Radar Chart, a 6-point scale per radius (varying from 0% to 125%) lets us position the veto value in relation to the target value taken as reference (100%). The two curves, red for veto values, green for target values, delimit the solutions space. The blue area reflects the values achieved by the current product. Its difference with the veto value represents the gap needed to close in order to reach the customer's region of interest, i.e., the solutions space.

Here is an illustration for Key Specification #5:

- The target value is 15 kW (100% satisfaction, green curve);
- The veto value is 20 kW (red curve). The customer wants to limit power consumption;
- Power consumption of the current product is 30 kW (blue area).

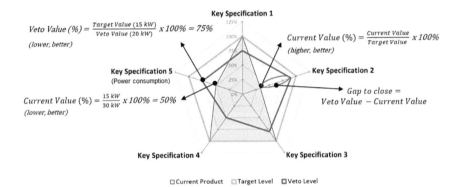

$$Veto\ Value\ (\%) = \frac{Target\ Value\ (15\ kW)}{Veto\ Value\ (20\ kW)} \times 100\% = 75\%$$

(lower, better)

$$Current\ Value\ (\%) = \frac{Current\ Value}{Target\ Value} \times 100\%$$

(higher, better)

$$Current\ Value\ (\%) = \frac{15\ kW}{30\ kW} \times 100\% = 50\%$$

(lower, better)

Gap to close =
Veto Value − Current Value

□ Current Product □ Target Level □ Veto Level

FIGURE 9.10
Product Radar Chart

Let's take an example of a white wine for summer (drink with moderation!). Five KVA were selected to assess the preference of two user segments: summer tourists and wine lovers. For example, the *Freshness*, considered important by summer tourists for a white wine, is characterised by three Key Specifications. The white wine sold today is too sweet: too high sugar content, 7g instead of the target of 3g, i.e., 43% from the target. To fully satisfy summer tourists, it will be necessary to review the wine making or select another white wine.

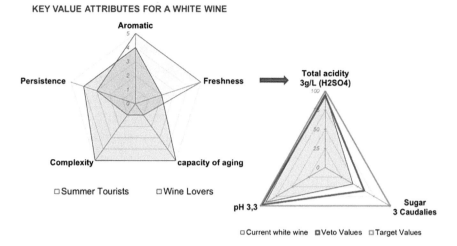

FIGURE 9.11
The White Wine KVA 'Freshness' is expressed into three Key Specifications

These Radar Charts provide clear guidance to engineers and focus their efforts on the right region of the solutions space.

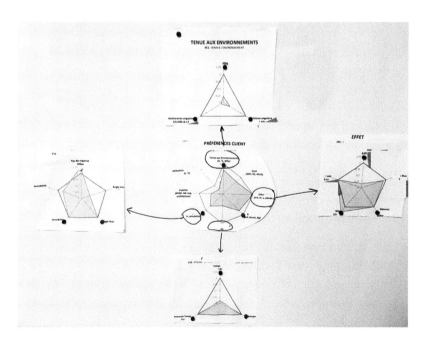

FIGURE 9.12
Example of Radar Charts on the Customer Wall

FROM TERRITORY OF CUSTOMERS TO TERRITORY OF PRODUCTS: THE CONCEPT PAPER**

> *The Concept Paper is an A3-page visual canvas that articulates in a coherent way the fit between the VoC and the product to deliver. This document will serve as a compass during development.*

The Chief Engineer is the owner of this Concept Paper. Large enough for essentials, too small for digressions, the canvas format[23] helps them frame their vision of the product, the rationale of its development, and the efficient way to deliver taking into account all the constraints. In that sense, the challenge is outlined: solving the trade-off between users' needs, business objectives, and company capability.

First drafts serve as a basis for exchanges between team members, which can lead to improvement as the thinking becomes clearer. Once validated, the Concept Paper is widely communicated to stakeholders to serve as a compass throughout the product design and development process.

Having this Concept Paper as a concise canvas makes it as understandable and actionable as possible. When done right, it inspires and motivates everyone to do the right thing.

This canvas is divided into distinct blocks, each embedding a piece of knowledge. By contrast, an empty block is indicative of a knowledge gap! The way the blocks are organised guides the reader through logical steps. Thus, by making the connection between all of them, each reader should be able to understand the challenge established by the Chief Engineer and deduce the implications for their own contribution to the product development flow.

The structure of the Concept Paper formalises the transition from the Territory of Customers to the Territory of Products:

- The left side focuses on the target customers, the problem to solve, and the competitors (external factors);
- In response, the right side defines the company strategy, scopes the product concepts, and establishes the project objectives (internal factors).

---

[23] In the same way, Alexander Osterwalder introduced a one-page Business Model Canvas (see Alex Osterwalder).

The fit between the left and right sides is driven by the product vision (message to the teams). The promise of this fit is expressed by the value proposition (message to customers).

Territory of Customers		Territory of Products	
Product vision			
Customer Segments		Company Strategy and Objectives	
Problem Scope		Product Key Specifications	
Key Value Attributes		Product Concepts	
Competitors		Project Tactics and Objectives	
Value Proposition			

FIGURE 9.13
The Concept Paper blocks as a canvas

Let's look into what each block is in more detail.

Product Vision

The product vision describes what the future product will be (definition and rough description) and the positive change it should bring about (outcome). It must be attractive to make the teams want to mobilise their effort around this product. It also has to be informative so that they understand where the main challenges or trade-offs lie. Thus, rather than explaining how the product will work, it is more about describing the product's attributes or features, and the benefits it should bring to customers and to business. These benefits will serve as a basis to establish the value proposition. Finally, this vision should guide each engineer in their design decisions.

Here are some basic examples:

- A robust wireless personal communication system integrated into the equipment of military vehicle drivers that does not hinder their movements;
- A sedan that uses less fuel than a city car (challenging contradiction assigned to Toyota engineers that led to the hybrid engine);
- 'Man-maximum, machine-minimum' (challenging metaphor[24] of a car short in length and tall in height. This 'Tall boy' product concept led to the urban Honda City).

---

[24] I. Nonaka and H Takeuchi. (1995). *The Knowledge-Creating Company*. Oxford University Press. Chap. 3.

Territory of Customers: The Problem Side

The next three blocks provide most of the customer insight needed to solve the value equation (refer to *Target Costing*).

Customers' Segments

Who is the product intended for? What are the common characteristics shared by these people? What are the corresponding customer segments?

You need to distinguish the segments from each other in order to characterise them with the right KVA. For example, an airline can target two segments of passengers, business passengers, and vacation passengers, with different demands and thus different KVA. Similarly, it may be useful to confirm whether the customers making the purchase transaction (Department of Defence) share a common KVA with the end users (the armed forces). A persona, as used in Design Thinking, may help model a given target segment.

Problem Scope

What are the top customers' problems worth solving? What task, goal, or objective are the target customers trying to accomplish,[25] and what obstacles or constraints block them from being realised?

The goal of great solutions is to reduce or even eliminate customers' wasteful activities. Understanding the true motivation of customers, i.e., the real goal, may lead one to consider that, finally, they do not want to engage in the *job* as proposed by the future product. For instance, do they want a drill, a hole,[26] or a shelf?

Key Value Attributes (KVA)

Which KVA and their relative ranking target customers' segment?

Competitors

Who are the most serious, aggressive competitors? What are their best alternative solutions? Why are they more competitive (price, features,

---

[25] aka *job to be done*, see Alan Klement. (2016). *When Coffee and Kale Compete: Become Great at Making Products People Will Buy*. NYC Press.

[26] As Theodore Levitt pointed out.

etc.)? 'Your true competition is not who you think they are, but who your customers think they are'.[27]

Competitors are always looking to challenge current solutions by offering more advantages on one or more KVA, or even offering others (refer to *Teardown*). The evaluation of competing products is plotted in the form of a Customer Radar Chart. Moreover, information on market conditions and new technology can advantageously complete this block.

The Products Territory: The Solution Side

Company Strategy and Objectives

What are the product policy and the business objectives in terms of pricing, profit, market share, time to market, level of sales, distribution, etc.? Which Target Cost? Which make or buy strategy? Which international footprint? Who are the potential industrial partners? The relative ranking between the company KVA can be expressed by a Company Radar Chart.

Finally, what is the direction that the teams will take and what is the plan they'll implement to achieve these business goals?

Product Key Specifications

This block sets the key specifications per KVA in the form of intervals where customer satisfaction is guaranteed. This can be displayed in a table or in a Product Radar Chart from which each functional department is able to deduce its technical feasibility domain (the set of its own accessible intervals) in the solutions space.

The 'wow effect' occurs when an excellent product or service experience exceeds customer expectations. For example, reducing the fuel consumption of a car to 2 L/100 km while the target value is specified at 3 L/100 km can cause a 'wow effect'.

---

[27] Ash Maurya: Why Lean Canvas vs Business Model Canvas? (leanstack.com).

Product Concepts

Once the solutions space has been defined, it is time to define the key characteristics of the target product, such as (not exhaustive):

- Its architecture (e.g., modular vs. integral architecture, distributed architecture), product breakdown structure, etc.
- Its main features, functions, technology, differentiators, trade-offs, etc.
- Its parts: parts with strong knowledge gaps, parts based on legacy or recurring parts.

A visual representation is very helpful, as well as a clarification of what the product 'is not'.

Project Tactics and Objectives

How to implement the strategy?

This block relates the Chief Engineer's tactic to the implementation of company strategy and objectives. It may concern planning, key milestones, project budget, or any other information, such as regulatory or export constraints.

Value Proposition

How can your proposed solution help your customers solve their problems better than those proposed by your competitors?

This block summarises the positive and differentiated experiences promised to the product customers for years to come. If multiple segments are identified, the value proposition should reflect this diversity.

CONCEPT PAPER

Owner:
Last Update:

Project/Product: **Robot New Generation**
Leader:

Product Vision

A **autonomous portable Unmanned Ground Vehicle (UGV)** enables to run various customisable missions .
Key challenge : autonomous navigation, positioning and motion control.

Customers Segments

The Armed Forces to perform Intelligence, Surveillance and Reconnaissance (ISR) missions in urban environments (tunnels and caves) and in open hostile terrain.
The Soldiers to conduct chemical/Toxic Industrial Chemical (TIC) and Toxic Industrial Materials (TIM) reconnaissance missions after natural or industrial disasters

Problem Scope

Access inside buildings, mines, subways, etc. or in open & chaotic hostile terrain
Lightweight, man portable and easy-to-deploy
Autonomous operation anytime under any condition.
They want more autonomy (automatic motion control & autonomous mapping and navigation).
Wide variety of missions.
All transmissions need to be secured (e.g. against cyber attack).

Key Value Attributes

- Mobility & Agility
- Resistant to environment
- Portable and easy to deploy
- Autonomy in operation
- Cyber secure

Competitors

The 510 **PackBot ®** from iRobot Company performs surveillance, reconnaissance, and detection.

Company Strategy and Objectives

Our product line Industrial Robot is key for our company.
Become the market leader in autonomous and intelligent UGV in 2024.
Strong support in R&D (x M€)
Time to market is for 2022 … (ROI, Market Share, etc.)

Key Specifications

Key Value Attributes	Solution Key Specifications	Sol. 80%	Sol. 100%
Mobility & Agility	Max. Speed (kph)	8	12
	Max. Slope (°)	40	50
	Ground clearance (cm)	8	12
	Turning radius (°)	0	0
Portable/Easy to deploy	Weight (no battery, no P/L) (kg)	15	10
	Maximum payload + battery weight (kg)	20	15
	Time to deploy (s)	120	90
	Width	40	35
	Length	70	60
	Hight	18	15
Modularity	Payload bays (Nb of simultaneous sensors)	8	12
Autonomy in Operation	Max. run time (hrs)	5	6
Cyber Secure	Refer to ISO/IEC/27032		7

Product Concepts

Caterpillar tracks concept for safe, stable and reliable motion - **Key trade-offs:**
- Energy available vs. processing accomplished by the robot
- Power consumption to steer vs. the limitation of weight of batteries to stay agile
- Manoeuvrability vs. a platform large enough to host all components
- Agility in uneven terrain: high slope vs. travelling speed

Project Tactic and Objectives

Topics - Constraints	Objectives	Comments
Target cost	xx k€	Hypothesis : see document xx
NRC	xx M€	Hypothesis : see document yy
Export Control, other	Refer to note …	
Program Planning	Refer to Master Planning	
Make or Buy	Refer to note …	

Value Proposition

Autonomously explore and diagnose all types of terrain in dangerous environments, more secured, faster and better than competitors without risking the safety of people.

FIGURE 9.14

A Concept Paper example

━━━━━━━

EXPLORING THE TERRITORY OF PRODUCTS

Exploring the Territory of Products means exploring the design space to find where the best solution lies. Unfortunately, most products are complex systems, so there is no direct path from the designer's intent to the outcome. By modelling this design space, the designer should gain better visibility on the different trade-offs to be solved and the knowledge gaps to be filled. They could then better control the primary effects of future decisions.

Causal Influence Diagram***

> *The Causal Influence Diagram is a powerful visual method to help engineers solve new design problems by characterising the relationships between design variables and expected performance.*

Designing a Problem-Solving Process

The Key Specifications along with other constraints express *what* the product must do. They frame the solutions space where designers are free to define *how* to best satisfy these specifications. By considering these Key Specifications as dependent variables, the freedom of the designer is then exercised in determining and combining the independent design variables. For example, the mass (dependent variable) of an object depends on the materials and dimensions (independent variables) decided by the designer.

This distinction between variables, obvious for hardware, is less so for software. What are the independent variables for software? Beyond decisions about the structure of the code (e.g., architectural styles and patterns[28]), software design decisions are mainly limited to the physical parameters of the hardware (e.g., memory size and type, number of inputs/outputs, CPU capabilities). Nevertheless, design variables

---

[28] S.T. Albino. (2003). *The Art of Software Architecture: Design Methods and Technique.* Wiley; E. Gamma and R. Helm. (1996). *Design Patterns: Elements of Reusable Object-Oriented Software.* Addison-Wesley Professional; M. Fowler. (2002). *Pattern of Enterprise Application Architecture.* Addison-Wesley Professional.

related to the software parameters can be defined (e.g., design patterns, processing, scheduling and resource sharing, communication protocols, virtualisation, redundancy, replication, security).

The relationship between design variables and specifications is worth modelling as a causal relationship, i.e. as an 'if *x* then *y*' statement (truth-functional operator). This means that a change in the values of the design variables (cause) leads to a change in the values of the specifications (effect). This causal relationship can be modelled as follows:

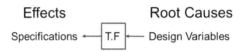

FIGURE 9.15
Basic causal relationship

The arrows symbolise this causal relationship that constrains the output values according to the input values assigned to the variables, through a Transfer Function (TF). This TF, considered primarily as a black box, expresses physical laws and mechanisms governing product behaviour and performance.

The way we use the concept of causality to characterise this relationship of dependency may seem naïve to some who are more accustomed to scientific causal statements. Indeed, this relationship is functional and therefore symmetrical. However, the designer's decisions do precede the desired effects of the product. The temporally asymmetric sequence of causality is therefore respected. This causal interpretation allows product behaviour and performance to be considered as deducible from design decisions. *In this sense, product design can be seen as a problem-solving process.*

These design decisions apply to both independent variables and TF. They transform the designers' knowledge into actions. Therefore, achieving the desired end, i.e., the full customer satisfaction (*final cause*), depends on the ability of designers to learn what is needed to make the right decisions (*efficient cause*), i.e., the right application of the right combination of independent variables on the right TF. The solution is considered elegant when it requires the least number of independent variables and TF (Ockham's razor principle). Finding this best solution can be challenging:

- Key Specifications (left side) can be numerous and sometimes antagonist requiring exploration and resolution of trade-offs;
- Design variables (right side) form a large design space to explore in order to determine the region corresponding to the best solution;
- Transfer functions (in the middle) can be complex to model.

To guide engineers, we suggest modelling this design problem through a Causal Influence Diagram (*CID*). This visual model should help structure the interactions between variables and identify which ones have a first-order influence on the expected effects. *CID* aims at seeing the problem in a systemic way by integrating conditions that could have been excluded by the linear *5 whys* method which assigns a single cause to each effect.

Model the Design Problem

Definition

CID is partially based on the Allen Ward's work[29] and the *QFD* (Quality Function Deployment). A similar diagram was also designed by the Kennedy family (11). *CID* stands for Causal Influence Diagram:

- *Causal* as the relationship between design variables and specifications. The causality can be modelled by mathematical relations;
- *Influence* as the multiple factors influencing specifications: designers' choices, manufacturing constraints, operations, etc.

As Ward wrote,[30] '*Causal influences* are the entities affecting the values a variable takes at any point in the design, manufacture, and operation of a device or system'. This name makes *CID* unique from other diagrams such as Influence Diagrams, Causal Diagrams, and System Diagrams.

---

[29] A. Ward and W. Finch. (1995). 'A Set-Based System for Eliminating Infeasible Designs in Engineering Problems Dominated by Uncertainty.' *ASME Sacramento, California.*

[30] A. Ward and W. Finch. (1996). 'Quantified Relations: A Class of Predicate Logic Design Constraints Among a Sets of Manufacturing, Operating, and Other Variations.' *ASME Irvine, California.*

As a problem-solving method, *CID* is worth using for both new and existing products. For new products, it helps engineers to formalise design problems and identify which variables influence which performances. It should be primarily focused on the flexible part of the product, the one impacted by the evolutions, where the gaps to be filled are located. For existing products, it is used to trace past causal design decisions and guide inferences between probable causes and the observed problem.

CID and the Scientific Thinking

Whatever the phenomenon to explain or to look for, it is not equally sensitive in all its variations. Because, even if the variables are linked, their sensitivity is not reciprocal. To avoid falling into a 'total correlation', it is necessary to consider each phenomenon described by a *CID* as a closed system which is not affected by minor perturbations. Thus, we must know how to neglect what has the least influence or no influence at all (e.g., the colour of a projectile does not modify its ballistic properties). To conduct a *CID* properly, we must therefore adopt a scientific thinking.

Mapping the CID

The *CID* makes visible the relationships between these blocks:[31]

- Key Value Attributes (KVA);
- Key Specifications – Performances;
- *Independent Design Variables* controlled by the designers;
- *Noise Factors*, other influencing factors difficult to control by designers;
- *Form Factors* (SWaP[32]). They are worth identifying in a specific block as constraints limiting the freedom of designers.

---

[31] See the *P-Diagram*.
[32] Stands for *Size, Weight, and Power.*

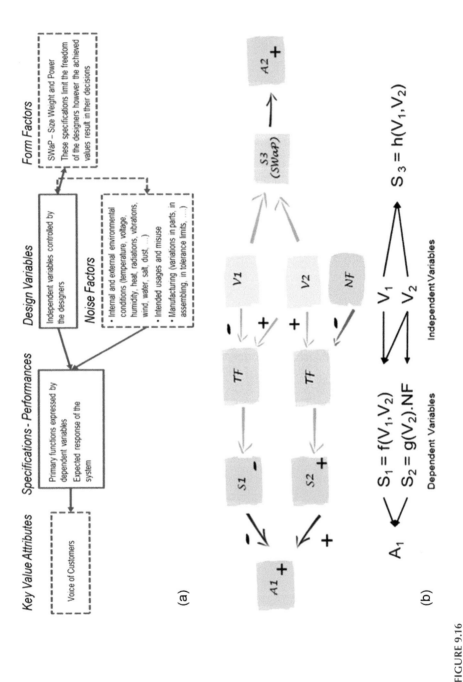

FIGURE 9.16

The different blocks and their visual representation

Here are the steps to build a *CID*:

- Engage experts and other key people in the drawing process. Each item is visually represented by a sticky note. It is best done in collaborative workshop sessions in front of the Product Wall;
- Develop from effects to causes. Begin with the highest priority KVA you want to satisfy. Attaching a sign + (–) to each KVA indicates that increasing (decreasing) its value reinforces the desired effect. For example, it is worth lowering the fuel consumption (–) while increasing the car comfort (+).

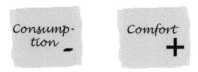

FIGURE 9.17
Indicate the preferred direction of evolution

- Identify and map out specifications, then the design variables that directly cause this KVA. Do these design variables have the effect you look for?
- Connect the KVA to specifications and variables. Show the relationships:
  - Arrows connect the variables together, from causes to effects;
  - Sign '+' on an arrow means a positive correlation between the design variable and the specification (both move in the same direction);
  - Sign '–' on an arrow means a negative correlation between the design variable and the specification (they move in opposite direction);
  - A question mark '?' means that the correlation is still unknown.
  - When the correlation function is already known, it can be written directly on the note (orange Post-it® on Figure 9.16).
- Take the next KVA, and so on.

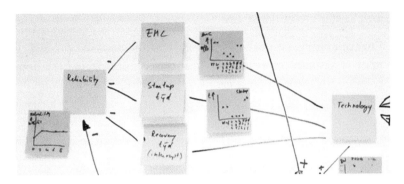

FIGURE 9.18
Part of *CID*

Application: Amateur Telescope

The objective is to visualise how the primary mirror[33] variables influence the image quality, size, and cost of an amateur telescope.

Initiate the CID

The *CID* starts from the highest-rated KVA (e.g., image quality). Image quality can be defined in terms of image brightness (proportional to the amount of light collected) and resolution (ability to distinguish between close objects). The brightness is proportional to the square of the aperture (design variable). For instance, a telescope with a primary mirror of 100 mm aperture collects four times as much light as a telescope with a 50 mm mirror. Therefore, a larger aperture contributes to image quality. The same is true for the resolution since a large aperture can resolve more details than a small one. The corresponding *CID* is as follows.

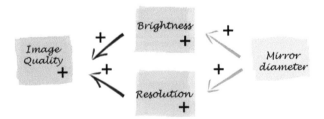

FIGURE 9.19
Initiate the *CID*

---

[33] The proposed exercise is just here to illustrate how to implement *CID*. It is not intended to describe precisely the physical principles of telescopes.

Trade-Off Identification

A trade-off exists when increasing a design variable improves one effect while worsening the other.[34] For example, the risk of coma optical aberrations increases with the diameter of the mirror, since it is caused by imperfections of the lens optical surface (the image of a point of light is rendered as a comet-shaped blur for a point away from the optical axis). Coma is antagonist to image quality. This trade-off is made evident by comparing the products of the signs for each path originating from the variable concerned. If these products are opposite, then a trade-off exists. Here the product is negative on the top arrows (aberration) while it is positive on the bottom arrows (brightness). This confirms that a trade-off exists!

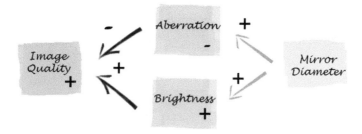

FIGURE 9.20
Trade-off identification

A trade-off curve may make the trade-off more explicit.

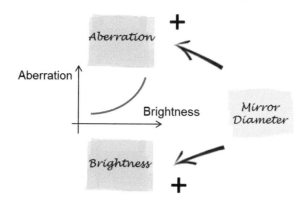

FIGURE 9.21
Make trade-off explicit with trade-off curves

---

[34] To be compared with the definition of TRIZ's Technical Contradiction.

Complete CID

New parameters produce new relations and reveal new trade-offs.

For example, the larger the focal length, the greater the size of the image. And increasing the size of the image spreads out the light, reducing its brightness. To maintain good brightness, the increase in focal length must be coupled with an increase in diameter. The larger these two parameters are, the larger and heavier the telescope is. Favouring the diameter – and the brightness, to the detriment of the focal length – and the magnification of the image, leads to a more compact instrument with a better stability.[35] This is true up to a limit. Above a given diameter (limit to be defined), the mirror becomes too heavy, erasing the gain on the overall dimensions.

The following CID makes visible these trade-offs. The intermediate variable *focal ratio* is given by dividing the focal length by the aperture. The diagram clearly shows that the smaller this ratio, the lower the magnification, the brighter the image.

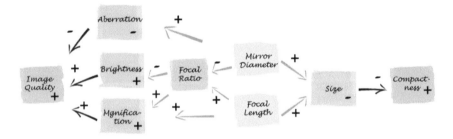

FIGURE 9.22
Complete the CID

If designers are unable to solve the trade-offs within the limits imposed (e.g., size of the telescope), they must introduce new parameters in the design (e.g., by adding extra optical elements to adjust the focal length).

What about Discrete Design Variables?

For discrete variables, the Transfer Function can be a list of discrete options (list of materials, component references) or geometric arrangements (unit form, number of cards, antenna patch location). For the mirror of the telescope, several materials are possible. For a fast temperature setting while guaranteeing a high image quality, a low-thermal expansion material

---

[35] A configuration adapted to extended objects (nebulas, galaxies) but which limits the exploitation of high magnifications for brighter objects (planets, moon, etc.).

for the mirror substrate is recommended (low surface deformation (< nm) as a function of temperature). The final choice of material (glass, quartz, ceramic, etc.) will also depend on their influence on other parameters such as mass or cost.

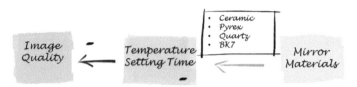

FIGURE 9.23
Make the discrete variables explicit

Identify the Noise Factors

Designers must also deal with Noise Factors that may limit the values accessible to the design variables or affect performance. Example of Noise Factors and how designers may compensate even eliminate their influences:

- Manufacturing/Production: manufacturing a mirror may introduce defects (e.g., flatness) and affect the image quality. The values of some mirror design variables (size, material) must be adjusted to mitigate the influence of tools, processes, expertise, and manufacturing practices. Co-engineering between design and production is therefore essential to clarify the influence of these Noise Factors and the limits they impose on design. This diagram shows the influence of manufacturing errors of the mirror on the aberration and the influencing design variables (red arrows).

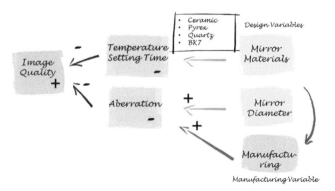

FIGURE 9.24
Add the constraints as limits

- Environment: image quality may be affected by atmospheric turbulence. Adaptive optics systems help mitigate the influence of these disturbances.
- Usage: image quality may suffer from misalignments of optical components. Facilitating collimation (lining up all components) can be achieved by adjusting mechanical variables (e.g., type and location of collimation screws).

For Large Systems?

For large systems, it can be useful to define one *CID* per subsystem. Interactions between subsystems are formalised either by interface variables (direct interactions) or by influences on the common performances between subsystems. The following block diagram shows multiple interconnected *CID* focusing on the image quality of an observation satellite.

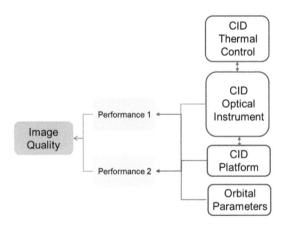

FIGURE 9.25
Connect *CIDs*

In contradiction with Ockham's razor principle, a complex *CID* with a large number of variables and interactions is more likely to produce inefficient architectures. For example, a vacuum cleaner operating with a dust bag or filter has many interactions between many design variables (refer to *User Value Stream Mapping (VSM)*).

What about Costs?

Design decisions directly influence the cost model of the product. Even though each design decision represents a small part of the overall product costs, its shadow, as it is projected on operational value streams, is the most important. By understanding the relationship between design and cost, you make better decisions and reduce cost accordingly (see *Target Costing*).

You must therefore monitor the impact of each decision on costs. In Figure 9.26, each line displays a design decision. The impact on recurring and non-recurring costs is reported in the columns on the right. The sticky note colour indicates this trend: green for expected impact, and pink for negative impact.

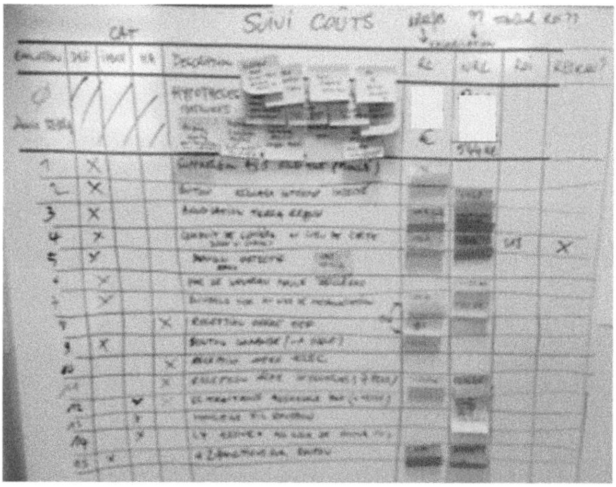

FIGURE 9.26
How design decisions impact costs

Establish the Transfer Functions

From Transfer Function to Model

While the identification of design variables and their influences (+/−) can be easily established, the characterisation of Transfer Functions requires a much higher level of expertise. Indeed, without deep expertise, engineers tend to grasp only the surface features of their design problems instead of their structure and underlying principles or theory. It is thus difficult for them to recognise a familiar structure under the appearance of a new problem, or to make inferences that allow them to discover a truly new structure for a new problem.[36]

For example, the Wright brothers had knowledge about the main geometric parameters of wing and how that influence lift (refer to *The Wright brothers – Learning then Designing*). However, they had not yet fully mastered the aerodynamic theory to understand the influence of aerofoil on lift. The aerofoil data they applied was wrong. Some experiments later, they discovered their error and were able to establish a model between the geometric parameters of the wing and the lift.

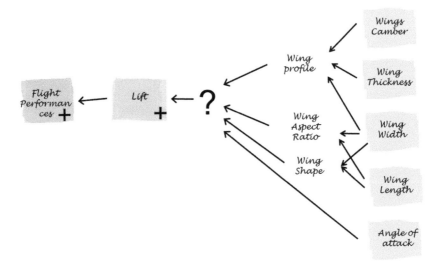

FIGURE 9.27
CID to determine the effect of wing geometrical parameters on the lift

When Models Exist

These Transfer Functions are either already described by predictive models, for example in the form of mathematical equations used to quantify physical phenomena, or by empirical models based on experimental results, such as the lift curves established by the Wright brothers.

For a given concept, the formal models can be used to predict product performance and behaviour for an arrangement of design variables. It then

---

[36] https://www.aft.org/periodical/american-educator/winter-2002/ask-cognitive-scientist.

becomes possible to use computational algorithms to search for the best design by optimising the objectives (performance) in given constraints (limits).

Note that rather than completely exploring the design space, the algorithm used by SBCE consists in gradually narrowing the set of solutions as the knowledge increases and the design progresses.

Once an analytical or physical model has been identified as the Transfer Function, its validity and accuracy must be tested in the configuration of the design problem to be solved. For example, the model can be tested at points for which valid solutions are known.

Model the Model

The *CID* is a simplified visual model of design and performance (i.e., solution) spaces and their interactions (Transfer Functions).

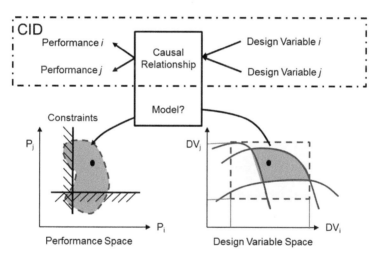

FIGURE 9.28
From performance space to design variables space

With *CID*, the engineers create a general multidimensional model in which the values of the design variables are free to be adjusted (concept of design space). Computer-based approaches such as multi-criteria/multi-objective optimisation algorithms and the processing power can then help to find the solutions that reach the target performance and satisfy the constraints. These solutions belong to the Pareto set and are visually expressed through the Pareto front. A Pareto front with two objective functions (optimisation on two criteria) is similar to a trade-off curve between two performances.

Be careful, however, that computer-based approaches do not put too much distance between engineers and their products. These software models can become black boxes for engineers who no longer see what variables govern the design problem. Unfortunately, an algorithm cannot suggest that another concept would be better. This the job of engineers!

When Models Do Not Yet Exist

If no known formal model has been identified, a knowledge gap is directly reported on the *CID* in place of the question mark seen previously.

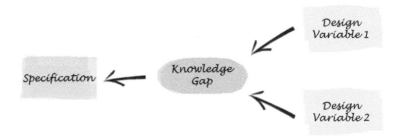

FIGURE 9.29
Make the Knowledge Gaps explicit

In this case, engineering teams must conduct more experimental investigations using engineering models (mock-ups, prototypes) capable of predicting what performance can be expected from a particular combination of design variables,[37] and thus build an empirical model to approximate an unknown relationship. Fortunately, the *CID* can guide them in their investigations by stimulating the formulation of hypotheses that infer causal *if–then* connections:

> *If* [I make this design decision] *then* [I should get this performance], i.e.
> *If* [I do this to this independent variable] *then* [this will happen to this dependent variable].
> Or, more generally: *If* [variable1] [verb1] *then* [variable2] [verb2].

---

[37] K.T. Ulrich and S.D. Eppinger. (2009). *Product Design and Development* (Chapter 6), Mznlnx.

For example, *if* [the coffee temperature] [increases] *then* [the sugar dissolution time] [decreases] (for the same proportion of sugar!).

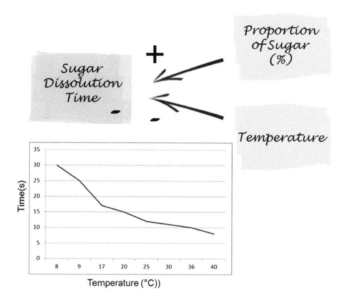

FIGURE 9.30
Solubility of Sugar in Water

After several experiments verifying this hypothesis,[38] it is possible to generalise these results and thus to conclude that the inferred model has a high probability of being true.

It may be necessary to explore the design space more broadly and thus to test several combinations of design variables. *DoE* (Design of Experiments) helps explore several causal relationships while minimising the number of experiments (Fractional Factorial Design). For example, the Wright brothers tested several dozen different aerofoils in their wind tunnel, since they were able to formulate their knowledge gaps in the form of hypotheses to be tested, and thus to focus their efforts on the right experiments. An experiment thus consists in formulating a hypothesis targeting the changes to be introduced in a controlled manner, thus avoiding successive, potentially unproductive trials and errors.

---

[38] 'An *a priori* idea, or better, a hypothesis, is a stimulus to experiment' Claude Bernard, founder of experimental medicine (refer to *Introduction to the Study of Experimental Medicine* published in 1865).

The rigorous formulation of hypotheses, sometimes considered tedious by engineers, is essential because it tests their understanding of design problems: 'How can I positively influence performance? What law or physical principle will do this? What experiment to test my hypothesis?' In this sense, *CID* stimulates hypothesis generation and experimental approaches to problem solving. It brings new questions that help engineers better understand how to solve a design problem. This helps make product design a *Questions Driven Design* approach where questions and then hypothesis are developed to test what engineers know … and don't know.

As a good application, an *MVP* (Minimum Viable Product (4)) allows you to test one hypothesis at a time. Each iteration tests a new hypothesis with a new *MVP*, thus increasing learning. In this sense, an *MVP* can be considered as a *PoK*, i.e., a *Proof of Knowledge*.

> *The challenge was to place an antenna patch on a very small receiver module placed at the end of a metal tube. While the link between antenna geometry and performance was well known, the small size of the antenna and the geometry of the host module required a revision of the engineering model. Three learning cycles formalised by three successive PoKs (a cork module, the same module reshaped with aluminium sheets, a last 3D printed module) allowed the model to adapt.*

MVP or *DoE* deserves to be structured in the form of PDCA loops.

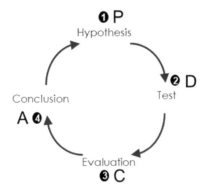

FIGURE 9.31
PDCA learning cycles as support for experiments

1 – **PLAN**: To answer an initial question, formulate a *hypothesis* that may explain the relationship between a design variable and the expected performance; propose the experiment as stimulated by the hypothesis;

2 – **DO**: Implement the *experiment* (analysis, prototypes, simulations, etc.);

3 – **CHECK**: *Evaluate* the result and compare it to the expectation;

4 – **ACT**: if the experiment confirms the hypothesis, adopt the inferred causal relationship. Otherwise, carry out a new cycle by adjusting the hypothesis, or even by proposing another one.

Several learning cycles may be necessary to verify[39] each hypothesis. The resulting process is, therefore, a continuous flow of learning cycles.

To Go Further

(i) Induction, deduction, abduction

The 'saw tooth model' explained by George Box illustrates the iterative cycle between theory and practice. If a model exists (based on a theory or a physical principle), then the result of the hypothesis is predicted by deduction. If the result is the expected one, then the fact that this model is the right one is made more likely. Otherwise, the model is refuted.[40]

Generating hypotheses, i.e., making inferences that best explain the evidence, is abduction. Physicians use this explanatory reasoning to select the hypothesis that best explains the patient's symptoms. Abduction can be analysed in two fundamental processes, formulation of hypotheses based on previous knowledge and evaluation of their plausibility (see also Bayesian theory).

---

[39] Observational evidence can never prove any general theories are true, but it can falsify them (see Karl Popper)

[40] George Box. (December 1976). 'Saw Tooth Model of Inquiry'. *Journal of the American Statistical Association*, 71(356), 791–799.

The term 'abduction' was coined by Charles Sanders Peirce, the founder of the philosophy of pragmatism. He wrote that 'Pragmatism is nothing else than the logic of abduction'. More precisely, abduction has the following logical form:[41]

- The surprising fact, C, is observed;
- But if A were true, C would be a matter of course;
- Hence, there is reason to suspect that A is true.

(ii) 'Try and Fail' vs. 'Test and Learn'

Try and Fail consists of modifying the values of certain variables in an intuitive way, hoping to find a solution that meets the needs. While it can be proven in certain circumstances, it should not replace the formulation of the hypothesis for several reasons:

- *Try and Fail* has only one plan to continue the tests until an explanation is considered satisfactory. This process may be repeated many times and ends when time runs out. Conversely, *DoE* aims to limit the number of experiments to explore the design space.
- *Try and Fail* generates little new knowledge, especially in the absence of constructive feedback. We don't know why we found a solution or why we failed. It is therefore difficult to infer the model able to predict other solutions. Conversely, formulating a hypothesis forces us to design an experiment capable of exploring the relationships between variables.
- As a corollary to the previous point is that it is not possible by *Try and Fail* to determine if the solution found is the best one.

Try and Fail is a mechanism used natively by the brain as a heuristic (system 1) that is helpful in many situations, for example in time-constrained conditions. But it can also lead to cognitive biases in unknown or unfamiliar conditions (lack of expertise, ignorance of relevant information while irrelevant information interferes in decisions). Conversely, *Test and Learn* can be viewed as an algorithm (system 2) following the rules of logic, i.e., a conscious, controlled, deliberate, and analytic cognitive process. By encouraging engineers to state hypotheses and reasons logically, the goal

---

[41] Pierce CP 5.189.

is to inhibit (system 3) the heuristic *Try and Fail* and activate the algorithm *Test and Learn* … and to make them aware of it.[42]

Make the Key Decisions Visible

On *CID*, each unknown element awaits a decision. Key Decisions (KDs) can be made about design variables, Transfer Functions, or even performance, i.e., anything that is still open or unknown. For example, once the region of interest for customers has been mapped, the decision on the best locations in the solutions space is still to be made.

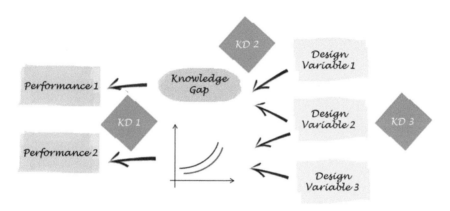

FIGURE 9.32
Key Decisions (KD) emerging from *CID*

By visualising decisions and knowledge gaps on the *CID*, you create the conditions for a *decision diagram* to emerge. Thus, starting from customers' interests (Key Value Attributes), *CID* makes KDs more apparent, whether they relate to performance, Transfer Functions, or design variables. This will serve as the basis for pacing the product development flow.

---

[42] Refer to D. Kahneman and O. Houdé.

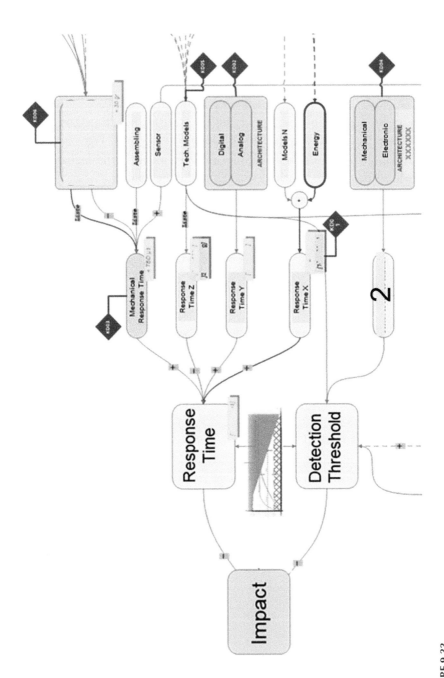

FIGURE 9.33
Part of *CID* with six Key Decisions

The Key Decision Diagram in Figure 9.32 is extracted from the previous *CID*.

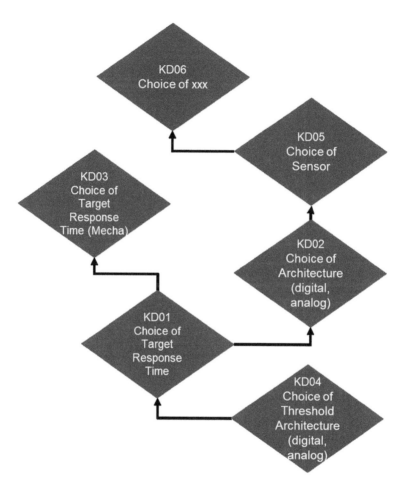

FIGURE 9.34
Key Decision Diagram emerging from *CID*

CID *and Software-Based Products*

CID is particularly well suited for hardware products, with physical variables. For 'pure software' products, there are no physical limits that would impose the identification of trade-offs (green coding aside). Once the KVA and performance targets have been established, it is 'enough' to develop the minimum software to get it into the customers' hands so that you can learn what they really need. Knowledge increases with repeated user experience measurements.

For embedded software products, there are real limits and certain things may not be feasible. Embedded software products have to obey physics. Indeed, the code performance depends in part on the physical parameters of the host hardware platforms (e.g., memory size, CPU power, number of inputs/outputs). Trade-offs are therefore imposed on the designers of these products as is the case for any material product.

Whatever the type of software, design variables related to operating systems, services, and software architecture (e.g., design patterns) can be reported in a *CID*. For complex software products, ATAM[43] may be an alternative.

Summary

CID allows you to uncover the influence and consequence of design decisions on performance and KVA. By encouraging questioning, it stimulates learning and focuses designers on what is key to designing the right products.

> *A CID clarified the origin of some pollution affecting the performance of a satellite solar panel. The size of the panel initially designed to withstand environmental pollution could be thus reduced by acting directly on the causes identified by the CID.*

---

[43] The Architecture Trade-off Analysis Method (ATAM) is a method for evaluating software architecture relative to quality attribute goals.

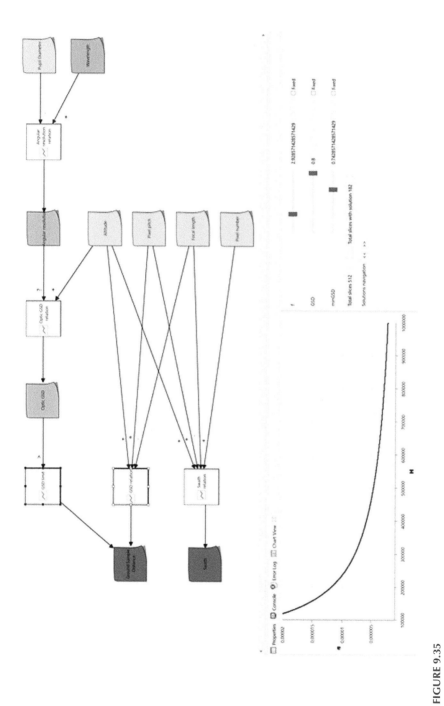

FIGURE 9.35

Example of tooled-up *CID*: Ground Sampling Distance (GSD) resolution

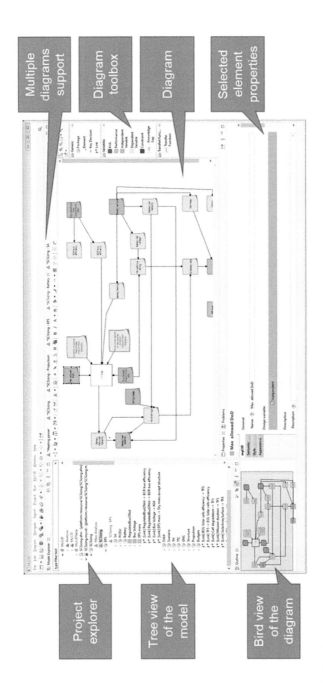

FIGURE 9.36

Overview of the Thales tool 'MyCID'

Trade-Off Curves**

> *A trade-off curve establishes a relationship between various conflicting parameters to each other. It helps engineers make comparisons between alternatives and guide their design decisions.*

Presentation

The term *trade-off* implies the loss of one quality of something in exchange for another quality. The concept of trade-off is linked to the concept of decision-making since it corresponds to situations where a choice needs to be made between two or more variables that cannot reach their respective expected value at the same time.

Satisfying multiple performances, while taking into account these trade-offs, requires the disentanglement of their underlying mechanisms, i.e., to highlight that this negative correlation between performances is due to common design variables. We have seen how *CID* allows us to surface these mechanisms.

By making these correlations visible, trade-off curves provide engineers with the knowledge needed to understand the sensitivity between decisions (shapes of the trade-off curves) and encourage the consideration of multiple design options (see paragraph *SBCE, the Lean Engineering Process*). Without trade-off curves, you may not have enough knowledge to make the right decisions.

You need to complete trade-offs with constraints, which are limits on the variables. Each boundary indicates where the eligible part of the trade-off curve is and where the possible choices between competing performances are. These trade-off curves map the eligible design space – the rest can be rejected – and pick the best spot.

These curves can be plotted accurately on the basis of mathematical models or approximated from experiments or simulations (e.g., extrapolations from measured points).[44]

---

[44] Ashby-type materials' selection charts are a good example of trade-off curves between various mechanical properties (H.R. Shercliff and M.F. Ashby. (2016). *Reference Module in Materials Science and Materials Engineering*).

Allen Ward[45] illustrates the principle of trade-off curves using the example from Sango – Toyota subcontractor.[46] The goal was to minimise both the noise emitted and the backpressure that it loads on the engine. Different muffler designs were tested to understand the best trade-offs.

The blue curve shows the true limit under the one the design is invalid (red plots). The shape of the curve indicates that any reduction in backpressure is paid for by an increase in exhaust noise. By playing on the volume of the muffler, it would be possible to move this curve and thus obtain a noise reduction without affecting the backpressure.

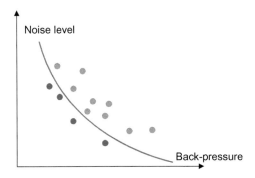

FIGURE 9.37
Typical trade-off curve

Application

Consider trade-off curves for the single-beam Klystron concept (a device used to amplify microwave through the kinetic energy of electron beams): the team wants to minimise the length while maximising the efficiency. The black dots are the measured points on current designs for the same concept. The dotted red line shows the true limit of this concept. The correlation between efficiency and size is represented by the blue line – efficiency increases with the number of cavities, which increases the size and mass. All these curves help to distinguish the safe region (green area) from the target region but are invalid with the current concept (yellow area). Gaining a few efficiency points close to the 70% limit is paid by a

---

[45] https://www.youtube.com/watch?v=hlAzjwntJdI.

[46] B.M. Kennedy and D. Sobek. (2013). 'Reducing Rework by Applying Set-Based Practices Early in the Systems Engineering Process'. *Systems Engineering* 17, no. 3.

faster increase in the Klystron size and a decrease in operating margins (closer to the limit). Other concepts must therefore be considered to move the limit curve up.

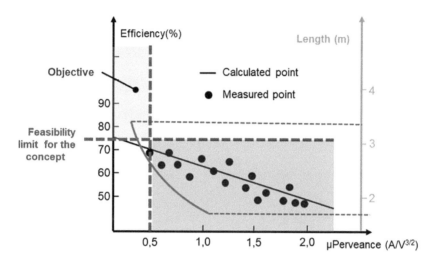

FIGURE 9.38
Examples of curves characterising the feasibility design domain of a Klystron

Combining trade-off curves allows a better targeting of the best regions of the multidimensional design space with respect to the weakest. Non-dimensional variables (for example, a combination of variables in the form of ratios) help to put more data on the curve. In this case, a point in space does not represent one solution but a continuous set of solutions. However, to understand a larger multidimensional space, visual modelling tools are necessary.

Support for Innovation

By visualising the boundaries that stand in your way, the trade-off curves focus you on the right new problems that need to be solved to reach the region you want to be in. Once these problems are solved, the generated data is again used to map the new limits, expanding the feasibility domain. This way, you direct your innovations to where you need them. For this reason, in particular, it is worthwhile to standardise trade-offs to better guide design decisions.

Moving the limits requires innovation since it is necessary to seek other effects for the users by playing directly on the causes, i.e., the design variables and the Transfer Functions, either:[47]

- By widening the ranges of admissible values for these variables;
- By organising these variables differently;[48]
- By introducing new variables;
- By a mix of the above proposals.

The result is generally the emergence of new concepts.

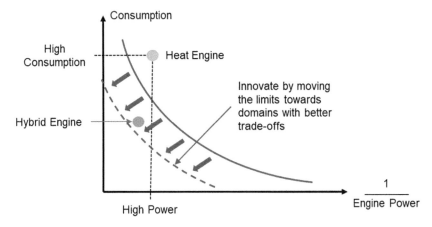

FIGURE 9.39
Moving the limit, guiding innovations

Conclusion

By visually capturing the evolution of knowledge, trade-off curves play the role of design standards effectively (see paragraph *Standards*):

- They aim to organise and visually display into reusable format what engineers know (and don't know) about key product variables' relationships and inform where the best known solutions are;
- They figure out the limits known today and guide engineers about what to do when they cannot design within the safe region, e.g., by

---

[47] See also the contradiction matrix and the 40 principles of TRIZ.
[48] See methods of creative resolution as ASIT.

changing the position and shape of the curves, or by making the curves irrelevant;

- They guide engineers in their design decisions. They are designed to be a decision-making tool particularly helpful coupled with Target Costing. As for the utility curves, it is essential to add cost model curves to the trade-off curves;
- They transmit knowledge to novice engineers;
- They serve as a support for consultation and negotiation between different parties.

Combining Radar Charts, *CID*, and Trade-Off/Limit Curves

Let us once again take the example of the telescope. Customer Radar Chart and Performance Radar Chart are shown below.

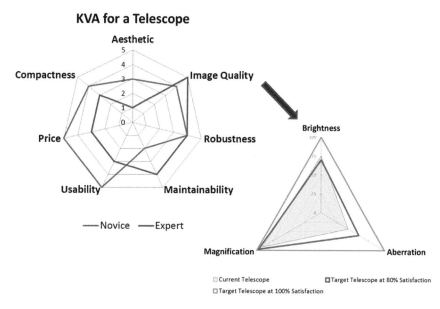

FIGURE 9.40
Relationship between the Customer Radar Chart and the Performance Radar Chart

The *CID* part corresponding to the 'image quality' attribute is as follows:

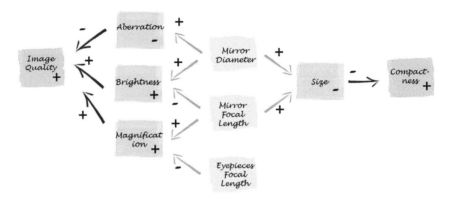

FIGURE 9.41
CID focusing on Image Quality

The shape of the trade-off curve visualising the two antagonistic performances, aberration and brightness, is as follows. The objective is to determine which telescope size can achieve the best trade-off.

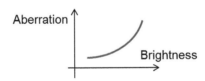

FIGURE 9.42
Aberration vs. Brightness

This curve potentially offers an infinite number of solutions!

By juxtaposing this curve with the utility curve dealing with brightness, we characterise its lower limit.

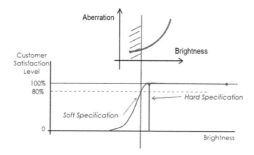

FIGURE 9.43
Brightness Utility Curve

These utility curves thus impose general constraints on performances. There are also other limits imposed on design variables. For example, the maximum telescope diameter is limited by the Target Cost. This last constraint limits access to superior brightness performances.

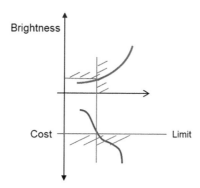

FIGURE 9.44
Cost versus Brightness

By gradually introducing new constraints, the admissible range of performance for the telescope diameter is bounded.

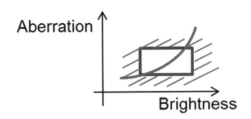

FIGURE 9.45
Accessible region for Aberration AND Brightness

Continuing in this way, the admissible region is reduced towards an acceptable solution. This process of convergence by gradually narrowing the set of solutions is known as SBCE (see *SBCE, the Lean Engineering process*). When there is no common design space between the target performance and the admissible design variables, there is no solution. It is therefore necessary to relax constraints or to innovate.

Teardown*

> **Teardown is an exercise that consists in taking apart a product, observing and analysing each element, how they relate to each other, to know as much as possible what it is made of and how it works.**

Origin

Curiosity is the primary motivation that pushes all children to want to take things apart to see what is inside, and sometimes to put them back together. However, Teardown is not only an item of sheer curiosity for children. As adults, some see it as an effective way to repair or improve existing products. This was the case with Sakichi Toyoda who disassembled and reassembled a large number of looms in order to better understand their mechanisms and explore new possibilities for improving the loom concept. Similarly, later, his son Kiichiro Toyoda 'purchased a new Chevrolet car and began disassembling it to analyse the vehicle's components'.[49] Subsequently, Teardown became a go-to method in the automotive industry and then widely adopted by major electronic and other manufacturers.

---

[49] History of TOYODA AUTOMATIC LOOM WORKS, LTD. – FundingUniverse.

Teardown Purposes[50]

Teardown is a method to take apart a product to reveal its functions, structure (interactions), parts, components, materials and technology used, manufacturing process, with the intention of better understanding how it works. This helps to uncover its strengths and weaknesses and thus pinpoint design improvements and cost-saving possibilities.

Teardown is primarily a competitive benchmark based on the analysis of competing products. It helps answer the question: how does the design, development, and manufacturing of your product compare? Finding out how other companies have solved the problems you or your customers face is one of the keys to staying competitive. On the other hand, it is also an opportunity to confirm if your products are still better than the competitors' newest products. The results of these comparisons should be used to make your product marketing strategies more effective.

However, Teardown is not limited to scrutinising the differences between two competing products. It is also an effective way to reverse engineering your own products. It enables you to uncover which past design decisions may have caused waste to your customers or your company. It helps stimulate new ideas to improve product design rather than simple design adjustments, or to reduce costs in combination with Value Engineering (see *Value Analysis/Value Engineering*).

Teardown is obviously appropriate for hardware products. However, how to disassemble a product with no moving parts like software applications? The same process, known as Software Reverse Engineering (SRE), applies to software. For example, decompiling and disassembling a compiled code or getting an original source code can provide information about its implementation, the technology stack used, the architecture, etc. SRE can also be used to detect and neutralise malicious code and malware like viruses[51] and give a better understanding of potential vulnerabilities in your systems.

---

[50] See R. Cooper. (September 1, 1995). 'When Lean Enterprises Collide: Competing Through Confrontation'. *Harvard Business Review Press*.

[51] For example, *Ghidra*, a software reverse engineering (SRE) framework developed by NSA's Research Directorate – Ghidra (ghidra-sre.org).

Connection with Lean Engineering

In addition to being widely used by Lean companies, Teardown also shares common traits with Lean Engineering practices and methods: it stimulates critical thinking, develops knowledge and skills, and improves decision-making. Moreover, its objective is the same as with Lean Engineering: 'maximising value creation while minimising waste for the entire system'.

Teardown allows engineers to test their own assumptions against a real product through exposure of facts and data, much like the *Genba Walk* does with the real place. During disassembly, a number of rich challenges and new questions arise that force engineers to use their critical thinking and problem-solving skills, and share their hypotheses and conclusions. For example, the strong points found in the competitor's best-in-class products can serve as a basis for transferring solutions to similar problems or stimulating new ideas.

In addition, Teardown is truly a hands-on approach to learning where engineers interact with the products. Driven by curiosity, they learn by doing. In this sense, it is part of necessary methods for effective product development and continuous improvement.

Teardown does not only develop individual skills and knowledge. Like most Lean Engineering methods and practices, it also develops teamwork (see definition). By co-locating engineers with different areas of expertise in the same room, e.g., in an *obeya*, around the same object, it encourages technical exchanges and learning conversations. This makes engineers reflect on the interdependencies between various design decisions and their influence on the product complexity, manufacturability, or reproducibility. They get thus a better feel that the best products result from solving the right trade-offs over the entire product life cycle rather than from optimising local decisions. In this way, Teardown contributes to eliminating poor engineering decisions and provides input for product and process improvement.

Finally, Teardown can also help to understand how your organisation affects the architecture of products. A complicated product is often the result of a complicated organisation!

The Proposed Method

We are not going to detail the Teardown process. Others have already done it very well.[52] We prefer to emphasise how Teardown can produce valuable

---

[52] Y. Sato and J.J. Kaufman. (2005). *Value Analysis Tear-Down: A New Process for Product Development and Innovation*, Industrial Press Inc.

learning experiences through the combination of doing and thinking, especially when interconnected with other Lean Engineering methods and practices, such as *CID* (Causal Influence Diagram) or Knowledge Briefs.

Teardown is analogous to typical problem-solving exercises. Engineers observe and disassemble a product as they dissect a problem.[53] They apply successive iterative cycles combining doing and thinking: make observations, state hypotheses/ask questions, take parts apart, make observations/analyse, build explanations, and so on. This is why we propose PDCA as a Teardown framework, as we do for *CID*.

PLAN
- Identify the problem and the product:
    - What problems are you trying to solve? Is it about a new design, a product improvement? What caused your product to succeed or fail?
    - What do you want to focus on? Teardown should always teach you something you didn't know before disassembling the product. So what knowledge gaps need to be closed? List your design issues and select the parameters to focus on: functions, technology, processes, components, etc.

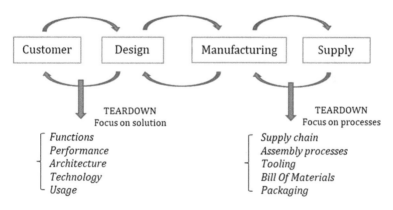

FIGURE 9.46
What does your Teardown focus on?

- What is the starting object? A complete product or sub-assembly? A best-class competing product? Any component that delivers functions that interest you? For example, once a necessary function is identified for your next product, you can evaluate

---

[53] Teardown is also an effective way to repair a defective product (i.e., *Genbutsu*).

through different products the many ways to achieve this function. Moreover, the same object can help answer a completely different set of questions depending on the perspective of the people concerned.

- Identify who should participate (design, production, marketing, purchasing, suppliers, etc.)
  - It is key not to rely on a single piece of expertise or points of view at the risk of missing elements that at first glance seem outside the scope. For example, an electrical engineer will preferentially focus on the electrical components and how they are powered, while a mechanical engineer will look at the product as a whole and how the parts fit together. The choice of participants is therefore essential.
  - Formulate questions which will drive your Teardown.
- Prepare for Teardown
  - Identify all modules, tools, devices, and processes that will be required to complete the Teardown. Prepare the video means to film each step.
  - Create your Teardown datasheets and templates. Use Knowledge Brief to properly document what has been done and learned to insure its reuse in technical departments or during future Teardowns.

DO

Do what was planned, that is, implement the Teardown according to plan. This means that the DO step should follow the Teardown steps through successive smaller PDCA loops, each combining doing and thinking. So, it is not a matter of trial and error, as every step is focused and intentional. We give an example with two loops.

- Display the product (first loop)
  - Observe (packaging, shapes, colours, connectivity, user interfaces, materials used), touch (handing, surface treatments), measure (dimensions, weight);
  - Take pictures;

FIGURE 9.47
Inside an electronic device

- Gather data (product datasheet, web source, BOM (Bill of Materials), installation manual, specifications, safety/security features);
- Run the product, conduct performance testing;
- Why is this product designed like this? Do you understand the design choices? Can you identify the constraints that led to these choices (cost, performance, certification standard, etc.)? Does this first step give information about the product's KVA or functions by making them legible and usable?
- Initiate the *CID* and the Knowledge Brief to note what has been learned. Adjust the next loop accordingly;

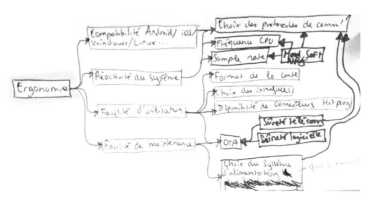

FIGURE 9.48
CID: Usability perspective of an electronic device

- Take apart the product (second loop)
  - Start filming;
  - How do the parts interact? Do you understand the architecture and how the parts relate to the system functions? Have you identified all the parts? Did you understand how well each part was implemented in the product? Have you discovered other ways to implement similar functions to those provided by your products? Do you confirm your preliminary hypothesis?
  - Establish the product breakdown structure and the functional architecture;

FIGURE 9.49
Handmade functional ground station architecture

- Are the materials appropriate? What manufacturing process and technology were used? It may be useful in this step to utilise the Design for Manufacturability and Assembly (DFMA) techniques;

FIGURE 9.50
Choice of the thread due to mechanical constraint (laser proximeter)

- Display all components. Note part costs, size, and weight. This data is to be used in Target Costing. Reconstruct the BOM;
- Provide a satisfactory explanation of your observations and analysis. Discuss the strong and weak points. Make your understanding of phenomena visible through the *CID*, the relationships between parts and functions, design decisions and performance, etc. Such evidence would indicate that you have a deepening grasp of the key product design variables.

CHECK

Examine the results achieved: review the *CID* and the Knowledge Briefs. Watch the film as many times as necessary. Complete if needed.

- Are the objectives from the plan reached? Are there still knowledge gaps? If so, what are they?
- Have you identified any new ideas or found alternatives that could improve product design through insights into parts, materials, functions, assembly, manufacturing, or provide the basis for transferring solutions to analogous problems?
- Do you need to refine and refocus your inquiries?

ACT

How to use all the data collected, your observations, your analyses?

- Are you considering adopting, adjusting, or abandoning a manufacturing process, the way functions are implemented, a technology, etc., to improve the design or development process of your future products? If so, which ones?
- How can you adjust your Teardown to make it more efficient?
- Are there any standards to develop or create?

Target Costing***

The purpose of target costing is to determine the Target Cost at which the new product should be developed and manufactured, and to achieve it using appropriate engineering.

Origin

The will to manage product costs was already present at Ford, which was determined to build simple, reliable, and affordable cars that every American worker could afford. The cost management procedures then progressed with the industrial expansion. During World War II, General Electric Co.[54] created Value Engineering (VE). In the 1960s, Toyota enriched VE with the idea of influencing and reducing product costs (*genka*) earlier in the planning (*kikaku*) and development stages. Target Costing (*Genka Kikaku*) was born. It has been combined with *Kaizen Costing*, the cost management part dedicated to the manufacturing of existing products. Rather than creating a formal structure, Toyota developed Target Costing as a part of the upfront engineering. This way, each employee felt responsible for the quality and cost of each product.[55]

As Target Costing refers to the competitive market, it is fundamentally customer driven. As such, it is close to the logic proposed by the value-based pricing process. For software products, this value-based pricing

---

[54] Lawrence Delos Miles was the creator of VE: Lawrence D. Miles – Wikipedia

[55] H. Okano. (2015). *History of Management Accounting in Japan: Institutional & Cultural Significance of Accounting.* Bingley.

approach is preferred. Like any other product, the perceived value of software products is defined by the value equation (see paragraph *Model and Make visible the Voice of Customers*). So software developers must first understand what trade-offs should influence software design.

Schematically, Target Costing covers two processes:

- The process of setting the Target Cost from the *Target Selling Price* and the *Target Margin*, and planning the new product.
- The process of achieving the Target Cost using appropriate engineering methods.

This chapter deals with the second point. Furthermore, several methods and practices detailed in this book can contribute to setting the Target Cost.

The Target Cost Equation

What should the product's Target Cost be for acceptance in the marketplace and to make this product profitable? This question can be expressed by this well-known equation:

$$Target\ Cost = Target\ Selling\ Price - Target\ margin$$

This means that the Target Cost can only be set once the Target Selling Price has been determined and the Target Margin established. It is the dependent variable. Marketplace and other market factors (i.e., company strategy, sales forecasting) determine the Target *Selling Price*, stakeholders, and financial markets influence the *Target Margin*.

Commuting this equation reflects different approaches where the product cost is not specified upfront but is determined once most of design decisions have been made. The cost is thus expected to be minimised as the design progress. The Selling Price is then obtained by adding the Expected Margin to this cost. It becomes the dependent variable, as in the cost-plus approach:

Target Selling Price = Expected Margin + Expected Cost

Connection with Lean Engineering

Target Costing belongs to the Chief Engineer since it requires the cross-functional management of all product related functions. The Target Cost and the target customer segment are communicated in the *Concept Paper* and displayed in the *obeya*.

The *Concept Paper* provides useful information about the company's product strategy. It is a determinant of the degree of effort devoted to Target Costing. Typically this effort is linked to the rate of new product introduction. The effort is also related to the degree of innovation of new products (*Product Takt*). The higher the degree of innovation, the lower the value of historical cost information for previous products. Product characteristics also influence target costing. A product with a long development cycle may require adjustments to the Target Cost according to market changes. A more complex product, with more components and based on different technologies, increases the effort of Target Costing.

Moreover, we have seen with Teardown that a product is first the sum of the functions it performs and the parts that make it up to perform those functions. However, a product is more than this sum. It is also the sum of the tasks performed to create, design, develop, manufacture, use, maintain, and dispose of it. All of these tasks have a cost, some of which are wasteful, and as such must be reduced or eliminated.

The fact is that most of these costly waste items are unpredictable, and therefore little considered, unlike direct costs. The risk is that they remain hidden despite their significant contribution to the total cost. Fortunately, Lean Engineering makes people aware of these waste costs, especially by making them dependent on engineering decisions. Indeed, most 'bad' costs are due to poor design decisions. So, the profit, and therefore the Target Cost, will depend on engineering's ability to make the decisions that create the right product, i.e., operational and customer value streams with minimum waste.

To guide their decisions, the engineers need to know the customer's KVA, which is the value that target customers assign to different product attributes. They also need to know the company KVA. Customers and company Radar Charts are central to Target Costing. They are also communicated in the *Concept Paper*. From this information, the objective is to reach the best balance between maximising the KVA and minimising the cost, as defined by the Value Equation. For engineers, this means identifying and resolving the right trade-offs between these (and other parameters). With each new decision, the current estimated cost variance with the Target Cost is re-evaluated. With this in mind, the management does not evaluate Target Cost progression from a central accounting system. They go to the shop floor, the lab, the open spaces, wherever design decisions are made (see *Genba Walk*).

The Proposed Method

Target Costing is applied to new design – Value Analysis (VA)/Value Engineering (VE) structures the loop between current and future products. It is therefore reasonable to consider that the related activities are part of routine design activities. Thus, describing the process of achieving the Target Cost appears to be roughly equivalent to describing the Lean product development process, with a strong focus on cost: for each decision, the current estimated cost is compared to the Target Cost. However, the path to get there is still the same: satisfy the KVA, Key Specifications, and constraints through good product design while limiting costly rework through earlier learning.

The first step of Target Costing must have defined a Target Cost per function from an estimate of the relative value of each function to the Target Cost. As for actual cost per function, it depends on the values of the Key Specifications, i.e., the performance, specific to each function. This dependency can be expressed by cost vs. performance curves over the intervals of interest. By identifying which design variables determine which performance, the *CID* provides information to plot these curves. At the same time, it may be useful to draw a *CID* starting from cost to confirm its main drivers.

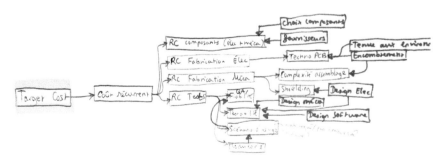

FIGURE 9.51
CID: main recurring cost drivers

By coupling these cost vs. performance curves with performance trade-off curves, it is possible to map the region where the trade-off decisions must be made.

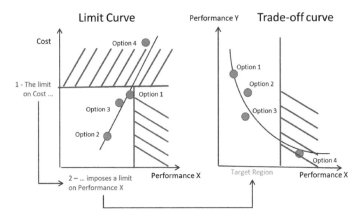

FIGURE 9.52
Coupling cost limit curves with trade-off curves

Conversely, it is possible to estimate for which function a small drop in performance would lead to a significant drop in cost, taking into account trade-offs between performances. Each point on a cost vs. performance curve represents an option in the solutions space. By selecting the values for a set of performances, the resulting option can be plotted on a Product Radar Chart. The result is a polygon where each vertex corresponds to the value of one performance on its own axis. As the area of this polygon is correlated with the cost, it can be used as a way to compare costs between options.

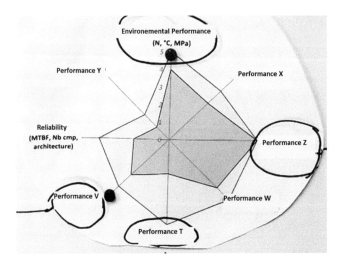

FIGURE 9.53
Stacked areas help to compare the cost of different options (blue and red)

Once the analysis has been carried out at the function level, the breakdown of each function into sub-assemblies and components makes it possible to focus more precisely on design choices according to the component-level Target Cost.

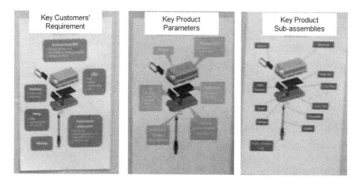

FIGURE 9.54
Exploded diagrams – from customers' needs to product sub-assemblies

By sub-assembly, the cost and specification impacts of each design decision are captured and displayed on the Product Wall.

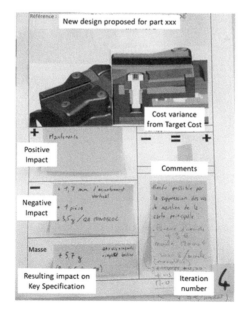

FIGURE 9.55
Impact decision sheet per sub-assembly

To get a global view, the components already identified and those whose options are still open are visualised in the *obeya*.

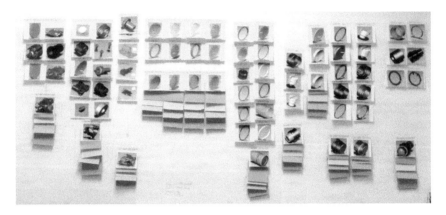

FIGURE 9.56
Product component-level breakdown structure

These decisions must take into account the impact on all operational value chains. For example, a new product that can be manufactured on the same production line as an existing product avoids new investments while offering increased production flexibility. Logically, the fewer evolutions there are, the lower the risk of making poor design decisions. Therefore, one should seek to maximise the reuse of standard solutions and, for new parts, rely on design and production standards. Product evolutions are relevant if they directly improve the user experience and/or reduce the cost of the product.

Interaction between cost and design decision is then closely monitored to detect any gap between the assigned Target Cost and the estimated cost for each sub-assembly and function. With these gaps visible, engineers can identify where to reduce costs and which parameters to focus on, while ensuring the product remains feasible (see SBCE).

Target Costing Issues

While Target Costing may seem easy to implement, common issues and misunderstandings can compromise its effectiveness:

- As the Target Cost is not directly correlated to the product value, all functions are considered equally important for the customer satisfaction. Conversely, if a certain function cannot be linked to a KVA, it is because it is not perceived as valuable for the customer or is not considered necessary for the performance or quality of the product. In this case, it might be better to simplify or even delete it;

- Rather than being consolidated from functional area contributions, the Target Cost is directly established by experts with little or no input from engineers and then imposed on development teams. Conversely, Target Costing is a collaborative exercise. It is about determining together which decisions will lead to the Target Cost and which trade-offs must be resolved to simultaneously maintain the value of the product. The objectives, progress, and results of this exercise are posted in the *obeya*, so that they are visible to all and can be referred to whenever a design decision is made;

- The Target Cost is set too late in the development, by which time a large part of the costs are already fixed. Conversely being able to set the Target Cost earlier with the goal of never exceeding it requires making fully informed design decisions (see *The Decision paradox*);

- The Target Cost is no longer monitored during product development. However, when it comes to complex products with longer development cycles, the early Target Cost established is subject to greater uncertainty. In this case, it is relevant to consider it as a draft Target Cost to be reviewed by an iterative process around the right trade-offs between Target Selling Price and product's features and performance;

- The Target Cost concerns an already mature product where the cost reduction margins are concentrated on the parts manufactured by suppliers. The risk is to generate an excessive pressure impacting the quality of these parts and ultimately the quality of the product. For example, this can lead to the use of cheaper components and materials that are less robust, less reliable, and more likely to fail during normal use. Conversely, the product must first be better before it is cheaper, i.e., create more value for the customer. This is the golden rule for successful companies:[56]

- Better before cheaper – in other words, compete on differentiators other than price.
- Revenue before cost – that is, prioritise increasing revenue over reducing costs.
- There are no other rules – so change anything you must to follow Rules 1 and 2.

So, go back to KVAs and check if they are defined to gain and retain customers through products that last longer. Share these KVAs with your suppliers and integrate them more closely into the design process.

Value Analysis/Value Engineering***

> *Value Analysis/Value Engineering aims to maximise the value offered to the customer in line with a Target Cost. While VA focuses on cost variances on current products, VE works to resolve these gaps on the engineering phase of future products.*

Origin

During World War II, the shortage of raw materials, parts, and skilled labour forced General Electric Co.[57] to create the Value Engineering (VE) concept of minimising costs without compromising the key product functions. After the war, Lawrence D. Miles improved his methodology which was named Value Analysis (VA). The value methodology gained in popularity and spread worldwide.[58] VE (or VA) 'focuses on improving value by identifying alternate ways to reliably accomplish a function that

---

[56] M.E. Raynor and M. Ahmed. (April 2013). 'Three Rules for Making a Company Truly Great'. *Harward Business Review.*

[57] Lawrence Delos Miles was the creator of VE: Lawrence D. Miles – Wikipedia

[58] SAVE International® SAVE International (value-eng.org).

meets the performance expectations of the customer'.[59] Value is commonly represented by the following equation:

$$Value = \frac{Functions}{Costs}$$

where *Functions* are the primary purpose of the product, i.e., what the product is supposed to do, also taking into account quality and emotional aspects, and *Costs* are all the resources needed to accomplish these functions. This equation reflects the same idea that the 'Value equation', from the perspective of the company rather than the customer:

$$Perceived\,Value = \frac{Benefits}{Sacrifices}$$

Therefore, the goal of VE (or VA) is to help you increase the *Perceived Value* of your products through its *Functions*. Combined with Teardown, you will be able to identify new *functions*, improve some of them, or even eliminate the weak ones. Related to Target Costing, you will do this to achieve your Target Cost.

Connection with Lean Engineering

Each product design decision also affects the design of the production flow. So, rather than discuss a potential hybrid Lean and VA/VE model for engineering, we prefer to explore Toyota's interpretation[60] of VE and VA, in which the former focuses on new products and the latter on existing products. In that sense, Toyota adopted the same partition applied to their cost management system: Target Costing as a cost reduction process in the design of new products and *Kaizen Costing* as a cost reduction process in the production and redesign of existing products. The goal is to leverage the latter to improve the former, and vice versa, in a continuous improvement loop.

---

[59] WSDOT Guide to Value Engineering (wa.gov).
[60] トヨタ企業サイト | トヨタ自動車75年史 | 研究開発支援 | 原価企画・質量企画・部品標準化 (toyota.co.jp).

Based on this interpretation, the main challenge of VA/VE is less technical than organisational. How to establish a dialogue between production teams busy with the problems of existing products and engineering teams busy with future solutions? Without dialogue, the risk is that they will repeat the same mistakes without knowing the consequences on manufacturing (or any other component of the operational value stream).

Just as the engineers visualise customer complaints on the Customer Wall, they should also be able to visualise operator complaints on a dedicated wall.

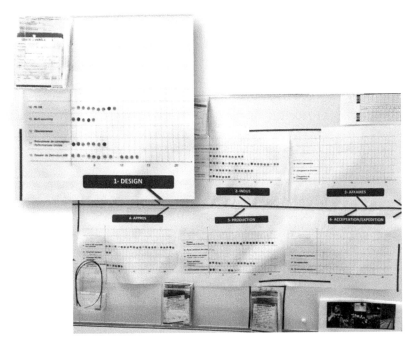

FIGURE 9.57
Problems Wall of a production line with a part dedicated to 'Design'

In the same spirit, defective products set aside in a red bin should be regularly analysed by engineers in collaboration with operators. Are they defects due to past poor design decisions? For engineers, the red bins are the place for collecting 'actual defective objects', i.e., the *genbutsu*. From them, you can observe, measure, or teardown the defective product to see the consequences of their own past bad decisions so they can improve the future ones.

By putting engineers in close contact with operators and focusing them all on the same problems, you create the conditions for a common professional language to be established between all collaborators and by doing so, you contribute to breaking down silos.

For software products, it is possible to see in DevOps[61] an application of VA/VE: operation and development engineers participate together in the entire life cycle of the service, from design to development process to production support. So, DevOps, as VA/VE, breaks down the silos between operations and engineering.

Did You Know Kaizen Costing?

As part of VE/VA, *Kaizen Costing* activities are of two kinds:
- Design changes are decided on the product when the difference between the actual cost and the Target Cost is significant after three months of production;
- After these three months, systematic *Kaizen* allow to reduce production costs (labour costs, material costs, etc.).[62]

HIT THE ROAD

In previous sections, we presented methods and practices to help you properly explore each territory. This section discusses how to best articulate them to establish what will be your new product flow. To do this, you need a leader, and the elements to map out the right path forward with confidence. Then it will be time to hit the road!

---

[61] A compound of development (Dev) and operations (Ops).

[62] Y. Monden and K. Hamada. (1991). 'Target Costing and *Kaizen* Costing in Japanese Automobile Companies'. *JMAR Volume 3.*

Chief Engineer***

> *The Chief Engineer (CE) decides the best path from VoC to the right product. They make key product decisions and lead the development flow to do it efficiently. They own the Concept Paper.*

Origin

The *Chief Engineer* is generally the person in charge of a product development programme. Depending on the company, their position in the organisation, their authority and their responsibilities may be different. At Toyota, the CE has a unique role with high decision-making responsibility.

Before using the term CE in 1989, Toyota used the word *shusa* to refer to these heavyweight product managers. Strictly speaking, *shusa* (主査) means 'chief examiner' (査 means to investigate, examine). The *shusa* were members of the programme team without authority until the Vice President Eiji Toyoda created a new role 'outside the organisation' in 1953. He explained it this way: 'On any matter you (*shusa*) think will be good for the vehicle you're responsible for, you can give your opinion to anyone in the company. Know that you have the authority to give your opinion'.[63]

Kenya Nakamura was the first *shusa* with this new role. In 1952, he was assigned to lead the development of the Crown, a car

The Heavy Weight Programme (Product) Manager

The term *Heavy Weight Programme/ Product Manager* (HWPM) was coined by Takahiro Fujimoto (Fujimoto and Clark (1991) 'Product Development Performance'. *Harvard Business School Press* to refer generically to powerful project/product managers with high decision-making responsibility that acts as both external and internal integrators. On the internal side, the HWPM integrate all the functional departments' contributions to the flow in a coordinated manner. On the external side, they capture customer needs and integrate them into a product concept. The CE at Toyota comes close to matching the HWPM.

---

[63] S. Hino. (2005). *Inside the Mind of Toyota: Management Principles for Enduring Growth.* Productivity Press. p. 182.

model intended for use as a taxi. The challenge was great: the Crown was to be the first true passenger car produced entirely in-house by Toyota.[64] His exceptional technical and leadership skills, along with the confidence of top management, allowed him to run his programme without having any hierarchical power over the teams working for him. In this way, he had full latitude to do whatever he felt good to get the job done, from VoC capture to concept and development to production launch. Thus, he handled as much responsibility for deciding the car's features as he did for its development process.

Kenya Nakamura's qualities and behaviour laid the foundation for a new model of technical leadership codified in ten precepts as a guide to succeed in a *shusa's* role.[65]

To summarise:

- *Shusa* represents the VoC and pushes a shared vision of the product;
- They are responsible for defining the product concept and orchestrates the teams activities from design to production;
- They lead their project through influence and technical skills. They have no hierarchical power.
- They are accountable for the success, or failure, of the product programme.

These precepts are consistent with the qualities emphasised by S. Toyoda. It is therefore not surprising that Toyota was the first company to develop this model of strong technical leadership, its founder being the first *shusa* in history.

---

[64] http://www.toyota-global.com/company/history_of_toyota/75years/text/taking_on_the_automotive_business/chapter2/section8/item3_b.html.

[65] https://www.lean.org/shook/DisplayObject.cfm?o=906.

The Famous Chief Engineer Tatsuo Hasegawa

Before joining Toyota after the war, Tatsuo Hasegawa was responsible for the design of the Tachikawa Ki-94 (interceptor aircraft) in 1943 at Tachikawa Aircraft Corporation. His experience as chief aircraft designer was a major inspiration for writing the Ten Precepts.[66]

In the 1950s, he assisted Kenya Nakamura, Chief Engineer of the Crown. He was appointed Chief Engineer in 1959 on the Toyota Publica released in 1961, and then on the Corolla in 1963.

Tatsuo Hasegawa explains the success of the Corolla (40 million units) by the intensive work done to understand what the public wanted, what their needs were, and how to satisfy them fully while bringing them pleasure, 'a car for everyone on the Earth'. He and his team have been pioneers in capturing the needs of their contemporaries and offering them appropriate technological solutions.[67]

Your Chief Engineer system

Why Would You Need a Chief Engineer (3) (12)?

To answer this question, let's look at how the CE system could solve some of the emblematic issues that many matrix organisations face, such as the coordination of temporary cross-functional teams, or the capture and reuse of knowledge. However, the CE system is not a one-size-fits-all approach, so it is down to you to determine how it can help you solve your own problems in the way you execute your projects.

Make the Organisational Matrix More Effective while Routing Engineers in Functions

Matrix organisations combine functional and project-based structures, with a wide spectrum of function-project balances. People attached to functions, e.g., engineering specialties and expertise, are assigned for a more or less long period to one or more projects. They have to juggle between the directive of their functional management and the requests coming from the project management. These multi-bosses issues do not only affect individuals, they also work their way to project management.

To facilitate cross-functional coordination and cooperation, some companies have adopted the co-location of project teams on plateaus.

---

[66] https://www.revolvy.com/page/Tatsuo-Hasegawa.

[67] *Summary of an interview with Mr. Hasegawa in 2000:* http://newsroom.toyota.co.jp/en/corolla50th/message/hasegawa/.

Although face-to-face is an effective way to exchange and collaborate, it comes at the cost of losing the transmission of information between functions deprived of their experts for much of the time. In addition, this plateau model can reinforce tension between projects and functions, particularly with respect to the availability and long-term assignment of key experts.

An effective system must balance strong integration of people's work in different functional areas with the development of deep expertise and knowledge in those areas that will benefit from that integration. This means balancing two types of flows (13):

- The *Product Flows* owned by the CE. They include all decisions, activities and tasks in the development process for producing profitable products;
- The *Knowledge*[68] *Flows* owned by the functional managers. They consist of capturing knowledge about markets, customers, technologies, capabilities, and supply chain and to channelling it to where it is needed into *Product Flows*.

FIGURE 9.58
Connection between products flows and knowledge flows

To make the intersections between these two types of flows efficient, we prefer a 'project *obeya*' rather than a plateau. This *obeya* frames the collaboration between the various functional experts and the CE. On the functions side, other *obeya* are dedicated to problem solving and knowledge development related to engineering specialties.

---

[68] By convention. It is rather a flow of knowledge and information.

Like in any matrix organisation, tensions may exist between the CE who makes the strong product decisions and the functional managers who provide the knowledge and people to do so. However, these tensions, primarily technical in nature, force the CE and the functional managers to share, and challenge information. While the CE can push the functional managers towards innovations, beyond the limits of what they know, the latter can in turn prevent the former from making potentially dangerous technical mistakes. This positive tension is fostered by set-based thinking, which provides more space to converge together on the best trade-offs in the design space.

Chief Engineer vs. Product Owner

Note the similarity with the term Product Owner used by Jeff Sutherland to describe the role of the Product Backlog Manager in Scrum. However, there is at least one major difference. In Lean, the CE is also responsible for defining and applying the product development process. In Scrum, the person who ensures that the process is understood and adopted by the team is the Scrum Master. The Scrum Master is more like a Process Owner. Where Lean sees one person, Scrum sees two!

Develop your CE System

By considering each project as a *product flow*, it seems logical that the Programme/Project Managers (PM) become the CE. However, changing the title of the role is not enough to make a new model of technical entrepreneurship.

How to go from PM to CE?

Answering this question starts with answering these: who defines the product vision? Who drives the right trade-offs? Who makes Key Decisions balancing VoC, business objectives, and company capabilities? Who is responsible for fitting all the parts of the system? Who defines the product flow process and runs the development? Who integrates the work of people? Who makes money and is accountable for the success of the project?

Many companies answer these questions by defining distinct positions:

- The *Product Manager* is responsible for formalising the VoC and proposing the best response to market's expectations, company's strategy and capabilities. They are also responsible for launching the product development throughout the life cycle;
- The *Programme/Project Manager* is in charge of the management and coordination of teams to complete the programme on time and within budget, with customer satisfaction. They apply the process defined by the company's quality reference system. On large projects, the PM groups work activities into Work Packages and assigns their management to Work Package Managers (WPM).
- The *Product (or Solution) Engineering Manager* is in charge of the design and development of the product, and the orchestration of the technical integration. They apply and adapt the process, practices, and tools as defined in the Quality Management System (QMS).

Unfortunately, this multiplication of positions encourages the dilution of responsibilities with several consequences:

- The split between the Product Manager who defines the product attributes without mastering its development phases and the Product Engineering Manager who develops the product without knowing the customers increases the risk of developing the wrong product. *A product vision without technical judgement is as useless as a product without a market vision*;
- The Work Package Managers, with the support of technical department heads, tend to optimise locally rather than globally. Much complicated architecture is the result of organisational silos;[69]
- The Product Engineering Manager doesn't bear the consequences of their technical decisions, which increase the risk of delays and additional costs.

---

[69] Work Breakdown Structure (WBS) is often based on Organisation Breakdown Structure (OBS).

Those who decide are rarely those who have the knowledge to do so with confidence, and those who manage the project are not those who make the product decisions. The CE system can be a solution to this dilution of responsibilities: one person to decide, act, coordinate, and be held accountable. Provided that, each CE represents the VoC and makes product decisions, since they have strong technical experience as opposed to 'professional' PM.[70] These multiple responsibilities require strong leadership but prevent 'multi-boss' problems. While it may be difficult to find leaders who combine all of these skills and responsibilities, it is not necessarily easier to find people who can share them effectively and who 'can think as one well enough to effectively implement this combination', as A. Ward said (3). And while the CE doesn't have to be an expert in all areas, they must have sufficient skills to interact with all functions and understand the trade-offs. The horizontal bar of the T is quite long for the CE (see Teamwork).

It is the responsibility of each company to set up the conditions necessary for the emergence of this unique technical leadership, starting with the adoption of Lean principles:

- As the internal representatives of the customers, your CE candidates must learn to go to the *genba*, first on the Territory of Customers. They must know how to formalise the VoC and the product vision in a Concept Paper. Then, they must know how to translate these VoC and product vision into product parameters and trade-offs.
- As product flow owners, they must be able to lead the development flow and integrate the work of all stakeholders in a coherent manner. They must know how to identify, articulate, and make Key Decisions. It is therefore necessary to develop, perhaps even more than for others, their ability to ask the right questions and to constantly adapt to changes.

---

[70] International reference bodies (PMI, INCOSE) promote Project Management as a profession, rather than a skill.

Pull, Flow, Cadence**

> *Flow is also a key concept in product development, where information is the primary flow unit. Less Work in Progress, smaller batches, fewer hand-offs, cross-functional teams, and paced learning cycles create the conditions for a faster development flow.*

Origin

In 1938, K. Toyoda proposed the first rudimentary implementation of Just-in-Time on the assembly line of the Koromo plant.[71] He defined it as follows:[72] 'What I mean by Just-in-Time is not simply that it is important to do something on time, but that it is absolutely essential to be precise in terms of quantity and not, for example, produce something on time but in excess, since excess amounts to waste'.

The actual successful implementation of Just-in-Time must be credited to Taiichi Ohno. In 1943, he joined Toyota Motor Corporation (TMC) to improve operations in its machine shop. He set up a production flow and experimented with a reverse information flow. After several adjustments, in 1948, a first version of the supermarket concept was born. The *kanban* system was fully tested in 1954 before being more widely adopted in 1956.[73]

The supermarket concept takes its name from the supermarkets seen in the United States where the goods arrive on the shelf to be picked by the customers. A minimum stock is essential to ensure that goods are available when customers need them. By analogy, this stock is called a supermarket on a Just-in-Time production line. When an item leaves the supermarket, a signal (*kanban* cards) is sent back to replenish the downstream process.

Since the items are transmitted – in accordance with the defined upper limit of the Work in Progress (WIP) – to the next point only when this

---

[71] http://www.toyota-global.com/company/history_of_toyota/75years/text/taking_on_the_automotive_business/chapter2/section4/item5.html.

[72] http://www.toyota-global.com/company/toyota_traditions/quality/may_jun_2004.html.

[73] M. A. Cusumano. (1989). 'The Japanese Automobile Industry/Technology and Management at Nissan and Toyota'. *Harvard University Press*.

point is ready to receive them, there is no need for central coordination. A pull system operates in a distributed mode (see p. 46).

In contrast, in a push system, once the items are ready, they are transmitted to the next point without taking into account either the real needs of the downstream process or the WIP level. This system must necessarily be centralised in order to coordinate activities and align production with planned requirements.[74]

Did You Know That?

The notion of *pull* is already present in 1915 in the book *Installing Efficiency Methods* by Charles E. Knoeppel. The author defined rules to avoid the downstream process waiting for the production of the upstream process (Extract from the book, p. 121):

'The method outlined also leads to an important principle which all should work to, and which will do much to correct the usual policy found in shops. It can be stated as follows:

The method to follow in getting the work through a shop is not to apply pressure at A towards B, but to draw at B from A. This means a 'pull' type instead of a 'push' type, as one man expressed it …'.

The Engineering Version

Planning and work in development projects are traditionally done in push mode. A centralised plan specifies, in detailed Work Packages (WP), what the tasks each individual has to accomplish are and when, without any WIP limits. In line with the plan, gate reviews interrupt the flow to check each WP deliverable. Any deviation generates actions that are added to nominal activities. Despite these checks, some problems will be detected only much later, once the deliverables are in the hands of their recipients. Solving them will lead to new actions and disruptions of the flow. From disruptions to interruptions, the schedule slips, requiring successive updates of the plan.

All these disruptions (*mura*) increase the workload (*muri*), leading to additional non-quality (*muda*). Aware of these degradations, managers reinforce their control by imposing more actions, reports, and reviews.

---

[74] Michel Baudin. (2004). *Lean Logistics*. Productivity Press. Chapter 10.

These countermeasures in turn add new disruptions. This is the vicious circle of product development.

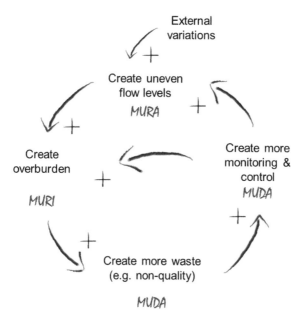

FIGURE 9.59
The Push mode generates the circle of evil in product development

This vicious cycle can be explained by the theory of queue, especially by the Kingman's law.[75] For stochastic processes such as new product development processes, the higher the utilisation of capacity (workload), the longer the waiting time (i.e., queue length). One should never ask to produce more than can be produced: queues occur when a system exceeds its capacity!

Usually, waste limits the potential of teams. Without the will to reduce the waste, maximising the workload to meet deadlines leads irremediably to slowing down the flow. If you thought that delay only starts when your people are 100% loaded, you were wrong! The average waiting time increases exponentially with workload. An 80% workload seems to be a good compromise between peak utilisation or underutilisation.

---

[75] https://www.allaboutlean.com/kingman-formula/.

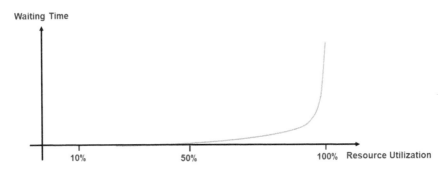

FIGURE 9.60
Waiting time as a function of resource utilisation

This gets worse with variations in work processing times and/or in the arrival rate. Slowdown starts at around 60% of resource utilisation. Therefore, planning close to 100% utilisation will further increase the development time of your products.

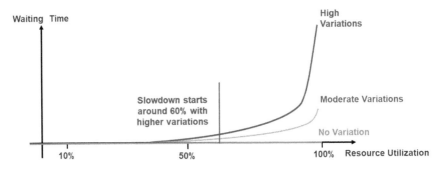

FIGURE 9.61
Waiting time increases with variations

Aware of the delays and team overload, the management usually chooses to add resources to increase the project capacity and get back on track. While this response may provide some temporary relief to the teams, it may ultimately worsen the situation. Indeed, the addition of more resources leads to more coordination and more hand-offs, i.e., more variations. As a result, all people are again overloaded, which makes the situation even worse.

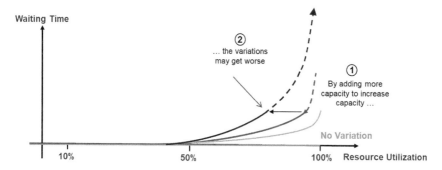

FIGURE 9.62
Variations increase by adding more capacity

This validates the relation between *muri* and *mura*. So, rather than focusing on people utilisation, start by reducing variations of the flow.

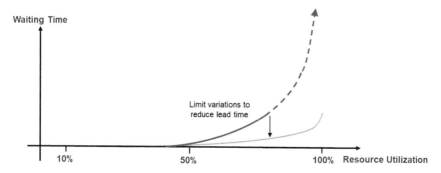

FIGURE 9.63
Reduce variation first

This is a shift from resource efficiency to flow efficiency.

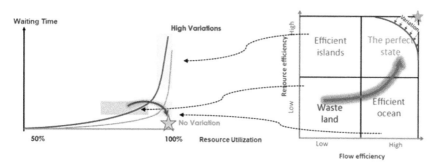

FIGURE 9.64
Kingman's law and the flow paradox

To support this shift, we propose three interdependent principles.[76]

Principle 1: Limit the Number and the Size of Flowing Items

This principle is stated by the Little's law linking the average number L of items present in the system to the average waiting time W that an item spends in the system and the average rate λ of items arriving at the system:

$$L = \lambda.W$$

This formula can be reformulated with flow-related terms:

$$WIP = Throughput * CycleTime$$

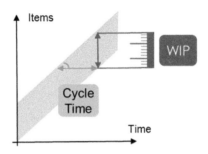

FIGURE 9.65
The Little's law

Strictly speaking, applying Little's law requires specific conditions that are not always perfectly met by engineering processes; Little's law[77] is defined for steady-state stochastic processes. However, it remains valid for any non-stationary development process under certain conditions:

- *Boundary condition: the finite time window of observation starts and ends with an empty system.*
- *Conservation (stable) condition: the number of arrivals equals the number of departures.*

---

[76] See (16), or M., and T. Poppendieck. (2006). *Implementing Lean Software Development From Concept to Cash*. Addison Wesley Professional. Chapter 5.
[77] Little's Law, by John D.C. Little and Stephen C. Graves, M.I.T

So using this law in product development contexts is less to accurately calculate one term from the others than to understand their mutual influence.

From this formula, it is easy to see that the flow accelerates when the WIP decreases, assuming a nearly constant throughput. And the WIP decreases when the size and number of flowing items decrease.

(1)   Get smaller batch sizes

In product development projects, the cycle time corresponds to the time elapsed between the identification of requirements and their fulfilment, or between the identification of knowledge gaps and their closure. The size of the batch is related to the work content to complete this cycle time.

How far to reduce this batch size? An answer is given by solving the trade-off between inventory costs and transaction cost:

- Holding or inventory costs[78] are related to the maintenance of inventory over a period of time. They increase with the batch size.
- Transaction costs correspond to the general costs of preparing and starting a new batch. This cost decreases proportionally as the batch size gets larger (fewer switching between batches).

The optimal batch size is set by the right balance between transaction and holding costs. The goal is to get closer to the green point of the U-curve.

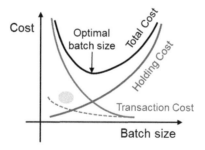

FIGURE 9.66
U-curve

---

[78] Costs related to storing and maintaining inventory over a certain period of time. See Economic Order Quantity – EOQ

For example, finding the right balance between the size of the tests and the preparation time between each test, or between the size of each increment of a document and the time to configure it and move to the next. Likewise, in Scrum, shorter sprints help reduce WIP and allow for more frequent feedback. The transaction costs of ceremonies and standing meetings must be thus reduced in proportion.

(2)   Limit the transaction (switching) costs.

<u>Fight Task Switching</u>

For individuals, multitasking and task switching can have detrimental effects on flow effectiveness and reduce productivity.

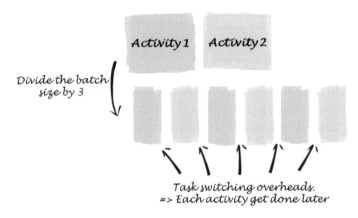

FIGURE 9.67
Overhead due to task switching for individuals

Task switching causes interruptions in the workflow and reduces concentration, especially when tasks involve diverse and unrelated tasks (context switching[79]). After each interruption, the working memory is reset to process new information. More switching leads to brain overload and mental fatigue. This form of *muri* can also create stress and affect the quality of work. In practice, it is therefore more efficient to have ten people working full-time on a project than 20 people working part-time

---

[79] https://www.fastcompany.com/944128/worker-interrupted-cost-task-switching.

on two.[80] Productivity increases by reducing the switching cost and the flow accelerates since the WIP decreases accordingly.

Unfortunately, avoiding multitasking is not always possible. In this case, try to focus on one task at a time and schedule-related tasks together to limit context switching.

<u>Fight Hand-Off</u>

Hand-offs are another source of transaction costs where switching takes place between individuals. They can generate much waste such as loss of knowledge, production of useless information or waiting. As long as you aim for lean development, you must fight against these hand-offs.

- Limit their number. Develop the versatility of your worker's skills. They will then be able to continue their activities further along the flow. For example, it is more efficient for a developer to perform all development steps for each *story* (analysis, coding, testing, integration, delivery).
- Reduce their impact. Encourage the collaboration between your workers and develop their ability to interact with other fields of expertise (see Teamwork).

Thus, multi-skilling and co-engineering help to fight against hand-offs that excessive specialisation and division of labour increase. Unfortunately, this division of labour still applies in knowledge work, with the following effects:

- Each discipline is busy maximising its own output (silo effect). WIP increases, slowing down the flow of development.
- Activities are divided between those who decide (managers), those who do (engineers) and those who know (experts), reinforcing the previous effect.

---

[80] In *Quality Software Management Systems Thinking*, Dorset House. (1991). Gerald M. Weinberg estimates a loss of 20% of time with a second task and 50% with a third one when they concern different projects (i.e., different flows)

The Division of Labour

With his pin factory, Adam Smith (*An Inquiry into the Nature and Causes of the Wealth of Nations*, 1776) demonstrated that a significant reduction in hand-off costs related to tool changes between two successive tasks could be achieved through the division of labour. In his logic, a single specialised task is assigned to each operator. The increase in their productivity is then paid for by their de-skilling. Lean fully opposes this model:

- People development. The division of labour, by overspecialising, impoverishes potential and demotivates human;
- Just-in-Time and agility. The division of labour eliminates the teamwork and the multi-skilling of team members that is needed to gain agility.

Yet this hard-living model still thrives on many production lines today.

Principle 2: Pace the development flow to level variations

Pace the flow with short cycles mechanically limits the work content and thus drives out variations from process (reduction of *mura*). In addition, more feedback accelerates learning and therefore continuous improvement. K. Radeka (14) describes them as Rapid Learning Cycles that set the pace of learning for the teams. Based on PDCA loops, they pull knowledge forward so that decisions can be made with confidence.

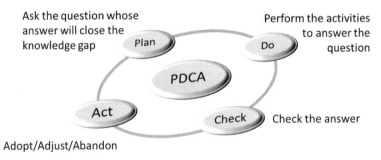

FIGURE 9.68
Rapid learning cycles as PDCA learning loops

In upstream stages, concurrent activities can make these learning cycles numerous and dependent on multifunctional teams. To ensure effective cross-functional coordination, they must be synchronised to the same heartbeat. By establishing this cadence through regular sync points, viewed as pull events, all parts of the system can be synchronised and the workload levelled.

The objectives and sequence of these pull events are approved by the Chief Engineer. As being late can delay the project, rescheduling a pull event must be avoided. The scope or performance should be adjusted instead.

New product development should therefore no longer be guided by phase gate thinking which tends to generate large batches and instil wasteful bureaucracy, but rather by successive PDCA-type loops. *Product development is a paced knowledge-based development flow.*

Principle 3: Apply a Pull Mode

In pull mode, each engineer adjusts their production directly to the demands of the immediate downstream recipient in the flow, respecting the WIP limit. Pull events make knowledge available to decide. The people doing the work know what knowledge (or any other artefact) is expected at the next event without the need for a rigid centralised plan.

These Three Principles Are Interconnected

The simultaneous application of these three principles of pull, flow, and cadence makes product development faster and more agile.

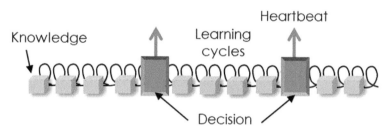

FIGURE 9.69
Pull, Flow, Cadence

The Knowledge-Based Decision-Making Method

The new product development flow moves at the pace of decisions! Ensuring you have the correct knowledge to close the gap, you will make the right decisions.

Drive and Secure Upfront Engineering through Key Decisions (KDs)

A decision describes a concrete, significant issue for which several potential options exist. A decision is key when its impact on the success of the project is major, i.e., when it is at an intersection where taking down the wrong path will have severe consequences. *A KD is costly to change!*

These questions provide criteria for assessing whether a decision is key:

- Impact on stakeholders' value and user experience? The Key Specifications and the Critical Items that are of primary importance to key stakeholders and have huge impact on product usability;
- What is unique? Any unusual requirements that will be more difficult to meet than the previous ones?
- Cross-cutting and systemic impact? Architectural significant issues that affect multiple parts of the system and their interactions.
- Large unknown? The larger the knowledge gaps, the greater the risk of making wrong choices. However, the unknowns about customers can be small and still have a strong impact.

These criteria narrow the focus only on the decisions that are truly key. The detail will come with the breakdown of the KDs into Knowledge Gaps (KGs). Once you have identified the KG, you can focus on closing these gaps to making KDs.

A: Identify the right Key Decisions

During workshops, each function collaborates to identify which KDs must be made to achieve the next objectives. They can be identified from customers' radars utility functions, *CID*, trade-off curves. A KD must be written down as 'choice of …'.

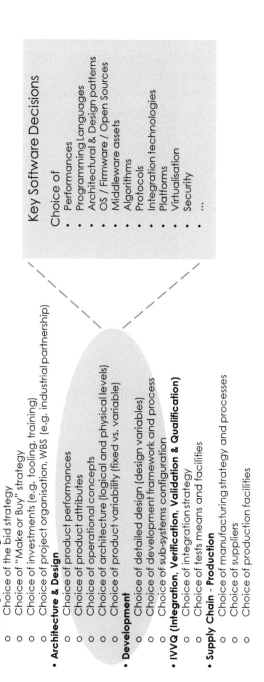

Key Software Decisions

Choice of
- Performances
- Programming Languages
- Architectural & Design patterns
- OS / Firmware / Open Sources
- Middleware assets
- Algorithms
- Protocols
- Integration technologies
- Platforms
- Virtualisation
- Security
- ...

- **Marketing**
  - Choice of the target market segment
  - Choice of Key Value Attributes
  - Choice of business strategy (e.g. pricing strategy)
  - Choice of product policy (e.g. shared assets)
- **Bid and Program Management**
  - Choice of the bid strategy
  - Choice of "Make or Buy" strategy
  - Choice of investments (e.g. tooling, training)
  - Choice of project organisation, WBS (e.g. industrial partnership)
- **Architecture & Design**
  - Choice of product performances
  - Choice of product attributes
  - Choice of operational concepts
  - Choice of architecture (logical and physical levels)
  - Choice of product variability (fixed vs. variable)
- **Development**
  - Choice of detailed design (design variables)
  - Choice of development framework and process
  - Choice of sub-systems configuration
- **IVVQ (Integration, Verification, Validation & Qualification)**
  - Choice of integration strategy
  - Choice of tests means and facilities
- **Supply Chain - Production**
  - Choice of manufacturing strategy and processes
  - Choice of suppliers
  - Choice of production facilities

FIGURE 9.70
Typical Key Decisions with a focus on software

B: Establish the KD flow diagram

As you make KDs, you gradually narrow down the solutions space. This means that you eliminate options that might have given you other alternatives on future decisions – after all, the word *decide* comes from a root meaning 'to cut off'. Thus, the outcome depends on the sequence of KDs that need to be taken, knowing that the objective is to converge towards the region where the best solutions will be found.

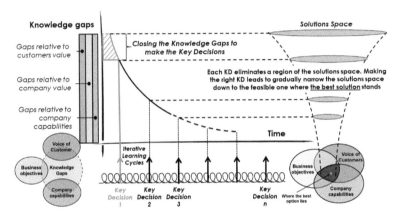

FIGURE 9.71
Narrowing down the solutions space by making Key Decisions

The KDs flow diagram visually shows how the KDs relate to each other and in what sequence they must be taken to achieve the next milestones. In the example below, the number of converters determines the choice of High Power Amplifier (HPA) converters, not the opposite.

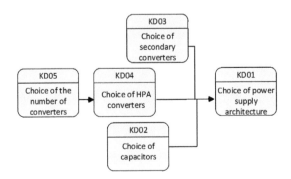

FIGURE 9.72
A Key Decisions flow diagram

In this other example, the choice to use.NET (Microsoft®) rather than J2EE (Oracle®) reduces the choice of possible app servers.

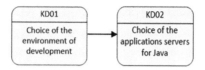

FIGURE 9.73
Example of conditional decisions

What is emphasised here is the level of dependency between KDs, which determines the sequence in which they will be taken. Other KDs can be added as you move forward. The KDs flow diagram can be posted on the Flow Wall to visualise at any time what KDs still need to be made.

C: Break the Key Decisions (KDs) down into Knowledge Gaps (KGs)

A KG is the distance between the knowledge you already have, and the knowledge you need to make a KD. To identify the right gaps you must pull the right set of questions to ask, such that those 'unknown unknowns' get uncovered. It is about testing the knowledge of individuals in the form of questions before they make KDs. A KG must be written as an open-ended question. Once the answer is accepted, the test is validated and the KG can be closed. This *Questioning Driven Engineering*[81] process drives product development.

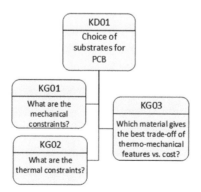

FIGURE 9.74
The KD Tree: relationship between KD, KGs and Data

---

[81] By analogy with *Test Driven Development* (TDD).

D: Map the Key Decision against the Milestones

A timeline can be added at the top of the KDs flow diagram to show successive learning cycles and pull events where KDs should be taken.

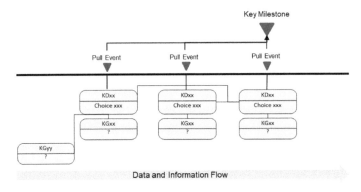

FIGURE 9.75
Map the KDs flow diagram against milestones

Integrate and Deliver Product Elements

Once the main KGs are closed, the number of KDs to be taken tends to zero. As you progress, more tangible elements replace the KDs. By symmetry with the upstream flow learning curve, this curve represents what happens downstream. A new product increment is delivered at each pull event.

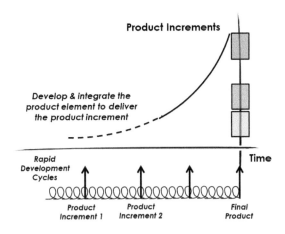

FIGURE 9.76
The product increments pace the flow in the same way as the KDs

Pull, Flow, Cadence: From Exploration to Delivery

New product development begins by continuously building new knowledge and integrating it to make KDs. It continues with the development of more tangible product elements and their integration in increments. In these later stages, there are fewer knowledge gaps to close. The cadence must be adapted to elements accordingly.

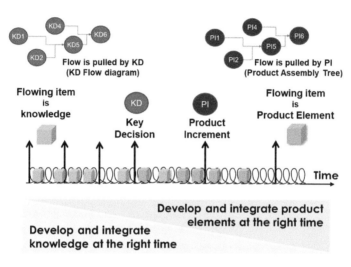

FIGURE 9.77
The product development flow as a reliable series of pull events

Thus, although the principles of pull, flow, and cadence apply regardless of the level of uncertainty, the previous diagram shows that it is important to adapt the process accordingly. To emphasise this adaptation, we sometimes represent the development flow through *4 EXs* moments.

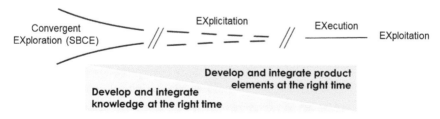

FIGURE 9.78
The four EXs of the product development and delivery flow

Make It Visible: The Pull-Scheduling Board

The conventional tools used to plan and manage product development projects are based on the division of labour represented by a succession of linked tasks (Gantt, Pert). This representation focuses attention on their completion as planned rather than on the availability of knowledge or elements as needed. This emphasises resource efficiency over flow efficiency. We prefer to focus on the flow efficiency.

We call the *Pull-Scheduling Board* the visual that focuses on flow. This visual lists the functions (or subsystems) on the vertical axis (one function per row), and the time intervals on the horizontal axis (e.g., one week per column). A colour is assigned to each row. Each new request is represented by a note of the colour corresponding to the function that needs it (the recipient). This note is placed at the intersection of the row of the function that delivers (the supplier) and the column corresponding to the due date.

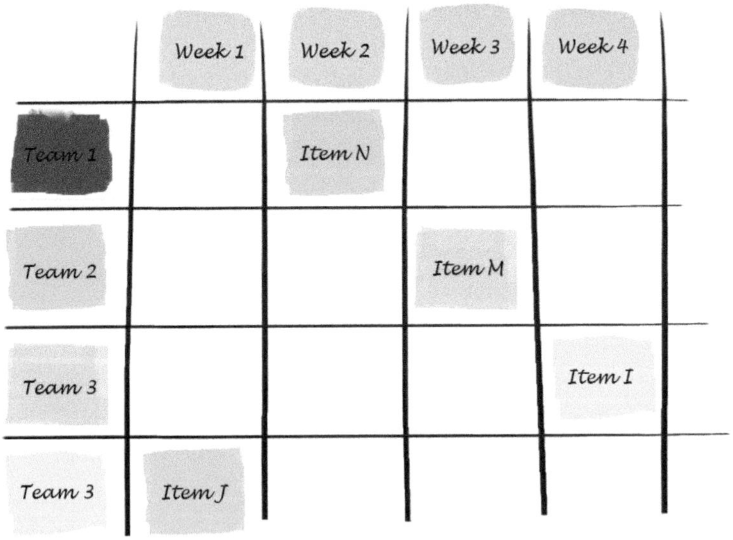

FIGURE 9.79
Pull-Scheduling Board

The Pull-Scheduling Board stimulates coordination across multiple teams and makes everyone's contribution to the flow visible. It can be viewed as a dynamic implementation of the KDs flow diagram (upstream) or the Assembly Tree (downstream).

The Pull-Scheduling Board applies the principles: flow, pull, and cadence.

1. **Flow:** the use of one note per request prevents flow overloading. Each supplier delivers just what is needed by the recipient. This works well if the delivered notes have a work content that does not exceed the duration planned by the recipients (see Little's law). For example, it is not appropriate to request a complete document. Instead specify the elements of the document that must be used quickly.
2. **Pull:** By design, the number of notes is limited (WIP limit). Each note is a signal posted at the intersection between one supplier and one recipient. The workload is therefore capped by the number of requests.

    By visualising all the notes on their own lane, the functions know what they have to provide Just-in-Time, who the recipients are, and agree with them on the exchange of information.

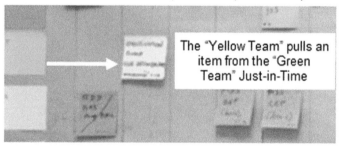

Each Post-it® represents an interaction between two functional teams (one team, one color)

The "Yellow Team" pulls an item from the "Green Team" Just-in-Time

FIGURE 9.80
Focus on an interaction of the Pull-Scheduling Board

3. **Cadence:** the shortest cycle corresponds to the time interval of one column. It is used to pace stand-up meetings and report on the progress of the work. The pull events are spaced far enough apart to allow knowledge gaps to be closed (usually a few weeks).

On top of the board, the master schedule defined by the company for the entire project is represented by a visual timeline. Each pull event, i.e., each KD or each increment, is linked to a milestone from this master schedule. For example, in the board below, the objective of the first milestone is to define the antenna patch architecture. To do this:

- The antenna function (green) has to decide on the patch configuration: it asks the R&D function (blue) for the result of the radiation diagram analysis.
- Then the antenna function has to decide on the transmitter power: it asks the manufacturing function (yellow) for a comparison between the 50 W and 100 W power transmitters. To do this, the latter asks the former for the environmental constraints.

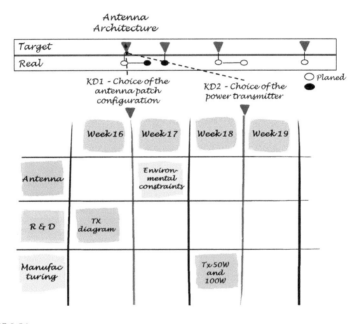

FIGURE 9.81
Back and forth between vision and execution

The Pull-Scheduling Board progress is tracked through regular stand-up meetings (one to two per week). During these status events, each new request posted on the board is an opportunity for a face-to-face conversation between suppliers and recipients. This conversation is 'the most efficient and effective method of conveying information within a development team'.

When a note gets completed, it is directly marked with a cross. When a note is unlikely to be delivered on time, it can be rescheduled, with the impact on workload and schedule clearly identified. To keep the pull events on time, their content must be adjusted accordingly.

	Week 16	Week 17	Week 18	Week 19
Antenna		Environmental constraints		
R & D	TX diagram			
Manufacturing			Tx 50W and 100W	

KD1 - Choix conf. patches antenne

KD2 - Choix puissance émetteur !

FIGURE 9.82
Stand-up result for week 18

A burn-up chart can be plotted to give the team general information about its speed of learning (and delivering). The vertical line shows the number of KDs (or increments) in absolute value and the horizontal timeline.

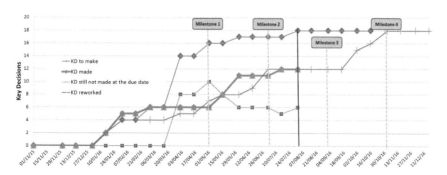

FIGURE 9.83
Example of Burn-up Chart to track KD progress

Pull-Scheduling Board vs. Kanban Board

The *Pull-Scheduling Board* and *Kanban Board* have similarities. Both are visual boards that make it easier for teams to manage their flow. They also have differences. While the former visually displays the interactions necessary for the constitution of the product, the latter visually depicts the progression of the product's constituent items at each stage of a process.

Understanding these differences allows us to choose the right board. The best part is that they can go hand-in-hand and be used at the same time. Figure 9.84 illustrates this complementary. At the top level, a Pull-Scheduling Board is used to manage the product flow. The Integration, Verification, and Validation (IVV) team pulls each new software increment from the software team (delivery every three weeks). To satisfy this request, the software teams, in turn, pull the content of each new increment from System Engineering (SE) and IVV team three weeks in advance. They manage their development flow with a *Kanban Board*.

This way of synchronising and visualising the flow between teams on the same project makes agility at scale effective.

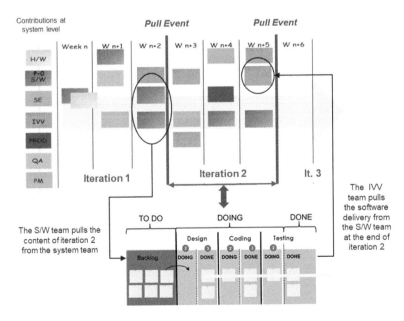

FIGURE 9.84
Product flow synchronisation at scale

Product Takt**

> *In engineering, the Product Takt is the pace of introducing new product release. To ensure its regularity, it is necessary to pace the flow of innovation and to level the resources accordingly.*

Origin

Takt Time is the time that elapses between two successive unit completions in order to meet the demand on a given production line.

For a production line, *Takt Time* is calculated as the ratio of available work time to the number of units demanded: doubling the amount of work time doubles the *Takt Time*. By extension, it is possible to calculate the *Takt Time* of any recurring activity. For example, if an after-sales service is expected to repair 160 products in 16:07 working hours, the *Takt Time* will be 10 hours.

Takt Is a German Word

Junkers is a German company that has been developing and producing warplanes since the beginning of the 20th century. Their first aircraft was the Junker J1 developed in 1915.

In the late 1920s, Junkers organised its production in such a way that the aircraft were moved simultaneously between each series of operations (today at Boeing, production lines move continuously with the operations). All these operations had to be carried out in the same time. This is called *Takt Time*. After 1933, Junkers was nationalised by the Nazis. The need for a high production volume forced Junkers to improve its system. Continuous improvement was used to reduce the *Takt Time* and increase production volume. Changes in *takt* were used to adjust production volume to demand. The Germans taught the *takt* system to Mitsubishi Aircraft in 1942 where it was established in the Nagoya plant in 1943 under the name *zenshinshiki* (前 進 式). At the end of the war, many engineers from the Japanese aircraft industry converted to the automobile industry taking the *Takt Time* with them, especially at Toyota.[82]

---

[82] Takt time – More about origins in German aircraft manufacturing – Michel Baudin's Blog.

Takt Time in Product Development

In product development, *Takt Time* is turned into *Product Takt*. While *Takt Time* is a time, *Product Takt* is the pace at which new products or new features are introduced to the market. Although it is mathematically equivalent, a pace does not accurately reflect how the available production time influences the time between two successive items. However, it emphasises the concept that is of interest in product development, i.e., delivering at fixed intervals.

In production, the question is 'how fast does your customer demand THIS product over time?' The objective is to determine the average time between each delivered unit of the requested product, in seconds or minutes. In product development, the question becomes 'how fast does a NEW product or NEW feature need to be released in order to fulfil market demand?' The objective is to determine the pace at which a new product or new feature is introduced on the market, in months, or even years. This *Product Takt* is the heartbeat synchronised to the market demand.

Faced with market pressure, the reflex is too often to develop a product to please too many users at once. Implementing more features and innovations for the chance to turn your product into a bigger success can make your product 'too much of a good thing'[83] rather than good enough (see also the concept of 'feature creep' – *Going for innovation*).

Rather than providing more than customers actually need or pushing features at the wrong time, you need to synchronise value delivery with value demand. How was your previous product perceived by customers? What and when do your customers consistently ask for what you don't yet provide? Do you need to add new products or upgrade existing ones? What is the *Product Takt* of your competitors? The knowledge gained from exploring the Territory of Customers should guide you in determining what customers truly need and when, and how your competitors are targeting your market. For example, how often should Apple release a new version of the iPhone® (e.g., for Christmas)? Toyota a new version of the Prius®? Canon a new EOS®? Adobe a new version of Photoshop®? Recurring events can also guide your *Product Takt* (e.g., a trade show).

---

[83] D.V. Thompson, R.W. Hamilton, and R.T. Rust. (2005). 'Feature Fatigue: When Product Capabilities Become Too Much of a Good Thing'. *Journal of Marketing Research.*

You need also to understand how quickly your market is able to adopt new technologies. The pace of technology change is accelerating today, fuelled by the digital revolution, with more players and fewer barriers to entry. With the combination of Internet of Things, Artificial Intelligence, big data, and robotics, each innovation can destroy a previously dominant technology, product, or service. However, disruptive innovations are not sudden events. They are even predictable (see box). Thus, rather than reacting once an innovation has been adopted by loading it on your product, it is better to reflect how to prepare and anticipate future innovations.

Since it is impossible to perfectly plan everything in advance, you must develop your ability to adapt to change faster. To do so, you have to think of a series of improvements rather than big revolutionary innovations, learn rather than follow, pace rather than rush.

The Disruptive Innovation by Clayton Christensen

Disruptive innovations are not events, but processes that can span several years. Before having a sweeping impact on the market, they take time to emerge. It explains why well-established players, too busy to defend their products and services, generally overlook disrupters. Why build castles in the air and compromise activities that are still profitable? When the improbable becomes reality, it is usually too late. Their market belongs to the disrupters! These incumbents are faced with two conflicting choices: to focus on their historical activities while neglecting to invest in innovations, or to invest in them at the risk of weakening their current business.

Pace of Innovation

The pace of innovation is the speed at which you improve your existing products or develop new ones to fulfil market demand.

It may be tempting to consider that shortening the development schedule creates positive pressure on engineers. By working harder, they should go faster and thus cut time to market! This way of thinking is counterproductive: under pressure, engineers prefer to hide problems rather than be slowed down.

Making deadlines more aggressive is not the silver bullet to speed up the time to market. Pressure is not a necessary condition to achieve this.

By enabling better next time, systematic and continuous learning is more likely a necessary condition for speeding ideas to market. In addition, learning earlier prior to decision-making prevents 'wishful thinking' and makes pressure to commit earlier unnecessary.

Lean product development stimulates this learning, especially by exploring the solutions space more broadly to expose knowledge gaps earlier, where good ideas lie. Likewise, it accelerates their implementation into marketable features by applying pull, flow, and cadence.

First, you need to focus your team's creativity on the limits that stand in the way of finding the right solution, and move the trade-off curves accordingly. The *CID* helps you visually connect ideas to these boundary curves and surface the knowledge gaps.

Next, you need to select which ideas should be prioritised based on value, organisational capacity, and business objectives. However, ideas may take a longer or faster time to be morphed into new features. This unevenness (*mura*) in workload may create overburden (*muri*) and then waste (*muda*) later in your product development, and more globally, in your organisation. To prevent future disruptions of your development cadence and thus complete all of the development steps on the planned schedule, you need to make your ideas available far enough ahead of the market need. You can even build a safety stock of 'ideas on the shelf' ready to feed a project on demand. Although not all new ideas will necessarily be integrated into new products, all those that will be must have been validated beforehand. A *Kanban Board* can help you effectively manage the backlog of approved ideas.

Finally, you have to decide how and when your product will carry the innovation.

- First, these decisions are guided by how well you balance the overhead of regularly refreshing a mature product with the cost of developing a new one at once. Rapid and regular introduction of new features contributes to reducing the length of learning loops, particularly by accelerating feedback from users in real conditions (4). Moreover, releasing a few features generates revenue right away with 100% certainty. It is better than expecting to capture a bit more in the future by offering more features with a new product. This can be analysed from the Cost of Delay perspective:[84]

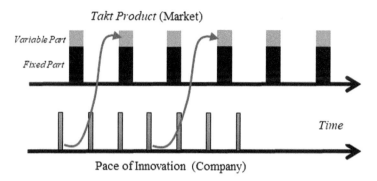

FIGURE 9.85
Pace of innovation

- Secondly, your ability to convert new ideas into innovative features or products on time depends on your ability to track the right balance between the business needs and your development capabilities. From one project perspective, there are three variables to be adjusted: capacity, time to market, and scope.
  1. Adjusting capacity would mean adding more engineers to high-priority ideas. Unfortunately, new resources are rarely operational instantly, amplifying variability rather than reducing it. Moreover, you risk pushing the problem elsewhere and making other projects slip.
  2. Postponing the deadline makes the *Product Takt* ineffective. By missing the date with the market, the product will go from leader to follower. Respecting *Product Takt* is not an option!
  3. Adjusting the scope of the product, e.g., reducing the variable part in favour of the fixed part, avoids workload adjustment while maintaining time to market. However, be aware that your company may miss out on more important business by removing some features.

---

[84] Cost of Delay helps you quantify the economic value of bring to the market a feature sooner as opposed to later.

To limit the risk of bad decisions, you should clearly state ahead in your Concept Paper what is necessary and what is optional.

In most organisations, for each idea, several products, and therefore several projects, may be candidates to bring to market. Once a project is selected, it is expected to have the resources to start development on the target market schedule. This requires that your workload needs to be established well in advance at the project portfolio level. To achieve this synchronisation of all your development activities across your project portfolio and allocate resources accordingly, you need to align all projects to the same cadence – again, we see how the concepts of pull, flow, and cadence are essential. To help you carry out this planning at the organisational level, we propose the *Visible Portfolio Planning*.

Visible Portfolio Planning*

> *The Visible Portfolio Planning is a visual board that includes the information essential to monitor and ensure cadence through your system.*

The *Visible Portfolio Planning* allows you to quickly visualise the number of projects in progress and their schedule. Its purpose is not to monitor the progress of each project in detail. Each project has its own *obeya* to help the project team members know where they are in relation to the objectives, and make the right decisions accordingly. The goal is to provide a comprehensive view of global resource requirements so that the engineering functions know when and where their support is needed. Armed with this information, your organisation can make the right decisions to maintain the development cadence and level the workload across the entire portfolio of projects.

Only the planned start and end dates of each project are shown, taking into account the drifts observed. Indeed, it is not always easy to level project start so that the specific resources are available. It is much more difficult to smooth the end … yet it is at this moment that congestion has the most consequences:

- Consequences on the launch of other projects (which will be delayed even before starting due to lack of resources);
- Consequences on the following activities. A production plant, for example, will never be able to simultaneously integrate the production launch of different products, endangering the availability on the market of all products.

It seems obvious to everyone that the company will not be able to absorb several large projects at the same time. But for this to happen, two essential conditions must be met:

- Projects must be staggered in time: their beginning, but especially their end;
- Projects must not be delayed!

The *Visible Portfolio Planning* code is simple. Circles mark the dates as initially planned, triangles mark the rescheduled dates. Circles or triangles are filled when activities are completed as planned and empty otherwise.

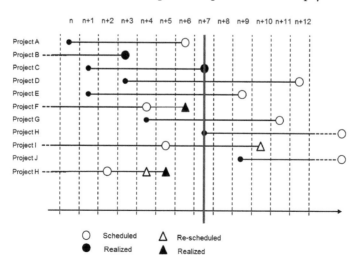

FIGURE 9.86
Visible Portfolio Planning: projects portfolio levelling

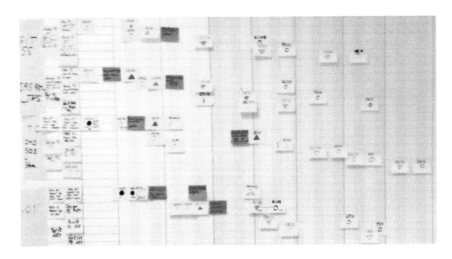

FIGURE 9.87
Visible Portfolio Planning in *obeya*

Each week, the Project Managers meet to:

- Confirm initial commitments and share rescheduling;
- Make decisions to maintain the workload levelling on the project portfolio.

This implies mutual transparency on the part of managers (PM and Functional Managers) regarding their respective difficulties experienced on their own project. To make this transparency effective, we suggest collecting in a *portfolio obeya* the key problems identified by each project. At regular intervals, all project managers meet in this *obeya* to select, in their turn, the top three of all these problems that affect the project portfolio the most, and make decisions accordingly. This escalation of problems from *genba* to this visual board is stimulated and fuelled by the *Genba Walks* performed by each Project Manager.

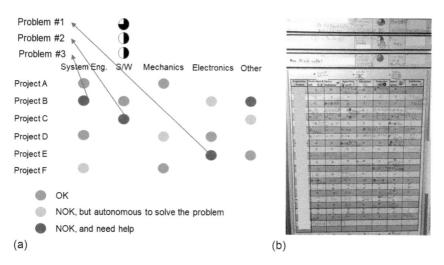

FIGURE 9.88
Top three problems detected in projects

Slow Build*

> *Slow Build simply consists of assembling one of the first products (prototype or pre-production) in order to deal with problems as soon as they appear. Slow Build is clearly dedicated to products intended to be mass-produced.*

Purpose

Here, 'build' does not refer to the software process of converting the source code into an executable programme. In this case, the 'slow build' is a problem that must be solved. Instead, we use the term 'slow build' to describe an efficient transition phase from product development to production. The reason for implementing 'slow build' aims at identifying and correcting residual product and process problems in production conditions before safely launching mass production.

In a typical production ramp-up, after the design freeze, the first step is to make adjustments in the pre-series. Then, the production manufacturing process is finalised before ramping up to the serial level, which can cause production interruptions. Any changes at this stage are costly in time and money. Thus, unrecognised problems in the development phases combined with insufficient maturity of the production process disrupt the start then the ramp-up of production.

The slow build simply consists of assembling one of the first products (prototype or pre-production) in order to deal with problems as soon as they appear through PDCA loops: each solution hypothesis is quickly tested directly on the production line. This gradual interaction between the product and the production processes helps you solve the residual product issues and determine how to efficiently produce it. The knowledge generated deserves to be captured in standards.

The exercise incites a dialogue between two functions which do not have the same technical vocabulary, one (engineering) using more justification by reasoning, and the other (production) being more on a practical and operational level. Both parties must be able to express themselves freely by listening to each other. This helps to establish a continuous flow between product development and production.

The Key Steps

- Identify who should be involved, beyond engineering and production (purchasing, suppliers?). As for any problem solving, the presence of an expert, here a senior operator mastering the production of similar products, is essential;
- Put yourself in the conditions closest to production, in a place that allows dialogue and exchanges between participants;
- Observe the product process, take notes on the observations (difficulties of assembly, tools, materials, everything interesting that is seen). You can film the steps and watch the film as many times as necessary;
- Note all the elements that should lead to the modification of technical choices or production activities.

In some ways, the Slow Build is similar to the Teardown. But this time, rather than understanding how the elements fit together for what purpose, it is about understanding why the elements struggle to fit together as expected.

10

The Path to Knowledge and Sustainability

We are in a world rightly qualified as *VUCA* (Volatile, Uncertain, Complex, and Ambiguous). The pandemic appeared in 2020 with all its effects, beyond its dramatic impact on the health of populations, confirms this statement.

While *Volatility* and *Uncertainty* require faster learning to better adapt to future unpredictable situations, *Complexity* and *Ambiguity* require more critical questioning of the current situation to better understand the interactions between elements and constraints. All these elements, whether attached to the environment or to agents, are interconnected. The more complex and volatile an environment is, the more difficult it is to obtain the information necessary to correctly predict the evolution of the phenomenon or to adopt an unambiguous common understanding.

Thus, the methods and practices presented in this section all have in common the objective of developing the problem-solving skills and critical thinking of each employee, conditions for agile adaptation to the *VUCA* environment. In addition, they ease the deployment of this agility across the company by paying particular attention to interactions between individuals.

That is why this path to Knowledge and Sustainability passes through the Territory of People Development.

DOI: 10.4324/9781003381945-12

───────

EXPLORING THE TERRITORY OF PEOPLE DEVELOPMENT

Exploring the Territory of People Development means exploring conditions that enable the establishment of a culture of continuous improvement (*kaizen*) to ensure sustainably increased performances in the long term. It is the job of management to create these conditions.

These conditions can take the form of regular sessions dedicated to individual or collective learning (*dojo, A3 Problem Report*), in particular to reinforce the mastery of Lean methods, tools, and practices. However, it is above all on a daily basis, through practices, reflection, and feedback, that behaviours can evolve in the long term. The members of a *kaizen* culture are its authors – people are the source of the main practices, values, and norms of their culture. Therefore, every day, everyone must proactively engage in exercising and developing one's creative and critical thinking, problem-solving, and decision-making skills, based on questioning, experimenting, and reflecting.

Thus, developing people means teaching them to think better about their work and to continuously improve it. Sustainability, even in a *VUCA* world, is ultimately nothing more than the consequence of this continuous development of all individuals.

Kaizen: Explore Further, Learn Deeper, Innovate Faster***

> *Kaizen is the driving force for developing people's knowledge by exploring and solving new problems, and in so doing, helps to accelerate the generation of innovations.*

Reminders

Lean always includes *kaizen*. In manufacturing, *kaizen* means that everyone should continuously[1] improve one's own daily work and performance, step by step, without the need to allocate costs (e.g., by properly identifying and removing what is unnecessary, i.e., everything that is better not to do, or *muda*). This implies that today the company

───────

[1] Here 'continuously' means 'all the time'.

should do better than yesterday, and tomorrow it should do better than today.[2]

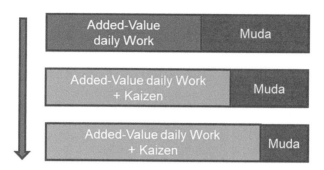

FIGURE 10.1
Introducing *kaizen* to facilitate daily work

In the same way, in product development, it is essential to improve every day what is just necessary, not only to avoid falling behind but also to get ahead of the competition, and keep it there. This means designing and developing better and more efficient solutions. To achieve this, *kaizen* must therefore concern with the improvement of processes and methods as much as that of products, the former serving the latter. This was the approach adopted by S. Toyoda, who always sought to improve looms and the means of producing them, driven by his inquisitive mind and ingenuity.

This way of thinking must be developed in each individual; the conditions for doing so must allow them to express it without roadblocks, for example, by facilitating experimentation and change, whether in daily work or in supervised exercises (see *Dojo* and *A3 Problem Report*).

Kaizen in Product Development

Where to start? Gear toward your true north, the one that indicates the best trade-offs between the satisfaction of your customers, your company, and any other stakeholder.

Start by questioning your work processes, methods, tools, or practices. What can you do to improve the performance of your engineering system?

---

[2] For more information, see Isao Kato and Art Smalley. (2011). *Toyota Kaizen Methods: Six Steps to Improvement*. Productivity Press.

Could you improve the efficiency of the flow between your *agile teams* and others? What about continuously reducing the Lead Time to deploy your software, for example, by improving your Continuous Integration (CI) process? Can you improve your test coverage? Why wait to write a script to automate these repetitive tests? Why not write tests instead of requirements? What if feedback was done more often? What if you started by reducing the inventory of defects, the WIP (Work in Progress)? What are all these indicators for? How can you better visualise your flow? Where your processes are meeting the standards and where you should improve them?

Each of these questions is intended to break a process standard (or a habit), i.e., to raise the bar by creating a new gap, rather than to get back to that standard by removing a deviation. So it's key that you teach each employee to look at their work better and ask the right questions, the ones that create those new gaps toward improvement. The support of a coach can be useful to develop the practice of questioning.

The same logic applies to product improvement. *Kaizen* seeks to establish a new level of performance, but this time in relation to the product. Therefore, it is about stimulating the creative thinking of each designer, and thus accelerating the continuous development of new knowledge needed to move the limits of design standards to extend the performance available to future products.

Pet Design

Some people sometimes use the term 'pet design' to describe designs that always reproduce the same technical choices, i.e., those to which their authors are most attached.

So, whatever the object of improvement is, an engineering with *kaizen* is an engineering where improvement is a daily concern for all. It is part of the work, every day! Thus, whenever an idea seems useful to improve the performance of your system or your products, then you should test it! Once again, rapid PDCA loops are the appropriate framework for producing actual improvements. You test your idea, and you act on it. *Without testing, any new idea will be a worthless opinion* and you will lose countless opportunities to improve your system and your products. In short, *kaizen* makes the practice of *Test and Learn* a routine of continuous, *incremental* improvements. To do this, you must tailor the size and number of PDCA loops to the size of the improvement! This can be learned through *dojo*:

- PLAN:
  - Question the current situation (or the standard) to discover what can be improved;
  - Derive a potential improvement;
- DO: test the improvement;
- CHECK: evaluate the new situation;
- ACT: what next? Adopt, adjust, or abandon the improvement?

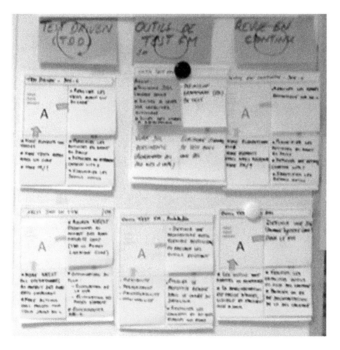

FIGURE 10.2
PDCA loop steps in *obeya*

Indeed, *kaizen* is not appropriate for more radical improvements which must therefore be dealt with differently – even though the accumulation over time of incremental improvements can lead to a radical improvement.

For example, breakthrough innovations occur more likely when science takes a hand, for example, through the introduction of new technologies (e.g., the marriage of massive MIMO (Multiple Input Multiple Output), and millimetre waves required for 5G can be viewed as breakthrough technologies, while 4G is the result of progressive technological innovations of its predecessor 3G). Engineering is an applied science, and so it depends on science for these radical innovations, regardless of the fact that for other improvements,

Kaizen and Kaikaku

To distinguish radical changes from continuous improvements, Toyota uses *kaikaku* (改革: massive changes or reforms) for the former, and *kaizen* for the latter. Both are useful. For example, it is not possible to convert a company to digital only by continuous improvements. It implies a transformation of business processes that is radical and reaches across an entire organisation. Thus, different structures are used depending on whether the changes are small or large scale.

it knows how to make good use of already acquired or standardised knowledge. This does not deny that engineering also involves creativity, and that notable innovations can result from the ability of designers to better manage the complexity of an architecture or solve better trade-offs. Moreover, a breakthrough innovation occurs more easily in a company accustomed to continuously testing and learning. Once a new breakthrough innovation has been adopted by customers, *kaizen* allows for the continued introduction of incremental improvements to ensure the reliability of the new dominant design until the next radical innovation, in line with *Product Takt* (Figure 10.3).

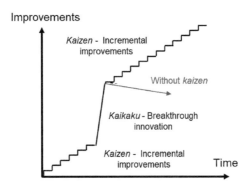

FIGURE 10.3
Overtime, *kaizen* sustains incremental and breakthrough improvements

Kaizen makes incremental innovations accessible, while encouraging the introduction of more radical innovations, even if it does not directly contribute to them.

In short, *kaizen* continuously improves the efficiency of your methods, practices, and products, and thus improves the overall performance of your company in a sustainable way. To do this, you must create the conditions for the continued development of more people who can produce these improvements. This is the purpose, among others, of *A3 Problem Report* coaching and *dojo* to develop skills and critical thinking as propaedeutic to *kaizen*. This will enable each individual to learn to continually challenge the *status quo* and to test new ideas more quickly, alone, or in teams. In doing so, you prepare your company to adapt more quickly to unpredictable situations.

Dojo, a Development System*

> *Dojo describes a mode of training supervised by experts or managers. Individually or in group, the objective is to continuously develop the skills and critical thinking of engineers so that they can better solve more complex problems and make better decisions.*

Origin

Dojo is originally a sacred place, used for teaching, worship, or ritual (from the Sanskrit term *bodhimandala*, a Buddhist monastery where monks and nuns study, practice, and teach the devotees the moral duties governing individual conduct). In Japanese, *dojo* (道場) literally means 'a place of the way'. Nowadays it refers to a formal training place for martial arts. Inspired by these training places, Toyota's training facilities are now aptly named *dojo*. They 'provide a space where people can gain and develop the fundamental skills they need for their jobs'.[3]

---

[3] TMUK's 25 Objects – 21: Dojo and Training – Toyota UK Magazine

Lean Engineering Dojo

Presentation

We have appropriated and extended this *dojo* concept to a process of hands-on training and critical thinking supervised by experts or managers. We propose two types of *dojo*:

1. The group *dojo*, inspired by the *dojo* practised by software developers. The objective of these group training sessions is to learn, improve, or refine workers' technical skills or methods (e.g., causal influence diagram (*CID*), problem solving) through purposeful practices in a collaborative environment.
2. The individual *dojo*, more similar to what can be practised in production. The objective is, for each manager, to regularly evaluate the level of expertise mastered by each member of their team on specific topics, and to initiate appropriate improvements.

Whatever the format, the objective is to develop and improve workers' knowledge and skills through practice and exchange. It is about strengthening the link between deliberate practice and skill level (experiential learning-by-doing). It is also about developing critical thinking by encouraging awareness of one's own knowledge and evaluation of one's own learning process in order to continuously improve them (metacognitive judgements).

The *dojo* outcome is the integration of new habits into individual behaviour to produce more appropriate responses. A habit is defined as a motor or cognitive routine that, once triggered, is performed without conscious supervision. It therefore requires less effort because it becomes the default pattern. By reflecting on their practices, especially through questioning or reflection during supervised exercises, each individual can become aware that they are applying unfortunate but comfortable habits, and that they need to break or improve them. To do so, *dojo* must apply effective learning strategies.[4]

- The *dojo* are done in a stable and predictable environment, unlike what may be experienced in operational contexts.

---

[4] P.C. Brown, H.L. III. Roediger, and M.A. McDaniel. (2014). *Make It Stick: The Science of Successful Learning.* Harvard University Press.

- The *dojo* are short (typically 20 minutes for the individual *dojo* and 45 minutes for the group *dojo*) and spaced over time. The contents are reviewed at multiple points in time. Associations that are often repeated end up having their own small network of specialised neurons, and the appearance of the stimulus automatically leads to the response that is commonly associated with it (*if* stimulus *then* response – see Standards). It is therefore the challenge of any learning process to develop a repertoire of automatisms for such stimuli which then allow us to act efficiently with a minimum of attention.

- The *dojo* mix related concepts, methods, and practices providing a high number and variety of experiences. For example, the study of several types of problems (caused or created gaps), or from different perspectives (customer, company, partners) at once favours learning to discriminate among types of problems and select the right method for each of them. This helps develop cognitive flexibility in order to be able to propose responses adapted to various situations. The contents and paces of *dojo* are defined according to the different standards and evolve with them.

- Sessions incorporate tests and feedback to make sure the participants reflect on what they have learnt. Moreover, quizzing is offered through appropriate online flashcards. These cards provide many opportunities to review key knowledge at a number of points in the learning process.

We support workers in cognitive thinking processes in order to train them to inhibit their wasteful intuitions and thus act more rationally.[5] This includes learning to ask good questions with the help of Critical Thinking Cards (refer to Is Lean asking questions or giving answers?). Thus, whether during *dojo* or during *Genba Walks*, these cards are often used to train individuals to become aware of one's own cognitive biases and to engage them in 'slower thinking'.[6]

---

[5] A Neural Network Framework for Cognitive Bias (nih.gov).
[6] D. Kahneman. (2012). *Thinking, Fast and Slow*. Penguin; O. Houdé and G. Borst (2015) 'Evidence for an Inhibitory-Control Theory of the Reasoning Brain'. Pubmed.

Group dojo

Similar to *Coding Dojo*,[7] widely used by software programmers, a group *dojo* describes a group training session where the members can practice and learn new skills or methods together. For example:

- Train to properly formulate hypotheses from various data. Formalising causal dependencies between independent variables and their effects in a consistent manner is helpful to better solve more complex problems (logical reasoning). How can an action on a given independent variable cause a fact to become true? What empirical evidence can legitimise this cause–effect relationship? And therefore what test can validate or refute this relationship?
- Train to master *CID* in various contexts through appropriate exercises. One of the objectives is to enable engineers to relate new information to what they already know and thus improve their ability to solve new problems. What are the impacts of this *CID* on changing technology, concept, target performance, etc.? What mathematical model can be used for this Transfer Function? Linking new knowledge to what they already know enhances their expertise.
- Train to correctly formulate Key Decisions as 'choices of' and Knowledge Gaps as open-ended questions. This limits the unconscious use of heuristics and therefore the risk of making mistakes in decision-making.

The advantage of doing group sessions is also that each participant is trained to listen to the opinions of others and to clarify their own statements. With the help of Critical Thinking Cards, it is possible to make judgements more objective and to limit worthless opinions.

The *dojo* can also be dedicated to practice and learning of more specialised topics such as those proposed in *Coding Dojo* (Test Driven Development, pair programming). Different formats can be proposed, such as those reported in the agile literature like *wasa* or *randori*.[8] The practitioners of these *Coding Dojo* claim that these formats not only give the opportunity to learn but also to teach: the collective nature and the animation would bring a dimension of co-training between participants.

---

[7] Bossavit and Gaillot. (2005). 'The Coder's *Dojo* – A Different Way to Teach and Learn Programming'. *6th International Conference, XP 2005*.

[8] E. Bache. (2013) *The Coding Dojo Handbook*. Leanpub.

However, these claims are partly based on the belief that novices could discover essential content or develop skills on their own. Unfortunately, good practices cannot simply emerge from the reflective action of participants. And just because there are skilled people in a group does not mean that the less skilled people in that group will automatically be able to recognise what a skill is and understand what skills might be beneficial. *Learning to practice a skill is not the same as practicing it.* In addition, another risk is that 'group think' replaces objective knowledge!

Thus, while *Coding Dojo* style can be effective, to avoid potential deception we recommend that group *dojo* be supervised by recognised experts who can identify the knowledge gaps and weaknesses of each participant and adapt the teaching methods, content, and pace accordingly.

Individual dojo

Individual *dojo* are regularly scheduled 20-minute exchanges between each team member and their manager, on a subject or practice related to their discipline. Typically, each day, an individual *dojo* is scheduled.

By assessing what is mastered or not for each individual, in particular by observing them perform a particular task, by questioning their mastery and their way of using standards, the manager identifies what needs to be improved or deserves to be standardised. In case of knowledge gaps are detected, the manager may choose to organise a specific group *dojo* or more personalised coaching. Regularly questioning each team member on different topics related to the expected competencies also helps to reactivate the relevant knowledge to make it stronger.

As we have seen with the practice of *Genba Walk* (see 'Lack of confidence'), the manager can be reluctant to face their own knowledge gaps when talking to their team members about the discipline they lead. However, no one expects them to be omniscient, but to be able to help them make better decisions and assess where they need to improve.

Conversely, the manager may want to show that they know and ultimately answer their own questions. Helping their team members to improve does not mean solving their problems for them. The knowledge gaps they detect during the *dojo* should guide them in identifying how to better develop their discipline.

Thus, it is the manager's responsibility to continuously develop the knowledge of their team. Individual *dojo* is a simple way to do this effectively!

Dojo and Kaizen

Whatever the formats of the *dojo*, they are obviously part of the continuous improvement process of engineering. In order for *kaizen* to spread, it is necessary to identify the habits that can be an obstacle to *change for the better.*

A3 *Problem Report*, an Efficient Way to Share, Coach, and Progress**

> **The A3 Problem Report** *provides a PDCA roadmap that helps people navigate through the problem-solving process.*

Origin and Purpose

A3 is the international term for a sheet of paper that stands at 11 × 17 in. Toyota adopted this standard size A3 for the problem resolution form after discovering its use during a visit to one of its UK plants. Others say that 'the idea to fit all information related to one project/problem on one sheet of paper dates back to quality guru Joseph Juran'.[9]

Larger than the 8.5 × 11 in. format, this A3 format is large enough to share just enough detail, images, drawings, and graphics to enhance communication, and it is small enough to limit verbiage and be easily copied and carried. Moreover, posted on a wall, the A3 can be read by several people at once. This advantage should be widely used in *obeya*. Although commonly used for problem solving, it can be extended to many other cases, such as work instructions posted above a workstation, technical communications, or reusable knowledge sharing. The A3 format is a good communication tool to share across the organisation what has been learned, and contributes to continuous improvement.

---

[9] The A3 Report – Part 1: Basics | AllAboutLean.com.

Conversely, using a single sheet to present a problem and its solution can be difficult and takes practice. For this reason, the *A3 Problem Report* is also used as a coaching tool[10] to develop the problem-solving skills of the problem solver by stimulating their thinking through questioning. To encourage this development, the coach must accompany the process of *trial and error* associated with any problem-solving process, and not eliminate it. It is a matter of taking into account the path taken by the learner, even if this path is the temporary path of error.

Thus, the *A3 Problem Report* does not solve problems by itself. It provides a framework that helps people navigate the problem-solving process. It fosters critical thinking and communication skills.[11] After capturing how the problem was solved, the *A3 Problem Report* deserves to be shared beyond the department where it was created (*yokoten* or horizontal deployment). Thus, it provides a reference point from which to move on to other questions.

Several variations of the A3 report can be used to differentiate between solving caused problems and solving created problems.[12] In the next sections, we propose a version that is well suited to product-related problems whose causes lie in past design decisions. However, whatever the problem to solve, the logic remains essentially the same.

A PDCA Story Board

To reflect the PDCA framework,[13] the A3 form is divided into two parts: the left side is about 'defining the problem', while the right side is about 'defining, planning, executing and checking the solution'. This emphasises the importance of laying the proper groundwork before attempting to solve a problem. Each column is made of successive boxes that fit the PDCA steps. The title, the owner of the problem, the coach, and the date of the last release are placed above.

---

[10] Refer to *Managing to Learn* (6).

[11] D.K. Sobek and A. Smalley. (2011). *Understanding A3 Thinking: A Critical Component of Toyota's PDCA Management System*. Productivity Press.

[12] T. Richardson. (2017). *The Toyota Engagement Equation: How to Understand and Implement Continuous Improvement Thinking in Any Organization*. McGraw-Hill Education.

[13] T. Richardson proposes to use the Toyota's 8 step methodology Create a Real A3, Do More Than Fill In Boxes – Lean Enterprise Institute.

This A3 form may suggest that problem solving is linear. This is *not* the case. Problem solving is an iterative and recursive process. It usually takes several PDCA loops before a solution can be confirmed and implemented.

Some Guidelines for Writing the Title

What is it about? What is the anomalous event, the incident, the gap?
A problem is the difference between what *is*, and what *might or should be*. Thus, the title should reflect this definition in a single sentence. A title that is too long may indicate a lack of understanding from the writer. Start with what you already know. The information needed for a more complete statement will be generated and reported in the first three sections of the A3 report. It will be always possible to rephrase the title after working on the current situation and objectives.

To help readers understand what it's all about on the first reading, there are a few rules to follow:

- Be clear about the entry point of the A3 report. Is it at the project, department, team level?
- Be clear about the nature of the problem – gap from desired state, improvement?
- Quantify the gap objectively. '*The defects rate of PCBA (Printed Circuit Board Assembly) is too high*'. Too high compared to what?
- Use unambiguous language. Is it really a '*Sensor performance drift*' or more precisely a performance loss? What means '*Optimisation of the number of tests*'. Too many tests or too few tests?
- Look at the problem from multiple perspectives: how do your customers, competitors, and employees see the problem? The response depends on the perspective you are asked to adopt. Everyone wants to make sure that they are not in a situation where their usefulness is less than it could be!
- Look at the problem at different levels:
  - Chunk down – make your problem more specific:
    - If the problem contains two or more ideas, break it down into sub-problems: ask questions such as '*what are parts of this?*' or '*what are examples of this?*'
    - Use words with a stricter meaning (hyponym), e.g., from electronics component to capacitor.

- Chunk up – make your problem more general:
  - Ask questions such as *'what's this a part of?'* or *'what's this an example of?'*
  - Use words with a broader meaning (hypernym), e.g., from capacitor to electronics component.
- Avoid a statement that presupposes a specific solution: *'Documentation level are too high and must be reduced'*, *'No one tests this software'*. Instead, if possible, use the metric that reflects the gap.
- Make your statement free of suggestion, speculation, opinion, etc. Stay focused on facts.

From Fact to Rumour

Facts: 15% of our products don't achieve the specified performance.

Inference: a significant percentage of our products are not tested enough.

Speculation: less efficient products are probably tested by inexperienced engineers.

Opinion: I think the reason products have poor performance is that the people in charge of testing are on too many projects at the same time.

Rumour: Paul told me that these products are less and less tested.

The Left Side: PLAN

(i) Business stakes – present the context

Why are we talking about this? Why is this problem worth solving?
As an entry door for the A3 report, this section presents why this problem is worth solving, especially in relation to the company's strategy and objectives. The impacts of the problem on customers, partners, or the company are explained. Developing people also implies clearly explaining why this problem matters and making economic sense of improvement actions.

(ii) Current state – grasp the situation

What observed facts are available to you? What do you know about the situation in which the problem has occurred?

- *Go* to the actual place where the problem originated, was discovered or as close as you can (*genchi*);
- *Look at* the actual defective part and the bad experience (*genbutsu*), and search for facts, clues, and data;
- *Ask* questions to the people closest to the problem. Use the question words 'what, where, how, how much, who and when' to characterise what is already known and circumscribe more precisely what remains to be learned – causality will be dealt with in a second stage.

Is the situation sufficiently quantified or is it still too qualitative? Collect and analyse the data (e.g., with exploratory data analysis), assess their quality (e.g., consistency), use correct metrics, and check for obvious errors. And beware of data averages, it can mask dispersions that are potentially useful for the analysis. Rephrase the problem statement if needed.

Is the situation sufficiently clear and precise? Represent it in such a way that you can effectively share your understanding (drawing, sketch, diagrams, graphs, …). Indicate whether the problem appears systematically or randomly.

Data are key at this stage. However, it would be a mistake to think that the more data you collect, the closer you are to solving the problem. You need to sort the wheat (relevant data) from the chaff (irrelevant data). And most of the relevant data are determined less by the problem itself than by the hypothesis of solution that may explain it. *Keep in mind that the data that will finally allow you to know the causes will be those that you will be able to produce from constructed experiments based upon your hypotheses.*

Once the gap is well characterised, it is time to look for an explanation, to suggest a hypothetical possible solution. This 'Current state' stage is therefore the starting point of the inquiry. 'Every inquiry whatsoever takes its rise in the observation', said C.S. Peirce[14] (we will see that inquiry also ends with observation). So, once you have a good description of the *Current State*, you are ready to move from the *ground* of facts to the *space* of hypotheses.

---

[14] A Neglected Argument for the Reality of God – Wikisource, the free online library.

(iii) Expected state – set the goal

Where do you want to be once the problem will be solved? What changes in metrics are expected, by how much, and when?
Agree on criteria and measures that will verify whether the expected state has been achieved. Reuse the metrics identified to characterise the current state. Progress towards the objective must also be measurable in order to quickly assess the relevance of corrective actions, and adjust them if needed.

(iv) Hypotheses – look for root causes

You need to enlist the cooperation of others, especially those who have a strong stake in the problem, either because they are directly affected by it or because their agreement will be needed to perform the required tests and then implement the selected solutions.

What is the root cause of the problem?
This is the step that involves engendering plausible hypotheses about root causes as explanations to account for the observed data. The root cause is the deepest cause in a causal chain that can be resolved by designers. A primary goal of causal explanation is prediction. Thus, root cause analysis (RCA) consists of keeping stepping back in time until the causal pathway shows the primary event (e.g., a design decision) that caused the observed event.

How do you know it is the root cause? What could have caused this cause?
Unfortunately, a single causal pathway cannot account for the multiple conditions that allow an event to occur. Depending on the starting chain you follow, you end up with a different root cause. The most famous illustration is the *5 Whys* method. It is simply asking the question 'why?' enough times until you get past all the symptoms of a problem and down to the root cause. In doing so, it may encourage the identification of a single cause, obscuring the fact that effects may result from a complex combination of causes.

This ease with which it seems possible to drill down to a single root cause, regardless of the complexity of the problem, is not compatible with a scientific approach. Forcing users to follow a single causal pathway should be disqualifying by itself. It supports your belief that one single root cause, to the exclusion of all others, is the *necessary* and *sufficient* condition to explain the observed effect. It creates the illusion of success: 'for every complex problem, there is an answer that is clear, simple and wrong'.[15] And even though it might work for single-event problems, this *5 Whys* method doesn't allow it to explain the behaviour of complex systems. It doesn't reliably give a full account of the different conditions for an event to occur.

In addition, how do you know that there are no more *whys* (infinite regress)? The succession of *whys* tends to lead you to answers that are no longer empirically demonstrable, or more embarrassingly, to the accusation of this or that person or function. Don't get intoxicated by the pursuit of *whys*!

What are all the other potential causes?
While starting your inquiry with a succession of *whys* is not recommended, it is nonetheless true that the search for a root cause must begin with a question; a cause is always a condition assumed unknown to the inquirer! A first *why* can thus acknowledge that a gap has been observed between a normal event and an abnormal event and requires explanation. However, even if this gap is unanimously validated, the answers to an open-ended causal question will differ depending on what the questioners already know. Background knowledge and prior beliefs frequently make a difference. Thus, several explanations can be proposed by a team, some of which are simply the result of a reasonable guess or hunch. *It is therefore more useful to welcome several explanations of causes in response to a single why question than to expect only one in response to successive why questions.*

Identifying the abnormal conditions whose presence would predict the observed event will be all the easier if the conditions of a normal operation are known and understood. Indeed, to understand *why* it does not work, it is better to have already understood *how* it works in normal operations! By representing causal pathways, the *CID* helps describe *how* each effect happens. It also becomes easier to reverse the problem to see how to cause it from a normal situation.

For example, one team noticed that an electronic board would randomly block during Linux boot. Three factors potentially responsible for this blocking were proposed in response to the question: *why* does the board block? Because of poor power supply coupling, wrong timing, or CMD (Command) errors. In addition, a certain temperature range was

---

[15] *Bon mot* from H.L. Mencken.

identified as a favourable condition for the problem to occur. How can the team judge whether these factors are informative or relevant? Before starting a potentially useless series of tests, establishing a *CID* allows one to focus the team's understanding of *how* each factor is able to predict the event. '*How* can bad coupling cause the board to be blocked?' Is there a model that correctly describes this causal relationship? If the design does not suggest such a relationship, then further investigation into this factor seems unnecessary as it is.

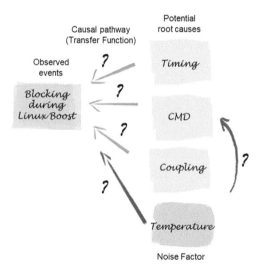

FIGURE 10.4
CID: express the causal pathway

While *why* questions may lead to speculations about possibilities when you run up against the limits of your knowledge, *how* questions trend to provide explanations based on prior knowledge and past experience. As soon as you ask the question '*Why?*' also ask the question '*How?*'.

In any case, whatever the answers to these questions, they are only provisionally adopted hypotheses about root causes. They deserve to be expressed as a conditional statement to make them more explicit:

If Causes are realised, *then* (observed) Event will occur.[16]

This statement makes it easier to check that the consequences of the suggested cause are appropriate to explain the observed event.

---

[16] C. Hempel. (1966). *Philosophy of Natural Science*. Pearson.

How can you select the right hypothesis as a root cause?

Inferring hypotheses from observed events, however, is not enough to guarantee the validity of your causal belief (abductive reasoning).[17] You must submit each hypothesis to experimental tests. The conditional statement makes the test definition obvious. However, no single hypothesis can entail, by itself, a test implication. You need to consider the conditions under which the hypothesis occurs: which factors to fix or vary, and which hypotheses other than the *test hypothesis* should be made.[18]

> **The Three Kinds of Arguments by C.S. Pierce**
>
> *Abduction* generates hypotheses; *deduction* makes predictions based on these hypotheses; *induction* eliminates hypotheses by testing via experiment the predictions generated by deduction.
>
> Thus, induction is an inference from a sample to a whole, while abduction is an inference from a body of data to an explanatory hypothesis.

Using the previous example: for a given temperature range (enabling condition), *If* the blocking of the board at Linux boot is caused by a poor power supply decoupling (test hyp.) *and* the Linux boot is error-free (auxiliary hyp.), *then* if the coupling is strengthened, the board will no longer be blocked.

Upon seeing the results of tests you either say that the *test hypothesis* has been confirmed or that it has been disconfirmed (deductive reasoning that fits the *modus ponens* pattern). However, a favourable outcome does not conclusively prove the hypothesis to be true and give a definitive causal explanation. You may need to test your hypothesis under a wide array of circumstances to assess how important the considered causal mechanism is to explain the observed situation (inductive reasoning).

---

[17] C.S. Peirce also terms '*retroduction*' this reasoning by which hypotheses are engendered from consequent to antecedent, Ibid.

[18] These additional hypotheses are called *auxiliary hypotheses* by C. Hempel.

The method used to identify the root causes are based on PDCA loops.

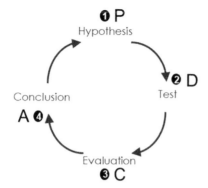

FIGURE 10.5
One short PDCA loop per hypothesis

1 – PLAN: formulate each hypothesis as a conditional statement between plausible causes and the observed event. Define the experiment implicated by this statement;
2 – DO: run the experiment;
3 – CHECK: measure the result and compare it to the expectation;
4 – ACT: if the experiment confirms the hypothesis, adopt the inferred root cause. Otherwise, run a new cycle by adjusting the hypothesis, or even by proposing another one.

There is one series of PDCA loops per hypothesis.

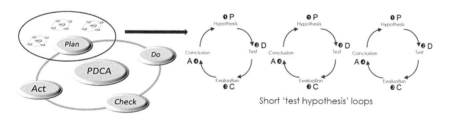

FIGURE 10.6
Move quickly through short PDCA loops to get to the root causes

You can organise your hypotheses in a table and number them to facilitate tracking in the following steps.

PLAN				DO	CHECK	ACT
Tentative hypothesis	Hypothesis statement	Independent variable	Dependent Variable	Tests Description	Actual results	Keep hyp.? OK/NOK
#1	If the coupling is strengthened then the board will no longer be blocked at Linux boot	Decoupling capacitor value	Frequency of board blocking	Test different coupling capacitors	Random blocking still present	NOK
#2	If a delay is added between each successive command in Flash, then the board will no longer be blocked at Linux boot	Additional delay	Frequency of board blocking	Test different duration	Partially reduced random blocking	OK (partial)

FIGURE 10.7
Example of hypotheses table

The hypotheses that you have selected will be the basis for countermeasures to fix the problem. The people affected by the problem should be aware of these results and have the opportunity to provide feedback. Once you have acquired everyone's buy-in, you can move on to the DO step.

The right side: DO

What countermeasures to prevent the problem from coming back?
A countermeasure is an action that prevents the problem from coming back by mitigating the impact of a root cause, or better yet, by eliminating it. Thus, once hypotheses are validated, implementing the countermeasures ensures that the successful result obtained during the experiments is reproduced and repeated in operational cases. They can act at different and multiple levels:

- On the independent variable(s), it may require a redesign of the product.
- On procedures of tests, control, installation, etc.
- On training, user manual, etc.

Therefore, propose at least one countermeasure per root cause.

This DO step has larger-scale consequences than previous steps, although much of the risk should have been eliminated by closing knowledge gaps during RCA. Thus, it may be better to put countermeasures into action one at a time rather than all at once while estimating their effectiveness, feasibility, impact, and cost/benefit first. Specify also who is responsible for doing what and when, and how the effects will be verified.

The right side: CHECK

What are the effects of countermeasures? What has changed? Do you get what you expected?
The measurement is done according to indicators defined in the *objective box* in order to compare it to the expectation. It should be performed on the *genba*, directly where these effects can be observed. The goal is to verify that the DO step worked as expected without generating side effects. If it did not, you may need to go back to the action plan or root causes (see ACT step).

What useful information can you take away from this problem-solving process?
Identify knowledge worth capturing in a reusable form to be shared and applied to other contexts in the future (refer to *Knowledge Brief*).

The right side: ACT

What do you need to do next?
From the CHECK result, determine whether to adopt, adjust, or abandon each proposed countermeasure:

- *Adopt* it when no significant value improvement is anticipated by running additional PDCA loops. Standardise the solution if needed.
- *Adjust* it if there is still room for improvement. Propose new actions to improve the solution. Go through a PDCA loop again, focusing more on the DO step.
- *Abandon* it when it does not meet expectations at all. Go back to the root cause analysis to see if additional underlying causes can be uncovered, then pivot to another solution, or even reconsider the objectives and problem statements. And go through PDCA loops again.

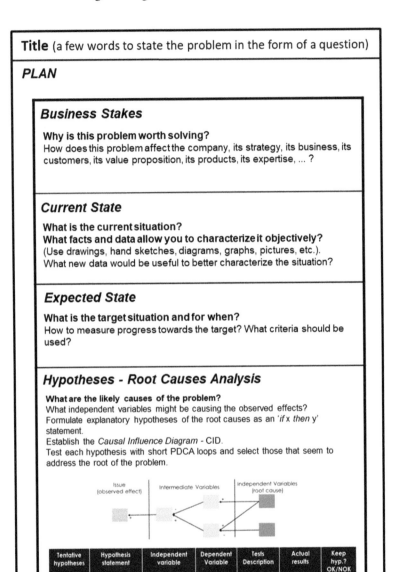

Title (a few words to state the problem in the form of a question)

PLAN

Business Stakes

Why is this problem worth solving?
How does this problem affect the company, its strategy, its business, its customers, its value proposition, its products, its expertise, ... ?

Current State

What is the current situation?
What facts and data allow you to characterize it objectively?
(Use drawings, hand sketches, diagrams, graphs, pictures, etc.).
What new data would be useful to better characterize the situation?

Expected State

What is the target situation and for when?
How to measure progress towards the target? What criteria should be used?

Hypotheses - Root Causes Analysis

What are the likely causes of the problem?
What independent variables might be causing the observed effects?
Formulate explanatory hypotheses of the root causes as an '*if* x *then* y' statement.
Establish the *Causal Influence Diagram* - CID.
Test each hypothesis with short PDCA loops and select those that seem to address the root of the problem.

Issue (observed effect)	Intermediate Variables	Independent Variables (root cause)

Tentative hypotheses	Hypothesis statement	Independent variable	Dependent Variable	Tests Description	Actual results	Keep hyp.? OK/NOK
1						
2						

FIGURE 10.8
A3 Problem Report Template and Guidelines

Owner	Coach	Date

DO - Propose the countermeasures & related action plan

Formulate countermeasures that can fix the root cause
Compare their effectiveness and impact as expected.

N°Hyp	Counter-measures	N° Counter-measure	Effectiveness/impact	Temporary/Permanent

Establish the action plan for each countermeasure

N° Counter-Measure	What	When	Who	Status O/C

Implement the selected countermeasures and monitor the action plan
Use the same criteria as defined in the 'Expected State' to track your progress.

Collect and document results.

CHECK - Results
Has actual result moved to expected state?
Have other problems been created?

Analyze how the change is working and compare the outputs to the prediction as a basis for learning.
Identify & summarize what was learned.

ACT - next step
What remains to be accomplished?

From the CHECK outcome, determine whether to adopt, adjust, or abandon your change: take the appropriate ACTion for next step ACT upon what has been learned.

FIGURE 10.8
Continued

XdB output Loss on Tube XXX

PLAN

Business Stake

Order Forecast
- m/month from July to Dec. 20xx
- n/month from Jan. to June 20xx

Customer impact: late deliveries
Business impact: loss of turnover, financial variances
Activity impact: activity weakening

Current State

From 20xx: N tubes Out Of Service (x€)
From Sept. 20xx: M tubes OOS
June 20xx : production shutdown

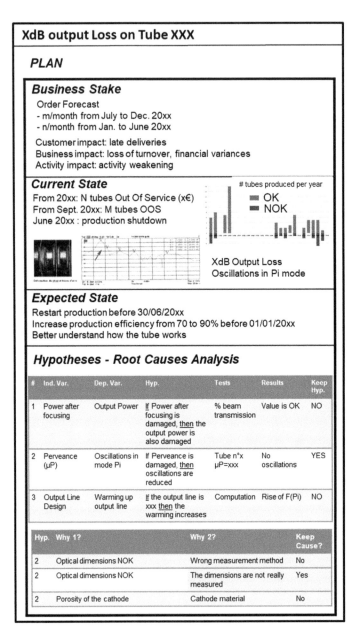

\# tubes produced per year
- OK
- NOK

XdB Output Loss
Oscillations in Pi mode

Expected State

Restart production before 30/06/20xx
Increase production efficiency from 70 to 90% before 01/01/20xx
Better understand how the tube works

Hypotheses - Root Causes Analysis

#	Ind. Var.	Dep. Var.	Hyp.	Tests	Results	Keep Hyp.
1	Power after focusing	Output Power	If Power after focusing is damaged, then the output power is also damaged	% beam transmission	Value is OK	NO
2	Perveance (μP)	Oscillations in mode Pi	If Perveance is damaged, then oscillations are reduced	Tube n°x μP=xxx	No oscillations	YES
3	Output Line Design	Warming up output line	If the output line is xxx then the warming increases	Computation	Rise of F(Pi)	NO

Hyp.	Why 1?	Why 2?	Keep Cause?
2	Optical dimensions NOK	Wrong measurement method	No
2	Optical dimensions NOK	The dimensions are not really measured	Yes
2	Porosity of the cathode	Cathode material	No

FIGURE 10.9
Example of *A3 Problem Report*

John	Julia	05/06/20xx

DO - Proposed the counter-measures & related action plan

Hyp	Counter-measures (CM)	N° CM	Effectiveness / Impact	Temporary / Permanent
2	Modify the optical dimensions to reduce Perveance	A	Expected prod. efficiency: 70%	Permanent
2	Ensure that the optical dimensions are measured and that the FRMs are properly filled	B	Expected prod. efficiency: 70%	Permanent
3	Remove the chamfers on the cells of the output line	C	Expected prod. efficiency: 90%	Permanent
4	Control the list of people certified for the shooping process	D	Expected prod. efficiency: 90%	Permanent

CM	When?	Who?	When?	Status
A	Update the optical dimensions plan	Technical Management	31/01/20xx	05/01/20xx
B	Check the dimensions before and after mechanical rework. Compare with the values indicated on the FRM	Manifacturing	30/06/20xx	01/06/20xx
C	Update the output line plan	Technical Management	31/06/20xx	15/03/20xx
D	Publish the list of certified people for the shooping process	Manifacturing	30/10/20xx	05/01/20xx

CHECK - Results

04/07/20xx
• The Y tubes produced are compliant
• 100% efficiency on these tubes (for this defect)
• Efficiency on outlet and inlet sections increased from 70-80% to 100%
• Better understanding of manufacturing defects
• Complete simulation of the tube
  - Cannon and electronic optics
  - Magnetic field
  - Interaction, RF performance and beam characteristics

ACT - next step

Create a standard for measuring optical dimensions and filling FRMs.
Implement verification and improvement of this standard (SIM – Short Intervalle Meeting)
Create a defects repository and update it as production progresses.

FIGURE 10.9
Continued

By logically articulating the PDCA steps in order to produce a discursive reasoning for the problem solver, the A3 report recognises problem solving as a method for developing individuals. It does this especially well as these steps do not follow each other in a purely linear way, as is usually the case, but are applied recursively locally (hypotheses) and globally (solution). Indeed, the content of the boxes (title, current conditions, hypotheses) might evolve as the investigation progresses, notably fed by the search for root causes.

The last version of the A3 report obviously does not include all the iterations. It captures in a reusable form what has been learned along the process. The successive intermediate versions, on the other hand, make it possible to follow the reasoning of the problem solver up to the result. This is why the configuration management of this document is key.

The use of A3 reports must be guided by the nature of the problem. It is not suitable for problems that a simple PDCA loop can solve, nor for complex problems that a single formulation cannot define definitively. Its use is also guided by the objective: individual coaching or team support? Thus, it is up to you to judge the relevance of using an A3 report, both on the nature of knowledge gaps and on the profiles of the problem solvers.

A3 Problem Report *and Kaizen*

Learning to solve problem to get back to standards or any previous state is very helpful to be more effective in closing the gap to a new level of performance (*kaizen*). It allows you to exercise your thinking skills to be more efficient to grasp the current situation, to understand the underlying causality, and to drive improvements accordingly.

Whatever the case, 'either changing what you do to meet an existing known way of doing something, or changing how things are done to solve a hitherto unsolved problem' to quote Tracey Richardson[19] (15). And while *kaizen* may require more creativity and a willingness to try new things, in both cases you have to close a gap by experimenting with changes one by one via PDCA loops.

MAP AND SHARE REUSABLE KNOWLEDGE

'Without standards there can be no *kaizen*[20]' this famous quote, attributed to Taiichi Ohno, means, to improve, you first need to know what is your starting point. So, instead of making random changes for the sake of change, to keep improving things, you need to identify and make explicit in a standard what you take for granted to be reusable, then improve the standard with new knowledge, and improve it further.

In engineering, perhaps more than anywhere else, to open the door to smarter and more creative solutions, the limits of current knowledge must be thus carefully identified and formalised beforehand, i.e., *the knowledge that reflects the current state.*

---

[19] How Does Asking Questions Create Change? – Lean Enterprise Institute.
[20] This quote specifically expresses the relationship between *Kaizen* and Work Standard.

Standards**

> *Lean standards are the basis for improvement. They capture reference knowledge in a rapidly reusable form, ensuring more predictable and higher quality outcomes.*

To respond appropriately to unpredictable changes, companies must be able to quickly exploit what they already know. By facilitating this exploitation, the standards contribute to making companies more agile.

In the past, explorers planned their missions based on the maps of their predecessors. As they explored new territories, they evolved these maps by transcribing their discoveries. Once home, they passed on their newly acquired knowledge in the form of these updated maps, to guide their contemporaries and successors.[21] The standards can be compared to the maps of the past. Once they have captured in a reusable form the valuable knowledge that the company has developed over time, they help engineers, on a daily basis, in their judgements and guide them in their decisions. Then, they evolve by integrating new learning.

These questions may help you assess which topics would be worth standardising in your technical departments:

- What knowledge is needed to make baseline design decisions?
- What problems recur?
- What decisions tend to be revisited in the absence of the right people?
- Which baseline activity leads to heterogeneous results depending on who is doing it?

Liker and Morgan (12) list three categories of engineering standards.

1. Design standards

They correspond to standard product architectures and component design (design checklists, design patterns, trade-off curves, *CID*), and reusable product components (building blocks, software libraries, common platforms). They structure the knowledge frequently (re)used in design decisions as a conditional '*if-then*' statement. For example, the trade-off curves, by making

---

[21] Inspired by *Maps and Exploration in the Sixteenth and Early Seventeenth Centuries*, Felipe Fernández-Armesto.

visible the effects already achieved by the interaction of selected design variables, provide engineers with the knowledge necessary to guide their design decisions. In the same way, the checklist mentioned below conditions the necessary design decisions for a good design of electronic boards.

1	Are the components in the preferred supplier list?
2	Is a voltage supervisor used?
3	Are class II ceramic or tantalum capacitors used (no gel electrolyte due to ageing)?
4	Is no reverse voltage applied to the tantalum capacitors?
5	Have the manufacturers' recommendations on decoupling been applied?
6	Have the powering up and down transitions been taken into account?
7	Have the ESD protection for I/O Ports been taken into account?
8	Have the testability (test points) been taken into account?
9	Have the programming interfaces (JTAG, …) been taken into account?
…	….

FIGURE 10.10
Extract of a design checklist for electronic boards

Thus, by making explicit how key design variables govern target performance, design standards act as a propaedeutic to more effective development of new knowledge and resolution of new design problems. They also provide opportunities to train engineers and assess their ability to use them wisely and to evolve them (see Engineering skill-set standards below).

2. Process standards

Traditionally, these processes describing how to coordinate, synchronise, and sequence engineering work are documented in the companies' Quality Management Systems (QMS) to guarantee their homogeneity across the company. So, how are Lean process standards different from these systems?

- First, on the intention. These systems set out the rules to be followed. Any deviation must be corrected since the success of an activity is conditional on compliance with these rules. Conversely, in a Lean standard, deviations are considered as opportunities to learn through problem solving. While the rules must remain stable, the standard evolves with learning.

- Second, on the use. On a daily basis, these systems are used as answer systems. These answers are calibrated to cover as many different cases as possible while maintaining homogeneity in their application. They consist of basic processes, instructions, roles, and gates checklists that are identical across the company. Thus, a QMS greatly reduces the available variety of answers, regardless of the variety of questions engineers have. By prescribing *a priori* the path to follow, it is intended to be predictive and robust regardless of the variety of situations. Conceivable in environments where stability is the norm, this logic becomes unsuitable where changes are the norm. Adaptation, and therefore agility, can only be a local answer to a local question. It is neither possible, nor desirable, that each singular question is subsumed under a single, common set of the same answers. Therefore, without denying the need to establish common rules, we propose to consider a limited number of principles and methods, especially those described in this book, and to capture part of the answers to local questions in process standards defined at the teams' level.
  - For example, following the few principles of implementation of a Pull-Scheduling Board is not sufficient to make it efficient for all teams. Each team must define its own standard for applying these principles and evolve it as needed.
  - In a similar way, each team using the KD/KG method (Key Decision/ Knowledge Gap) makes explicit in a standard how to apply it depending on the context, the product, the knowledge gaps, etc.

  In this sense, a Lean system can be seen as a system of questions since it questions each team on the best way to date to apply the principles and methods according to its own situation. 'How do we relate this new problem to this principle? How is this method applicable? Should this new case be standardised?'
- Finally, on their establishment and management, corollary of the previous point. The QMS and their evolutions are managed centrally, at the quality department level. This way of proceeding is a legacy of Taylor's scientific management theory and its ceaseless quest for 'the one best way', modernised into 'best practices'. In contrast, a Lean process standard is established locally by the teams. However, these local standards do not define a common language for all employees of the same company to interact in a consistent manner, often across borders. The challenge is thus to find the right balance between common principles and local standards.

JOB INSTRUCTION SHEET	Job Name: Create a new ticketing data index		Takt time: 5 days	Cycle time: 186 min	Date: Feb 2017	Dept./Location: Hub	Prepared By: xxx	Supervisor: xxx
#	**Step**	**Tool**	**Quality check & Note**					**Time (min)**
1	Remote log on to Hub workstation PC3 (login:?) with Team Viewer	Team Viewer	Local log on to hub workstation PC3 to find out Team Viewer ID & Password of PC3. Note: Team viewer passwords are changed everytime workstation is restarted or service is restart					2
2	Start WampServer on Hub workstation PC3		**Check WampServer icon in Windows task bar is visible and online (orange in color, tooltip: WAMPSERVER - server Online)**					1
3	Connect and login to Ticketing Data server (login: ?) with internet explorer - http://info.com.xx	Internet Explorer						3
4	Download latest period of ticketing data onto data backup folder of Hub workstation PC3 H://CENTAI/...	Internet Explorer	**Check number of files downloaded match the time period** Check ticketing data download file size is as follows, else restart download: •SD_FARE file > 125,000 KB •XDS_TXN file > 7,000 KB If download does not start, reinstall Juniper VPN application from website link.					35
5	Copy ticketing data onto data production folder of Hub workstation PC3 - H://Program Files/wamp/_data		Ticketing data are later fetched from production folder of Hub workstation PC3 by algo script run in step 8					5
6	Remote log on to production Hadoop server hadoop1 (login: devel) with Team Viewer	Team Viewer	Local log on to production server hadoop1 in servers room to find out Team Viewer ID & Password of production server hadoop1					2
7	Download timetable onto data folder of production Hadoop server hadoop1 /home/devel/dataTransfer/timeTable	Team Viewer	Timetable file is provided by xxx Timetable file must cover same time period as ticketing data folder download in step 4					5
8	Run Algo script to cook and index the new dataset Home/devel/script/runAlgorithm.sh ...		**Check for script successful message:** *output data exported* D: download ticketing data into HDFS and parsing p: push ticketing data to elastic search ...					120
9	Check new dataset index is created in production Elastic Search cluster http://elastic1.9200/^plugin/head	Chrome or Firefox	**Check for new Elastic Search Indexes named as:** results_metrics_[ticketing data foldername] platoccu_[ticketing data foldername]					3
10	Check new dataset index is available in production Kibana data visualisation http://218.189.207.163/#	Chrome or Firefox	Check data graphs in ticketing dashboard do not have overlap or missing days / data					10

FIGURE 10.11

Example of Job Instruction Sheet (Ticketing creation process steps)

3. Engineering skill-set standards

They formalise which technical expertise and skill engineers continuously need to develop to be capable to do their job correctly. These standards are intended to continuously grow the base of the *T* on specific technical expertise (refer to T-shape – *Teamwork*). They are part of training and development paths defined by each technical department.

While repeated applications of design and process standards in a variety of situations help enhance effective learning, this is not sufficient to move from mere knowledge to true mastery. Developing expertise requires exposing each engineer to new and increasingly complex problems on a regular basis. To do so, engineers must be trained through repeated exercises using different supports (design standards), methods, and technics (refer to *dojo*). After having developed new knowledge and understanding *offline*, apprenticeship as closely as possible to the products they work on helps them to transfer them to their workplace.

In Summary
Capturing and organising in a quickly reusable form what you already know is a necessary condition to accelerate the learning of what you need to better design better products. Progress on the path to Knowledge can be tracked in terms of the number of standards created, used, and improved.

Application: The Knowledge Brief**

> *The Knowledge Brief (KB) is an example of a standard formalised in the form of an A3 sheet.*

Definition

A Knowledge Brief is an A3 sheet used to capture the knowledge produced by the closure of a Knowledge Gap in a quickly reusable form. It can concern a customer, a product or its components, a technology, a practice, or a method. The KB structure must be adapted accordingly. A KB is also a good template to share trade-off curves or *CID* (as a Design Standard).

Compared to an *A3 Problem Report*, a KB does not provide solutions to a problem but makes explicit what has been learned and what deserves to be shared. In this sense, KB and *A3 Problem Reports* can be complementary. For example, a KB can be used to decontextualise, or even generalise for wider reuse what has been learned while solving a specific problem.

Models of Knowledge Brief

The Knowledge Brief model depends on the nature of the Knowledge Gap (KG) considered and therefore on what needs to be learned to develop new products.

Customer Knowledge Brief
This Knowledge Brief is related to Knowledge Gaps about customers, their uses, and their preferences.

Decision Knowledge Brief
This KB makes the possible options explicit. The goal is to capture information about each option and present comparative analyses based on evaluation criteria. The number of options can be reduced by using Set-Based Concurrent Engineering (SBCE), rather than picking the one that seems best at the outset.

KG Knowledge Brief

This KB captures what has been learned or still to be learned to guide decisions. This knowledge can concern applicable physical laws, key technologies or processes, mathematical formulas, configuration guidelines, and key points of architecture.

Guidelines

- A KB focuses on a particular type of knowledge, thus avoiding the dilution of information. Depending on the topic and purpose, specific questions and statements guide the writer.
- A KB captures knowledge on a single A3 sheet. As with the *A3 Problem Report* or Concept Paper, the A3 format is large enough to capture the essentials and too small to leave room for extraneous material. Simplifying the writing also means simplifying the reading.
- A KB is understandable and usable, even modifiable, independently of its author.
- A KB is reliable and validated by peers to inspire confidence in users.
- A KB is accessible and identifiable. Information is of no value if it cannot be found on demand, Just-in-Time.
- A KB is produced in the product development flow. It is not an additional activity like the *lessons learned* activities done at the end of projects. Capturing knowledge to share is part of the engineering job.

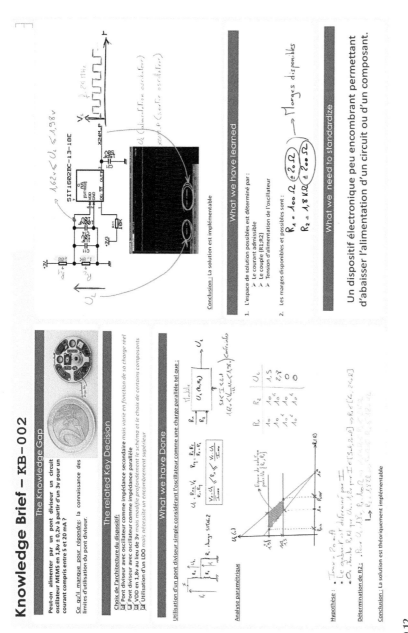

FIGURE 10.12

Example of KG Knowledge Brief

Standards and *Kaizen*

Establishing Lean standards limits the temptation to reinvent solutions to problems already solved and the risk of repeating the same mistakes. Thus, the time that was not spent reinventing the wheel is reinvested in improvement and innovation, i.e. *kaizen*. Standards and *kaizen* are therefore directly intertwined! *While the standard captures knowledge, kaizen fuels it.*

11

SBCE, the Lean Engineering Process***

We have described most of the methods, practices, and tools of Lean Engineering that are useful for exploring all or part of the different territories and taking the best itineraries. This section aims to go further by presenting a system that combines them in a coherent way, transforming conventional engineering into Lean Engineering. This coherent system is the SBCE.

The Set-Based Concurrent Engineering (SBCE) is the process at the core of Lean in Engineering. This approach consists of establishing as soon as possible the accessible design space by identifying trade-offs and interactions between variables, then developing the knowledge required to gradually narrow down this space towards the best solution.

ORIGIN AND DEFINITION

Set-Based Design

The term Set-Based was coined by Allen Ward. In his thesis,[1] he described how a set of algorithms (a compiler for mechanical design) could converge to the best solution in a design space after successive eliminations of options that did not satisfy the constraints.

During study trips to Japan in 1992 and 1993, while interviewing Toyota engineers and suppliers to understand their success factors, he discovered a strong analogy between the compiler convergence process and the

---

[1] Allen Ward. (1989). 'A Theory of Quantitative Interference Applied to a Mechanical Design Compiler.' *MIT Artificial Intelligence Laboratory.*

DOI: 10.4324/9781003381945-13

Toyota product design and development process. As a starting point for design activities, all functional departments propose a set of options from their respective area of expertise. This increases the probability that a combination of subsystems will fit well together to achieve the best solution. As the design progresses, each department progressively narrow down their respective set by eliminating the weak options, until the optimal fit is obtained. This similarity to the process used by his compiler led Ward to call this design process 'Set-Based Design'. This term is not used by Toyota.

Converging on the optimal solution by dropping the options that do not satisfy successive cut-off criteria is simpler than determining which of these options should be selected on the basis of a set of criteria weighted according to their influence on the solution's performance. Moreover, it is illusory to think that the selection of a solution on a few local optima can lead to a globally optimal solution. *The optimal solution is the result of the resolution of trade-offs and not of the sum of local optima.*

Unfortunately, traditional organisations apply this Point-Based Design, with the intention of selecting the best point in the solutions space very early on. Since the probability that this point actually corresponds to a working solution is not 100%, designers might iterate around this point to find a solution that works, without being able to guarantee it is the optimal solution!

In addition, since all design decisions are made with respect to this single point, each deviation from a subsystem leads to changes in all the others, requiring the implementation of a long and often costly change management process. In contrast, by communicating a set of options relatively independently, each of the subsystems reduces the need to interact with the others: *they look for intersection rather than for interaction.* The dependency between design decisions is thus less with Set-Based Design than with Point-Based Design. This enables the implementation of concurrent engineering.

Concurrent Engineering

Concurrent engineering is opposed to sequential engineering. Driven by increasingly rapid time-to-market, Japanese car manufacturers adopted this configuration massively in the 1970s. Here again, Toyota was the pioneer (as early as the 1960s[2]). The main benefit of concurrent engineering, as identified by Hirotaka Takeuchi and Ikujiro Nonaka, is the reduction in development cycle times. In their famous article,[3] which inspired Jeff Sutherland, creator of Scrum,[4] they use the analogy of rugby versus a relay race to illustrate this overlapping of activities. They also find some drawbacks, such as the high number of simultaneous contributors, which makes managing the process more complex than a sequential process. American car manufacturers, who have adopted this configuration have not been able to reap all the expected benefits. Toyota has overcome some of this complexity by adopting the Chief Engineer system.

One of the most famous achievements of concurrent engineering involves product design and industrial design activities at Toyota. This arrangement makes it possible to define, upfront, a set of options considering each party's limitations, tolerances, and trade-offs.[5] The objective, as stated by Ward, is that the design choices should lead to the development of a profitable production flow (3).

Engineering departments also work concurrently, each on their own subsystem, and communicate regularly to ensure that there is always an intersection between the respective sets of options. Coordination and information sharing are organised in *obeya*.

Set-Based Concurrent Engineering

Principles

We summarise here the SBCE principles as defined by Ward and his colleagues.[6]

---

[2] Jeffrey K. Liker, John E. Ettli, and John Creighton Campbell. (1995). *Engineered in Japan: Japanese Technology-Management Practices*. Oxford University Press. Chapter 8

[3] H. Takeuchi and I. Nonaka. (1986). 'The New Product Development Game.' *Harvard Business Review*.

[4] https://www.scruminc.com/scrum-godfathers-takeuchi-and-nonaka/.

[5] This concurrent approach was formalised and structured by Chihiro Nakao in the form of the 3P process (*Production Preparation Process*)

[6] D.K. Sobek, A.C. Ward, and J.K. Liker. (1999). 'Toyota's Principles of Set-Based Concurrent Engineering.' *Sloan Management Review*.

Map the design space and communicate: the objective is to map out the feasible design space:

- *Define the feasible regions*: based on the Concept Paper, the functional departments determine their respective feasible region of the design space according to the constraints and objectives applicable to their own subsystem (refer to *CID*). Each region is expressed as a set of discrete options or/and as ranges of values.
- *Exploring trade-offs by designing multiple options*: the functional departments explore their region simultaneously and relatively independently, especially by varying the values of variables on the trade-off curves. Exploring these trade-off curves helps determine where the Key Decisions lie to eliminate the weakest options.
- *Communicate sets of possibilities*: each functional department communicates about its set of options to inform others of the possibilities accessible to them, and the constraints to be respected (e.g., interfaces).

Integrate by intersection: the objective is to integrate the options of all parties revealing the feasible intersections, i.e., the solutions workable for all.

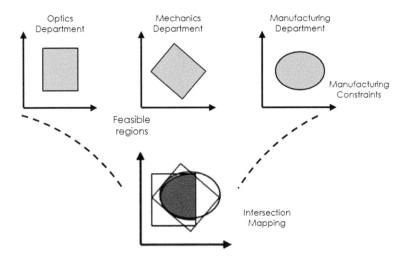

FIGURE 11.1
Convergence by mapping the intersection of feasible regions

- *Look for intersections of feasible sets*: the functional departments look for overlapping feasible regions, i.e., those where there are options that are acceptable to all (points or ranges of values). The other options are eliminated.
- *Impose minimum constraints*: constraints, or specifications, are expressed as ranges to leave enough room for interfacing subsystems to adjust with limited risk of rework. By imposing its decisions too early, a subsystem can generate blocking constraints for other subsystems, making it impossible to establish a common region. *Local optimisation makes the process iterative rather than convergent!* It is therefore necessary to impose a minimum of constraints. For example, Toyota provides its suppliers with specifications with tolerances of up to 30% for the first prototypes and reduced to 5% for the following ones.
- *Seek conceptual robustness*: a robust design is a design whose performance is not compromised when certain requirements vary, whether they are related to the subsystems directly at the interface or to the needs expressed by the customers. Robustness allows exposure to greater variability without having to develop new options. It is the basis for product standardisation.

Did You Know That?

Nippondenso, Toyota's main supplier of radiators and alternators, used Set-Based Design for a new alternator model in the 1970s. The engineers began by determining the target performance from which many concepts were created, tested, combined, modified, and improved to define a set of options. After four years, three concepts were selected, each represented by five prototypes. In the fifth year, a single solution was selected as the basis for a family of 700 alternators (M.M. Andreasen, C.T. Hansen, and P. Cash. (2015) *Conceptual Design: Interpretations, Mindset and Models.* Springer).

Establish feasibility before commitment. At each step, Key Decisions are made with less uncertainty once the feasibility of the options has been established, thanks to the knowledge acquired regularly.

- *Narrow sets gradually while increasing detail*: as the level of detail increases and uncertainty decreases, it is possible to reduce the ranges of values or the list of discrete options accessible to design variables. Thus, by making Key Decisions that gradually eliminate the weakest options, each functional department narrows down its own region to converge to a spot that is compatible with the spots of the other functional departments. For example, in Figure 11.2, the range of accessible values is reduced after two successive decisions.

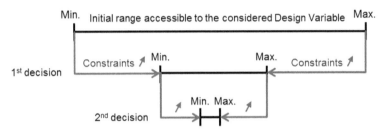

FIGURE 11.2
Convergent decision-making process

- *Stay within sets once committed*: once established, the accessible options (points or ranges of value) are no longer modified. There is no question of introducing new ideas that would expand the design space and could affect the robustness of the final product.
- *Control by managing knowledge at Integrating Events (IE)*: the convergence process is paced by IE that brings all the subsystems together where the convergence criteria act as filters to eliminate the weakest options. At each step, one or more convergence criteria may be tightened. For example, margins on specifications are reduced (from 30% to 5%) to target specifications. Compatibility between subsystems is assessed and incompatible options are eliminated. The remaining options get refined a little more up to the next IE. The decision to eliminate regions of the design space is then made according to the acquired knowledge at each step. IE pace the decision-making convergence process. (IE is the terminology used in SBCE. IE corresponds more generally to what we have called Pull Event.)

SBCE is a convergent decision-making process that aims to eliminate options (ranges of values or set of discrete options) over time rather than choosing one upfront, until the best solution is found.

Evolution of the Design Involved in Making a Mass-Production Hybrid Car

To select the best design for its hybrid engine, Toyota started with a set of 80 options and narrowed it down to four. Driving simulations were used to eliminate one of the four options on the basis of fuel consumption. Production potential and technological maturity were then used to eliminate two of the three remaining options. The last option was taken as a reference for the Toyota Hybrid System.[7]

The So-Called SBCE Paradox

Allen Ward and his colleagues describe[8] this engineering process as the second paradox of Toyota (the first one is the TPS): how 'delaying decisions, communicating ambiguously and pursuing excessive number of prototypes, enables Toyota to design better cars faster and cheaper?'

The first proposition of this paradox corresponds to the Decision Paradox which expresses that it is more effective to delay decisions until sufficient knowledge is acquired to make them with confidence. The second proposition expresses that it is better to leave room for interpretation, rather than imposing categorical requirements too early, such that the product performance is not compromised beyond the minimum requirements in the presence of future variations or uncertainties.[9] The last proposition is the corollary of the previous two. Allowing time to learn with more freedom allows for a broader exploration of the design domain and thus the generation of more options earlier. The paradox is therefore in appearance only.

Set-Based Design just acknowledges that it is precisely upfront that the designers' freedom is the greatest and the learning cost the lowest. The

---

[7] Hideshi Itazaki. (1999). *The Prius That Shook the World: How Toyota Developed the World's First Mass-Production Hybrid Vehicle*. The Nikkan Kogyo Shimbun, Ltd.

[8] D. Sobek, A. Ward, J. Cristiano, and J. Liker. (1995). 'The Second Toyota Paradox: How Delaying Decisions Can Make Better Cars Faster'. *Sloan Management Review.*

[9] Jawad Qureshi. (2009). 'Set Based Robust Design of Systems – Application to Flange Coupling'. *CIRP Design Conference.*

real paradox is in the Point-Based Design. Instead of taking advantage of this low learning cost, this design approach forces decisions to be made when knowledge is incomplete, and thus incurs a debt to be repaid at a high price.[10]

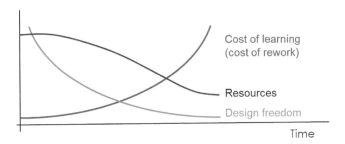

FIGURE 11.3
Evolution of the cost of learning as a function of time

To decide better, you need to learn more deeply, and to learn more deeply, you need to explore more widely, and this is in a collaborative way. These are the conditions for a more robust design. Therefore, investing in knowledge upfront always pays off, both for the project in question and for all subsequent projects that benefit from this reusable knowledge. So, SBCE always pays off more than it costs.

Set-Based Design Is Not 'Multi-Points-Based' Design!

SBCE is often seen only as a way to process several options simultaneously. While increasing the number of options increases the probability of having a solution that works, this probability is higher if the options help to delineate the region of the design space where to find the best one.

When the Wright brothers or Toyota build prototypes, they don't choose them from anywhere in the design space. They target those that generate the knowledge useful for establishing the relationships governing product performance in the form of trade-off curves. Thus, each option contributes to delineating the region of accessible solutions that meet the needs and constraints. Once this region has been correctly mapped, it remains to refine each candidate option a little further and to apply the cut-off criteria to converge on the best one.

---

[10] https://www.youtube.com/watch?v=K9IN28A7FLU.

The word 'set' in Set-Based should therefore not be understood as 'the set of points randomly picked out from the design space to find a solution', but as 'the set of points useful for establishing the limits of the accessible design space'. These two figures illustrate this difference.

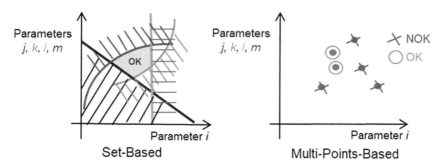

FIGURE 11.4
Set-Based versus Multi-Points-Based

This understanding of the true nature of SBCE is unfortunately missing from most of the literature that tries to explain it. Yet this is what makes it so special and effective (13). Let us illustrate this point with the design of a new system composed of several subsystems.

A somewhat elaborate approach would be to first generate several alternatives per subsystem, and then force the selection of an optimal alternative based on a set of criteria. For example, Pugh's matrix uses the scoring of criteria to create an optimal hybrid solution from the combination of the best elements of each alternative. Unlike SBCE where the best option emerges after successive elimination of all its competitors, each elimination being based on a few criteria, the Pugh matrix applies a set of criteria at once to establish the best alternative. Not to mention that the evaluations are made while the knowledge gaps are not yet characterised, the hypothesis that the sum of local optima necessarily leads to the global optimum is more than doubtful. In addition, the methods using these pairwise comparisons fail to identify whether there is a region of the design space common to the options of different subsystems.

The 'Multi-Points-Based' approach, by forcing one to pick the best option up front among a set extracted from the design space, does not create the conditions for a better knowledge of this space. In doing so, it leaves teams unaware of where the best solutions to their problems lie.

Without this knowledge needed to make trade-off decisions properly, they put themselves in a position to make bad decisions, without even being aware of it.

SBCE, THE LEAN DESIGN, AND DEVELOPMENT PROCESS

The SBCE articulates most of the Lean methods, practices, and tools in a coherent way.

- *Concept Paper*: as the compass document, it provides guidance on where the design needs to be, primarily through key performance expressed as ranges or sets. Starting with rough targets, imposing minimal constraints, allows better designs to emerge as learning progresses.
- *Obeya:* as a place for sharing and collaboration among the multidisciplinary teams involved in SBCE, it accelerates the ideas generation and makes visible the trade-offs and intersection of options.
- *Causal Influence Diagram (CID)*: it models the design space to be explored by the different parties and guides the decision-makers to the right trade-offs and design variables.
- *KD/KG*: Key Decisions are made based on convergence criteria, according to the sequence defined by the Key Decision Diagram. All options that meet the criteria move on to the next Integration Event. They remain in the set until the closing of Knowledge Gaps leads to their elimination.
- *Key Decision Diagram*: derived from the *CID*, it visually structures the dependencies and priorities between Key Decisions to drive the convergent decision-making process and design space narrowing.
- *Pull Scheduling Board*: by making the decisions flow and Integrating Events explicit, it facilitates synchronisation, learning coordination, and decision-making across the project.
- *Trade-Off Curves*: at the heart of the SBCE, they visually display the areas where there are feasible options common to all parties.
- *Knowledge Briefs*: it captures in a reusable form the knowledge acquired from the options that succeeded and the ones that did not.
- *Problem Solving and Kaizen*: they accelerate learning and continuously improve practices and processes.

Part Three

Compose Your Itinerary

Now that you know the vocabulary, the pathways, the territories, the principles, the practices, and the tools, you get ready to compose your own itinerary taking into account the culture of your company, your environment, your customers, your partners, your products, and so on.

However, there are still two questions to address before you leave.

1. Where are you starting from? To help you answer this question, we suggest a simple grid to identify your starting point in each *territory*, enabling you to select appropriate practices that fit your gaps and related challenges, in addition to the must-haves (the 'practices' considered as must-haves are *obeya*, *kaizen*, and *Genba Walk*).
2. What gaps do you want to close first? And therefore, what methods, tools, and practices are best suited to do so efficiently? To help you answer these questions, we present a table that summarises them in the order in which they appear in this book, in line with the progression in the *territories*.

12

The Customer/Product Matrix

To start, you will logically choose a candidate product (or a product line) and identify where the knowledge gaps are. The purpose of this matrix is thus to position you according to what you already know and what you still need to learn, both about your customers (*Territory of Customers*) and your products (*Territory of Products*).[1]

		The problem to solve: the customer need	
		Well known	Not well known
The proposed solution: the product	Well known	A	C
	Not well known	B	D

FIGURE 12.1
Fit matrix

---

[1] Inspired by the article *Lean Product Management* of Greg Cohen, 2011.

DOI: 10.4324/9781003381945-15

Four types of situations can be identified:

A – You know your territories pretty well. The challenge is to improve your existing products. *VA/VE* can allow you to increase the perceived value while *Product Takt* will help you to better manage and then reduce time to market.

B – The *Territory of Customers* is pretty well known, but you still need to explore the *Territory of Products* (*market pull*). The challenge is to design new products or to significantly enhance existing ones. Exploring new areas is thus necessary. *CID*, *Teardown*, *Trade-off Curves*, and *Standards* will help you to identify the limits of your current designs to better push them and propose incremental improvements through rapid *learning PDCA loops*.

C – The *Territory of Products* is fairly well known while you lack information about the *Territory of Customers* (*techno push*). In other words, the solution is known and is looking for a problem. In this case, the solution is usually a radical innovation, resulting from breakthrough technologies capable of opening a door to a new market. This is why *techno push* is considered a crucial innovation practice. Thus, your gap is more related to the *Territory of Customers*. Its deeper exploration through *Customer Genba Walks* should identify customers mature enough (*pilot customers*[2]) to test concepts, through *short PDCA loops*, in the early stages of new product development. Also, since the deciding factor here is to make explicit the problem that is solved by the technology, with the support of a *CID*, try to go back to *KVA* to which your solution would be an appropriate answer.

D – This situation refers to the research and technology challenges; it is not the focus of this guide.

---

[2] See also Geoffrey A. Moore. (2014). *Crossing the Chasm, Marketing and Selling Disruptive Products to Mainstream Customers.* Harper Business.

13

Summary Table

As a reminder, each practice, tool, or method presented in this table is rated from 0 to 3 stars. These stars are awarded on both their impact and their difficulty. The most powerful ones but requiring more experience are identified by three stars (***). The easiest ones to access are identified by one star (*). It is your responsibility to adjust and evolve their rating based on your own experiences.

In addition, we suggest which emblematic wastes and gaps these practices, tools, and methods are targeting in priority. Although this mapping is somewhat reductive, it has the virtue of making visual that it is difficult to pretend to do Lean in Engineering without a large coverage.

Thus, while it may be wise to choose a particular place to start your journey according to your needs, it is by following *itineraries* that cross all *territories* that you will create the conditions for effective and sustainable Lean Engineering.

Neither *obeya* nor *kaizen* or *Genba Walk* is listed in this table. This is because we consider them to be the foundations of Lean in Engineering, without them, all other practices will have only limited impact, with the risk of seeing them wither and eventually disappear.

DOI: 10.4324/9781003381945-16

	Rating	Customer - Product				People		Process	
		Not expected features	High cost of ownership	Delayed market entry	Lack of vision	Lack of expertise	Reinvention	Reworks	Poor process flow
Customer complaints	*	▓							
Walk on the user's premises	***	▓							
Walk in the user's shoes	**	▓							
Customer VSM	**	▓							
KVA - Customer Radar Chart	*	▓							
Product Radar Chart	*	▓							
Concept paper	**				▓				
CID	***	▓	▓			▓			
Trade-off curves	**	▓						▓	
Tear down	*	▓				▓			
Target costing, VA/VE	***		▓						
Chief Engineer	***				▓				▓
Pull, flow, cadence	**							▓	
Takt Product	**			▓					
Visible Portfolio Planning	*			▓					
Slow build	*								
Dojo	*		▓						
A3 problem solving	**						▓		
Standards	**						▓	▓	
Knowledge Brief	**						▓	▓	
SBCE	***	▓	▓	▓	▓			▓	

FIGURE 13.1
Summary table

14

Enjoy Your Journey

All that's remaining is for us to wish you a travel as pleasant as ours. Test, make mistakes, progress, and above all have fun!

The Lean bet always wins.

Enjoy …

DOI: 10.4324/9781003381945-17

Bibliography

Many books, sites, and articles have been referenced throughout the book. We have selected in this bibliography some reference books.

1. Cécile Roche. *Le Lean en Questions*: L'Harmattan, 2016.
2. Cécile Roche. *A Little Lean Guide for the use of Managers*: L'Harmattan, 2013.
3. Allen C. Ward. *Lean Product and Process development. 1ère édition*: Lean Enterprise Institute Inc., 2007.
4. Eric Ries. *The Lean Startup, How Constant Innovation Creates Radically Successful Businesses*: Portfolio Penguin, 2011.
5. Katie Anderson. *Learning to Lead, Leading to Learn*: Integrand Press, July 14, 2020.
6. John Shook. *Managing to Learn: Using the A3 management process*: Lean Enterprise Institute, 2008.
7. Michael Ballé, Daniel Jones, Jacques Chaize, Orest Fiume. *The Lean Strategy*: McGraw Hill Higher Education, 2017.
8. Michel Sailly. *Démocratiser le travail: un nouveau regard sur le lean management*: Les éditions de l'atelier, 2017.
9. Mary and Tom Poppendieck. *Lean Software development, an Agile Toolkit*: Pearson, 2003.
10. Niklas Modig, Pär Ahlström. *This is Lean, Resolving the Efficiency Paradox*: Rheologica Publishing, 2012.
11. Michael N. Kennedy, Brian M. Kennedy, Penny W. Cloft. *Success is Assured*: New York: Productivity Press, 2018.
12. James M. Morgan, Jeffrey K. Liker. *The Toyota Product Development System*: New York: Productivity Press, 2006.
13. Michael N. Kennedy, Kent Harmon, Ed Minnock. *Ready, Set, Dominate: Implement Toyota's Set-Based Learning for Developing Products and Nobody Can Catch You*: CreateSpace Independent Publishing Platform, 2008.
14. Katherine Radeka. *The Shortest Distance Between You and Your New Product, 2de édition*: Chesapeake Research Press, 2017.
15. Tracey and Ernie Richardson. *The Toyota Engagement Equation*: McGraw Hill; 1st edition, July 31, 2017.
16. Donald G. Reinertsen. *The Principles of Product Development Flow: Second Generation Lean Product Development*: Celeritas Pub, 2009.

Photographs taken at *Toyota Commemorative Museum of Industry and Technology* by Cécile Roche (pp. 77, 78, 81, 82).

The obeya map was created by Johanna Guillaume. A detailed version is available on the Institut Lean France website https://www.institut-lean-france.fr/medias/2018/02/lean-map.html.

Index

Note: Page numbers in **bold** refer to titles.